Paradise Regained.

The Biblically Annotated Edition

Praise for Paradise Lost: The Biblically Annotated Edition

"When the Bible has to share time and page space with Homer, Virgil, Ovid, Tasso, Ariosto, and so on, there are only so many times an editor can include a note pointing readers to a biblical passage. The advantage of an edition like Stallard's, which limits its annotations exclusively to the Bible, is that it can afford to be far more exhaustive and detailed."

—Jeffrey Shoulson, *Milton Quarterly*

"Focusing exclusively on biblical allusions and references, Stallard calls attention to Milton's intense biblicism and to the qualities of the biblical culture in which he lived and wrote. Stallard's edition will help to introduce a new generation of readers to the history, scope, and nature of the Bible as the preeminent literary influence in the Renaissance [...] Stallard places his notes beneath the text on each page. This position provides quick access for readers, and visibly illustrates that the Bible is indeed the deep structure of Paradise Lost. Stallard demonstrates this principle through judicious editorial choices and insightful annotations. This timely and welcome edition will prove valuable for all readers of Paradise Lost."

—David Gay, *Renaissance & Reformation/Renaissance et Reforme*

"Stallard's edition is a valuable resource to scholars of the seventeenth century, but not one limited to the rarified sort of research characteristic of academia. What Milton writes of Bible study in his Treatise of Civil Power (quoted in Stallard's preface) could just as easily pertain to the Biblically Annotated Edition itself: 'It is useful for teaching...even those learned and wise.' [...] At the very least, any library at an institution where Milton's writing is taught ought to procure a copy of this edition, and instructors tasked with the responsibility of familiarizing their students with the incredibly dense verse of Milton's epic, owe it to themselves to keep an edition close by. Stallard's contribution to Milton scholarship through the production of this meticulously edited text cannot be underestimated."

—T. Ross Leasure, *Reformation*

JOHN MILTON

PARADISE REGAINED.

THE BIBLICALLY ANNOTATED EDITION

Edited by

Matthew Stallard

MERCER UNIVERSITY PRESS
MACON, GEORGIA

MUP/ P716

Published by Mercer University Press
1501 Mercer University Drive
Macon, Georgia 31207

29 28 27 26 25 5 4 3 2 1

Books published by Mercer University Press are printed on acid-free paper that meets the requirements of the American National Standard for Information Sciences—Permanence of Paper for Printed Library Materials.

Printed and bound in the United States.

This book is set in Palatino.

Cover/jacket design by Burt&Burt.

Library of Congress Cataloging-in-Publication Data
Names: Milton, John, 1608-1674, author. | Stallard, Matthew S., 1970- editor.
Title: Paradise regained : the Biblically annotated edition / John Milton ; edited by Matthew Stallard.
Description: Macon, Georgia : Mercer University Press, [2025] | Includes bibliographical references and index. |
Identifiers: LCCN 2024054752 | ISBN 9780881469653 (paperback)
Subjects: LCSH: Jesus Christ—Temptation—Poetry. | Bible—History of Biblical events—Poetry. | English poetry—17th century. | Milton, John, 1608-1674. Paradise regained. | Milton, John, 1608-1674—Sources. | Bible—In literature.
Classification: LCC PR3563 2025 | DDC 821/.4—dc23/eng/20250129
LC record available at https://lccn.loc.gov/2024054752

CONTENTS

Acknowledgments / viii

Introduction / ix

Appendix A / li

Appendix B / lii

Appendix C / liii

Appendix D / liv

Abbreviations / lxiv

PARADISE REGAINED

Book I / 1

Book II / 51

Book III / 85

Book IV / 125

Bibliography 169

Index 181

MERCER UNIVERSITY

MERCER UNIVERSITY PRESS

Endowed by

TOM WATSON BROWN
and
THE WATSON-BROWN FOUNDATION, INC.

For Cara Stallard
"Union of mind, or in us both one soul"

ACKNOWLEDGMENTS

I am indebted to many fine people for providing the encouragement and motivation to complete this edition. I am especially grateful to my son Brody Taze Stallard who was relentless in monitoring my progress every step of the way. Brody always "believed." Cara, my supportive wife, was an invaluable sounding-board and supporting ear that I needed to complete the project. My daughter-in-law Robin Stallard provided generous insights in our long discussions about the poem. Many thanks to Miriam Intrator of the Ohio University Mahn Center Archives for assistance in navigating the archive's digital initiatives. Special thanks also to Daniel Linke from Special Collections at Princeton University. The following amazing people, past and present, offered research support, comments and other essential assistance: Beth Quitslund, Roy Flannagan, Edward Jones, John Shawcross, Joseph Wittreich, Stanley Fish, Leland Ryken, Jameela Lares, Charles Durham, David Hopkins, Jeremy Webster, Robert Ingram, Linda Rice, Sherrie Gradin, Todd Snyder, William Breeze, Robert Ingram, Josephine Bloomfield, Marsha Dutton, Rebecca McNeer, Joseph McLaughlin, Paul Jones, Kasia Marciniak, Robert DeMott, Regina Schwartz, Jill Ingram, Linda Zionkowski, Samuel Crowl, Eric LeMay, Kevin Killeen, David Wanczyk, David Ainsworth, Timothy Hodor, David Urban, T. Ross Leasure, John Michael Drew, Nicole Reynolds, Carey Snyder, Loreen Giese, Miriam Shadis, Candace Stewart, Elizabeth Koonce, Chester Stallard, Helen Stallard, Ward Buckner, Ginger Buckner, Lavonne Baker, Penelope Flickinger, Grant Stallard, Liam Stallard, Gavin Stallard, Anjeli Rivera, Esther Thomas, Timothy Thomas, Siena Thomas, Alexandria Thomas, Eden Thomas, Sandra White, Joshua Westfall, John Hibshman, Richard Castrop, Will Tevis, Jeff Houtz, Jeff Morris, David Swartz, Ben Stewart, and Marc Jolley.

INTRODUCTION

Shortly after the publication of the first edition of *Paradise Lost* (the ten-book version) in 1667, John Milton (1608–1674) turned his attention and poetic efforts to the subject of Christ's temptation in the wilderness recorded in the Gospels. The result of this meditation was *Paradise Regained,* which was licensed for publication in 1670. This places the appearance of *Paradise Regained* directly between Milton's 1667 *Paradise Lost* and the 1674 *Paradise Lost* (the twelve-book version). As was true with *Paradise Lost,* Milton drew heavily upon biblical sources in *Paradise Regained,* and it is a fair assumption that his creative process for bringing the Gospels to life was similar to his approach to dramatizing the epic of the Garden of Eden recorded in Genesis.

In my preface to *Paradise Lost: The Biblically Annotated Edition* published by Mercer University Press in 2011, I argue, and I believe the edition amply demonstrates, that the Bible for Milton possesses the highest *ethos* and contains the most desirable idiom for poetic expression. Likewise, *Paradise Regained: The Biblically Annotated Edition* is overflowing with biblical allusions and connections that, when properly recognized, fill the text with insights into the theological thinking of Milton and place the intellectual exchange and engagement between Jesus and Satan firmly within the historical context of the English Reformation.

For this edition, I employed as my copy-text *Paradise Regain'd... To which is added Samson Agonistes* (1671) held by the Department of Rare Books and Special Collections, Princeton University Library. It is my sincere desire that this new edition of *Paradise Regained* will help both scholars and students to better enjoy Milton's biblical echoes in one of his finest poems.

In 1665, Thomas Ellwood, one of Milton's amanuenses for *Paradise Lost,* upon reading a completed manuscript commented to the author: "Thou hast said much here of Paradise lost: but what hast thou to say of Paradise found?" According to Ellwood, who is the only source for this conversation, Milton said nothing in response to his impertinent question. Milton had been Ellwood's teacher and there was a thirty-one year age difference between them. At the time of the remark, Ellwood was twenty-three and Milton was fifty-four. Allegedly a year later, Milton credited Ellwood with prompting the writing of *Paradise Regained*. After the completion of his second epic, Milton returned to Ellwood and quipped to him: "This is owing to you: for you put it into my head by the question you put to me at Chalfont, which before I had not thought of."[2]

Whether or not Ellwood was the catalyst or wellspring to get Milton pondering the implications of a "paradise found," there is ample evidence that Milton had some years earlier considered writing a longer poem about Jesus. In the *Trinity Manuscript* dated to 1642, Milton listed among other topics for biblical tragedies that he considered taking up in poetic verse "Christ Bound," "Christ Born," and "Christ Crucified."[3]

To be sure, the subject matter of *Paradise Regained* pairs well with *Paradise Lost,* and I do not object to calling *Paradise Regained* a thematic sequel in the sense that the poem plays out the implications of *Paradise Lost*. The big question in *Paradise Lost* is why is there human suffering in the world and what is God going to do about it? The answer provided in *Paradise Lost* is that a group of insurrectionist angelic Sons of God deceived the first pair of humans into rebelling against God and that God's solution to the resultant misery and woe was to appoint another Son of God, Jesus Christ, to intervene as Sacrificial Lamb, Messiah, High Priest, and King of God's Kingdom.

The big question in *Paradise Regained* is related and is critical to the panacean solution offered in *Paradise Lost*: who really is a Son of God?

---

[2] For a full account of the Ellwood episode see William Riley Parker, *Milton: A Biography*. 2 vols. (Oxford: Clarendon, 1968), 597–98.

[3] *The Complete Prose Works of John Milton*, ed. Don M. Wolfe, 8 vols. (New Haven: Yale University Press, 1953–82), 559, 580.

Satan claims in *Paradise Regained* that Jesus has no more claim to the title "Son of God" than Satan has, and therefore Satan is just as qualified as Jesus to redeem humankind. When tempting Jesus, Satan begins the first and last of his challenges with the taunt: "If you are the Son of God." Most Milton scholars who have weighed into the identity of the Sons of God described in *Paradise Lost* Book XI suggest that Milton might be confused on the subject as well. The consensus of scholarly opinion is that in discussing the events of Genesis 6:1–4 in *Paradise Lost,* that Milton is referring to human descendants of Adam's son Seth, but that when he discusses the same scripture in Book II of *Paradise Regained,* Milton flips the script and is referring to Angels. This claim of Miltonic uncertainty disrupts the thematic continuity from *Paradise Lost* to *Paradise Regained.*

To grapple effectively with the question of Son-hood in *Paradise Regained,* it is essential to arrive at a clear understanding of the identity of the Sons of God in *Paradise Lost* or at least make the attempt. It is my contention that Milton *is* consistent and that the term "Sons of God" refers to angels and not men in both *Paradise Lost* and *Paradise Regained.* This reading is completely in keeping not only with Milton's personally mined Biblical sources but also with the received interpretative tradition of the early Christians, the medieval scholastics, and Renaissance reformers. Understanding the shared identity of the Sons of God in Milton's epics is not only important for grasping the power of Milton's answer to the big question in *Paradise Regained* but also has broader implications for the shared thesis of *Paradise Regained* and *Paradise Lost,* which is that God has the right to rule all of his Sons.

In John Milton's second edition of *Paradise Lost* (1674), the archangel Michael provides a vision for fallen Adam that depicts in encompassing detail the many consequences brought by Adam's fall upon the descendants of Adam and Eve.[4] Michael places drops "from the well of life" in Adam's eyes which enable Adam to see distant

[4] All references to *Paradise Lost* are taken from *John Milton,* Paradise Lost*: The Biblically Annotated Edition*, ed. Matthew Stallard (Macon: Mercer University Press, 2011).

future events.[5] After beholding the pitiful plight of his many children who contend with ageing, death, disease, and violence, Adam tearfully repents. In the third visionary episode which is drawn from Genesis 6.1–4,[6] Adam is presented with the following educational scene:

> After these,
> But on the hither side, a different sort
> From the high neighboring hills, which was their seat,
> Down to the plain descended; by their guise
> Just men they seemed, and all their study bent
> To worship God aright, and know his works
> Not hid; nor those things last, which might preserve
> Freedom and peace to men; they on the plain
> Long had not walked, when from the tents, behold
> A bevy of fair women, richly gay
> In gems and wanton dress; to the harp they sung
> Soft amorous ditties, and in dance came on:
> The men, though grave, eyed them; and let their eyes
> Rove without rein; till, in the amorous net
> Fast caught, they liked; and each his liking chose;
> And now of love they treat till the evening-star

---

[5] *Paradise Lost* 11.416.

[6] Genesis 6.1–4: "So when men beganne to be multiplied vpon the earth, and there were daughters borne vnto them, Then the sonnes of God sawe the daughters of men that they were faire, & they tooke them wiues of all that they liked. Therefore the Lord saide, My Spirit shall not alway striue with man, because he is but flesh, and his dayes shalbe an hundreth & twentie yeeres. There were gyants in the earth in those dayes: yea, and after that the sonnes of God came vnto the daughters of men, and they had borne them children, these were mightie men, which in olde time were men of renoume" (Geneva Bible, 1560). In the editorial preface of my edition of *Paradise Lost,* I argue that the 1560 Geneva Bible was the translation preferred by John Milton in the composition of the poem (vii–xxxvi). That these scriptures culled from the Genesis account are the source for Milton's postlapsarian "Sons of God" incident is generally conceded by Miltonists.

Love's harbinger appeared; then all in heat
They light the nuptial torch, and bid invoke
Hymen, then first to marriage rights invoked;
With feast and music all the tents resound.[7] (11.573–92)

Adam, who has just previously witnessed the graphic presentation of traumatizing scenes of murder and death by disease, is cheered up and encouraged by this panorama of courtship, marriage, and celebration. Michael makes no attempt to prepare Adam for each episodic vignette. Events play out before Adam's eyes, but the names of players are not provided. Adam cannot hide his enthusiasm for the anonymous "bevy of fair women" and "just men" in this joyous tableau. He says to Michael: "much better seems this vision, and more hope / of peaceful days portends, than those two past."[8] To Adam's surprise and chagrin, Michael rebukes and corrects Adam. According to the stern warrior angel, all is not what it seems. Pulling back the veil, Michael turns expositor of bad news and explains that the "grave men" are special and that "the bevy of fair women" are wicked. The identity of the women is not in doubt. Michael reveals "those tents thou saw'st so pleasant, were the tents / of wickedness, wherein shall dwell his race / who slew his brother."[9] In context, Adam has just witnessed the graphic murder of Abel by Cain: "[Cain] smote him into the midriff with a stone / that beat out life; he fell; and, deadly pale, / groaned out his soul with gushing blood effused."[10] Clearly, the women are descendants of Cain, but who are the men? Michael provides additional details:

To these [female descendants of Cain] that sober race of men,
  whose lives
Religious titled them the Sons of God,
Shall yield up all their virtue, all their fame

[7] *Paradise Lost* 11.573–92.

[8] *Paradise Lost* 11.599–600.

[9] *Paradise Lost* 11.607–09.

[10] *Paradise Lost* 11.445–46.

Ignobly, to the trains and to the smiles
Of these fair atheists, and now swim in joy,
Erelong to swim at large; and laugh, for which
The world erelong a world of tears must weep.[11]

Michael differentiates these "grave men" from all other humans by calling them "Sons of God." Who are these "Sons of God"? This question has received many disparate and thoughtful answers.

If one consults the popular modern editions of *Paradise Lost*, there appears to be little doubt and certainly no controversy as to the identity of these "men of a different sort": the "Sons of God" are descendants of Adam and Eve's third son Seth. Who exactly is Seth? What is known of him from the Biblical sources? Details in the Biblical narrative regarding Seth, however, are scant.[12] Nonetheless, Flannagan confidently glosses 11.576: "The men are the 'Sons of Seth,' or 'Sethites,' not the descendants of Cain."[13] Hughes declares: "A tradition stemming from Genesis 6.2–4, represents the sons of Seth as de-

---

[11] *Paradise Lost* 11.621–27.

[12] The following is a comprehensive list of all Biblical references to Seth in Genesis as translated by Robert Alter (*The Five Books of Moses: A Translation with Commentary*. New York: Norton, 2004). Genesis 4.25, 26: "And Adam again knew his wife and she bore a son and called his name Seth, as to say, 'God has granted me other seed in place of Abel, for Cain has killed him.' As for Seth, to him, too, a son was born, and he called his name Enosh. It was then that the name of the Lord was first invoked." Genesis 5.3, 4: "And Adam lived a hundred and thirty years and he begot in his likeness by his image and called his name Seth. And the days of Adam after he begot Seth were eight hundred years, and he begot sons and daughters." Genesis 5.6–9: "And all the days Adam lived were nine hundred and thirty years. Then he died. And Seth lived a hundred and five years and he begot Enosh. And Seth lived after he begot Enosh eight hundred and seven years, and he begot sons and daughters. And all the days of Seth were nine hundred and twelve years. Then he died." Seth is included in the genealogies found in the Hebrew history of 1 Chronicles 1.1 and in the Christian Greek scriptures at Luke 3.38. There is not much in the way of substance in any of the foregoing references aside from Seth's being born, begetting, and dying. There is nothing here to sustain the assumptive designation "Sons of God" for his immediate progeny.

[13] Roy Flannagan, *The Riverside Milton* (Boston: Houghton Mifflin, 1998), 677.

servedly called the "Sons of God" until they were lured from their mountain homes to marry and beget a giant race on the daughters of Cain."[14] The modern editors do not waiver in their determination that the "Sons of God" are "Sethites."[15] Likewise, Miltonist commentators have amassed an overwhelming consensus of published scholarly opinion in support of this view.[16]

I must write, however, from the enemy camp by suggesting an alternative reading of the "Sons of God." I would like to unimaginatively assert that the "Sons of God," are indeed, "Sons of God." More specifically, they are the angelic "Sons of God." I will make my case for this understanding of the text by addressing the following questions: 1) What is the exegetical history of reading the "Sons of God" in the book of Genesis as either angels or Sethites? That is to ask, is this a fanciful leap to suppose that the "Sons of God" are angels or is there solid precedent for this assertion in the pages of theological history? 2) Why has the Sethite reading of *Paradise Lost* prevailed so pervasively and conclusively in recent editions and commentary? 3) Why might an "angelic" reading provide a viable and rational alternative approach to this rich yet thorny text? 4) Finally, what are the potential critical ramifications of such a reading?

Genesis 6.1-4: Angels

With the emergence of "document theory" at the end of the nineteenth century, schools of Higher Criticism came to recognize that Genesis 6.1-4 should be understood as the product of a single author. Whereas much of Genesis bears the earmarks of compilation, these

---

[14] Merritt Y. Hughes, *John Milton: Complete Poems and Major Prose* (New York: Odyssey, 1957), 446.

[15] See also: Gordon Teskey, ed., *Paradise Lost: A Norton Critical Edition* (New York: Norton, 2004); Alastair Fowler, ed., *Milton: Paradise Lost*, 2nd ed. (New York: Longman, 2006); Barbara K. Lewalski, ed., *John Milton: Paradise Lost* (New York: Wiley-Blackwell, 2007).

[16] Jameela Lares, *A Variorum Commentary on The Poems of John Milton*, Vol 5 Part 8, "*Paradise Lost* Books 11–12" Ed. Paul J. Klemp (Pittsburg: Duquesne University Press, 2012) 135–138.

four verses are conceded to belong intact, as they are, to a particular originary redactor or text known as "J-1." Bissel places these four verses of text between the genealogy from Adam to Japheth found at Genesis 5.1–32 known as "P" and the beginning of the Noah story at Genesis 6.5–8 known as "J."[17] Therefore, it is appropriate to examine these verses as a group and does not corrupt the interpretative possibilities to do so. Whereas it is now a commonplace to accept that there is something distinct and different in the style of this insertion of the "J-1" fragment in Genesis 6.1–4, many readers of antiquity likewise take note of the unusual character of these verses for manifold reasons and comment upon them and speculatively expand the contexts.

The ancient Jewish apocryphal and pseudepigraphal book of *Enoch,*[18] recounts in what amounts to a thorough exegesis of Genesis chapter 6 "the descent of angels to take human wives" during the "days of Jared," a fifth-generation descendant of Adam, before the Flood.[19] The father of Noah, Lamech, suspects that his suspiciously strong and robust newborn son could be the product of a sexual dalliance between his wife Bitenosh and a sexually promiscuous fallen angel:

> Then I decided that the conception was at the hands of Watchers,[20] that the seed had been planted by Holy Ones or Nephil[im…] I was in a turmoil because of this infant. Then

---

[17] Edwin Cone Bissel, *Genesis Printed in Colors Showing the Original Sources from Which It Is Supposed to Have Been Compiled with An Introduction* (Hartford: Belknap and Warfield, 1892) 6.

[18] Found among the some 972 fragments of the so-called "Dead Sea Scrolls" discovered from 1946–1956 near Kirbet Qumran. For a complete discussion of the relationship between Milton's works and the Book of Enoch see Arnold Williams, "Milton and the *Book of Enoch*: An Alternative Hypothesis." *The Harvard Theological Review* 33/4 (1940): 291–99

[19] Michael Wise, Martin Abegg, and Edward Cook, ed., *The Dead Sea Scrolls: A New Translation* (London: Harper Collins, 1996) 77.

[20] Neil Forsyth provides a full treatment of the historic tradition of the "watchers" as angels in *The Old Enemy: Satan and the Combat Myth* (Princeton: Princeton University Press, 1987) 349–58.

> I, Lamech, hurriedly went into my wi[fe], by the Lord, the Great One, by the King of all Et[ernity [...] have you conceived] [by one of] the Sons of Heaven? Tell me every detail truthfully [...] [in truth] make it known to me, without lies. Was this [...] by the King of Eternity. You are to speak with me in utter truth, without lies.[21]

The fragment 4Q180-181 that was retrieved from the West Bank caves and which is believed to be a portion of a much longer Jewish predestinarian work known as *The Ages of the World* broadens the context of Genesis 6.1–4 and 1 Enoch 6–11 by naming specific angels who corrupt humanity: "The prophetic interpretation concerning Azazel and the angels wh[o went in to the daughters of man,] [so that] they bore mighty men to them. And concerning Azazel [who taught them] [to love] iniquity and caused them to inherit wickedness all."[22] Another fragmental clutch of texts known as *The Book of the Giants*, 1Q23 Frag.1+6, indicates that these angels also engaged in bestiality and selected certain animals to detain for this purpose: [two hundred] donkeys, two hundred asses, two hundred [...] rams of the flock, two hundred goats, two hundred [...beast of the] field from every animal, from every [bird...] [...] for miscegenation."[23] In a manuscript that is in particularly poor condition, the anonymous redactor records that this sexual activity with animals produces monstrous offspring in addition to the "giants" stipulated in the Genesis narrative:

> [...] they defiled[...] [...they begot] giants and monsters[...] [...] they begot, and behold, all [the earth was corrupted...] [...] with its blood and by the hand of [...] [giants] which did not suffice for them and [...] [...] and they were seeking to devour many [...] [...] they would arise [...] lacking true knowledge [...] because [...] [...] the earth]grew corrupt...] mighty [...] [...] they were considering [...] [...] from the

21 *The Dead Sea Scrolls: A New Translation,* (Jubilees 4:22) 76.

22 *The Dead Sea Scrolls: A New Translation,* 238–39.

23 *The Dead Sea Scrolls: A New Translation,* 247.

> angels upon [...] [...] in the end it will perish and die [...] [...] they caused great corruption in the [earth...] [... this did not] suffice to [...] they will be [...][24]

The Book of Jubilees or *Leptogenesis,* the oldest extant copies of which date to 100 BCE, tells a similar tale: "By the tenth generation, Adam's race had hugely increased. Lacking female company, the angels known as "Sons of God" found wives among the lovely daughters of men."[25]

It is possible, but not certain, that the Christian Greek Scriptures of the Bible refer to this incident with the "Sons of God." The author of 1 Peter speaks of "the spirits[26] that are in prison which were in time passed disobedient, when once the long suffering of God abode in the dayes of Noe, while the Arke was preparing, wherein fewe, that is, eight soules were saued in the water."[27] Jude writes of "the Angels also which kept not their first estate, but left their owne habitation, hee hath reserued in euerlasting chaines vnder darkenesse vnto the iudgement of the great day."[28] Although no certainty of meaning can be attached to the verses in 1 Peter and Jude, both New Testament epistles curiously resonate with the narrative of angels assuming the guise of men by acting "in times past disobedient" during "the days of Noe" "which kept not their first estate, but left their own habitation."

Flavius Josephus clearly understands the "Sons of God" to be angels who forsake heaven to cohabitate with women. His musings permit us to view Noah fearfully working to counteract the iniquitous environment nourished and fostered by the angel's influence in the days before the Flood:

---

[24] *The Dead Sea Scrolls: A New Translation*, 248.

[25] Robert Graves and Raphael Patai, *Hebrew Myths: The Book of Genesis* (Garden City: Doubleday, 1963), 100.

[26] To render ἄγγελων as "spirits" is not justifiable. Clearly, the sense is "angels" here.

[27] 1 Peter 3.19, 20, Geneva Bible 1560.

[28] Jude 6, Geneva Bible 1560.

> For many angels of God accompanied with women, and begat sons that proved unjust, and despisers of all that was good, on account of the confidence they had in their own strength; for the tradition is, that these men did what resembled the acts of those whom the Grecians call giants. But Noah was very uneasy at what they did; and, being displeased at their conduct, persuaded them to change their dispositions and their acts for the better; —but, seeing that they did not yield to him, but were slaves to their wicked pleasures, he was afraid they would kill him, together with his wife and children, and those they had married; so he departed out of the land.[29]

For centuries, rabbinic scholars have shown great interest in this portion of Genesis (see Appendix A of Genesis 6:1–4 in the Masoretic Text). Robert Graves provides an exhaustive account of various rabbinical interpretations of this frequently debated text and points to a number of readings from the midrash tradition that support the signification of angels in the text: "By the tenth generation, Adam's race had hugely increased. Lacking female company, the angels known as 'Sons of God' found wives among the lovely Daughters of Men."[30] Although this take on Genesis chapter 6 is not the only interpretative option in play among early Rabbi commentators, it is widespread in the *midrashim*. The *Yalqut Shimoni* compiled by R. Shimeon Hadarshan during the first half of the thirteenth century CE provides names for many of these fallen angels such as "Shemhazai" and "Azael" who plead with God to be permitted to descend to the earth to dwell in order to "sanctify [God's] name." They are indulged to go to earth but are "at once overcome by lust" and father "two monstrous sons named Hiwa and Hiya, each of whom daily [eat] a thousand camels, a thousand horses and a thousand oxen."[31]

---

[29] William Whiston, trans., *The Works of Josephus Complete and Unabridged*. "The Antiquities of the Jews." 1748. (Peabody; Hendrickson, 1988) 3.1.73, 74.

[30] Graves, 100.

[31] Graves, 100.

Early Patristic theologians also devoted considerable discussion of the Genesitic "Sons of God," and many of them favored a seraphic interpretation[32] (See Appendix B for the Greek *Septuagint* text). In commenting upon these verses in 160 CE, Justin Martyr claims, "The angels transgressed this appointment and were captivated by love of women. And they begat children."[33] Ireneus, writing about 180 CE, explains that God is compelled to bring the Noachian Flood in order to destroy the hybrid and reproductively sterile monstrous offspring of angels and humans: "In the days of Noah, he justly brought on the Deluge for the purpose of extinguishing that most infamous race of men then existent, who could not bring forth fruit to God. For the angels who sinned had commingled with them."[34] Clement of Alexandria was also of the same mind. Writing about 190 CE in *Christ the Educator* he declares: "The mind is led astray by pleasure, and the virgin center of the mind, if not disciplined by the Word, degenerates into licentiousness and reaps disintegration as reward for its transgressions. An example of this for you is the angels who forsook the beauty of God for perishable beauty and fell as far as heaven is from the earth."[35]

Commenting upon the Genesis account at the threshold of the second century, Tertullian (160–220 CE) credits the fallen angels with teaching the metallurgic arts and other refinements to humans.

> Those angels who invented them [jewelry, etc.] are assigned under condemnation to the penalty of death. They are the

---

[32] For African and Near-Eastern clerics no interpretation of the *Septuagint* text was required because the Alexandrine *Septuagint* does not render Genesis 6:3 from the Hebrew with οἱ υἱοὶ τοῦ θεοῦ (the sons of God). Rather, the Alexandrine text employs οἱ ἄγγελοι (the angels). See *The Septuagint Version of the Old Testament with an English Translation and with Various Readings and Critical Notes* (Grand Rapids: Zondervan, 1970).

[33] *The Ante-Nicene Fathers* (ed. Alexander Roberts and James Donaldson; 1885–1887; repr. 10 Vols. Peabody: Hendrickson, 1994), 1.190.

[34] *The Ante-Nicene Fathers*, 1.516.

[35] *Fathers of the Church: A New Translation* (Washington, D.C.: Catholic University of America Press, 1947) 3.2.14.

> same angels who rushed from heaven on the daughters of men [...]. If it is true, they laid bare the operations of metallurgy, divulged the natural properties of herbs, promulgated the powers of enchantments, and traced out every curiosity, even to the interpretation of the stars. They conferred appropriately—and as it were peculiarly—upon women that instrumental means of womanly ostentation: the radiances of jewels, [...] the dyes of orchil with which wools are dyed, and that black powder itself with which the eyelids and eyelashes are made prominent.[36]

Interestingly, in Tertullian's interpretative construal, he lays emphasis upon the corrupting influence of the angels whereas Milton seems to suggest that the Cainite women lured the angelic "Sons of God."[37] Magic seems to have played a role in these seductions: "I lay down this one proposition: that those angels, the deserters from God, the lovers of women, were likewise the discovers of this curious art of astrology. And on that account, they were also condemned by God [...]. For we know the mutual alliance of magic and astrology."[38] Regardless of the potency of the uncanny power wielded by these fallen angels to disarm the unwary "Daughters of Men," Tertullian insists that the angels were not typically drawn to chaste virgins: "If it is on account of the angels—those whom we read of as having fallen from God and from heaven because of lusting after females—we can presume that such angels yearned after bodies that were already defiled and were relics of human lust."[39]

Commodianus, writing about 240 CE, also suggests that the angels were perhaps unwittingly captivated by the beauty of women but could not return to heaven after forming ill-joined unions and promulgating a race of tempestuous gargantuan hybrids:

---

[36] *The Ante-Nicene Fathers*, 4.14, 15.

[37] *Paradise Lost* 11.581–97.

[38] *The Ante-Nicene Fathers*, 3.65.

[39] *The Ante-Nicene Fathers*, 4.32.

> Such was the beauty of women that it turned the angels aside. As a result, being contaminated, they could not return to heaven. Being rebels from God, they uttered words against Him. Then the Highest uttered His judgment against them. And from their seed, giants are said to have been born. By them, arts were made known in the earth. They taught the dyeing of wool and everything that is done. When they died, men erected images to them.[40]

It would seem that even if these angels desired to repent, the way to heaven is closed to them after engaging in forbidden intimacies with humans. Commodianus postulates that the angels could not help themselves "such was the beauty of the women."

Julius Africanus does not seem as confident in his assessment that the "Sons of God" are angels, but he is intent on covering his discursive bases. He speculates in 245 CE:

> When men multiplied on the earth, the angels of heaven came together with the daughters of men. In some copies, I found "the Sons of God." [...] However, if it is thought that these refer to angels, we must take them to be those who deal with magic and sorcery, who taught the women the motions of the stars and the knowledge of things celestial. By the power of those angels, they conceived the giants as their children, by whom wickedness reached its peak on earth. Finally, God decreed that the whole race of the living should perish in their impiety by the deluge.[41]

In the same manner as his theological precursors, Julius Africanus insists that the angels directly promoted wickedness in human society, encouraged debauchery, practiced debasing magic, and perpetrated acts of egregious and senseless violence. Likewise, their degenerate offspring follow the poor example of their fathers, bringing

[40] *The Ante-Nicene Fathers*, 4.203.

[41] *The Ante-Nicene Fathers*, 6.131

ruin to that antediluvian civilization, through their wicked offspring. Therefore, God brings the Flood.

Not all the Ante-Nicene fathers, however, agree with this assessment that the angels were universal corrupters in the pre-Deluge world. Lactantius, writing c.304–313 CE, maintains that the angels were not lured to earth by beauty, nor were they drawn out by their own selfish longings, but rather, they came to earth because they were dispatched on a noble divinely sanctioned mission to edify debased human society.

> God, in His foresight, sent angels for the protection and improvement of the human race—lest the devil [...] should either corrupt or destroy men through his subtlety. Since He had given these angels a free will, He admonished them above all things not to defile themselves with contamination from the earth and thus lose the dignity of their heavenly nature [...]. However, while the angels lived among men, that most deceitful ruler of the earth, by his very association, gradually enticed them to vices and polluted them through sexual relations with women. Thereafter, not being admitted into heaven because of the sins into which they had plunged themselves, they fell to the earth.[42]

Lactantius does not clarify who is meant by "the most deceitful ruler of the earth." Whether this is Satan or an unruly human is mere conjecture. It is also not clear as to why this episode should provide a favorable measure for God's "foresight." The results, however, are the same: the ethereal Sons of God have sexual relations with women.

Into the early fourth century, the angel reading of Genesis 6.1–4 remained the dominant interpretation, although new peculiar details begin to creep into the traditional narrative. Consider, for example, the pseudonymous work *Disputation of Archelaus and Manes* composed around 320 CE: "Certain of the angels, refusing to submit themselves to the commandment of God, resisted His will. And one

---

[42] *The Ante-Nicene Fathers*, 7.64

of them indeed fell like a flash of lightning upon the earth, while others, harassed by the dragon, sought pleasure in sexual relations with the daughters of men, and thus brought on themselves the deserved recompense of the punishment of eternal fire.[43] Certainly, this author feels compelled to join the imagery of Luke's Gospel and Revelation with the account of the Genesis "fall" of the "Sons of God."[44] Why exactly fleeing from "the Dragon" would fire up cherubic sex drives is not explicitly stated, nor is "the Dragon" precisely identified who seems in this reckoning to be a fully separate entity from Satan who "falls like lightning from the heavens."

By the mid-fourth century CE, the angelic reading of Genesis 6 is a firmly entrenched exegetical assumption and is earnestly endorsed by Ambrose (340–397 CE) in his treatise *On Noah*: "'The giants (Nephilim) were on the earth in those days.' The author of the divine Scripture does not mean that those giants must be considered, according to the tradition of poets, as sons of the earth but asserts that those whom he defines with such a name because of the extraordinary size of their body were generated by angels and women."[45]

In summation, the view that the "Sons of God" of Genesis 6 are angels is evidently pervasive among the Apostolic fathers of the Church. Many others could be named who likewise endorse this reading include Origen,[46] Cyprian,[47] and Athenagoras.[48] More than

---

[43] *The Ante-Nicene Fathers*, 6.205.

[44] "I watched Satan fall like lightning from heaven" (Luke 10.18, The New Jerusalem Bible). "Then a second sign appeared in the sky: there was a huge red dragon with seven heads and ten horns, and each of the seven heads crowned with a coronet. Its tail swept a third of the stars from the sky and hurled them to the ground [...] "And now war broke out in heaven, when Michael with his angels attacked the dragon. The dragon fought back with his angels, but they were defeated and driven out of heaven. The great dragon, the primeval serpent, known as the devil or Satan, who had led all the world astray, was hurled down to the earth and his angels were hurled with him" (Revelation 12:3,4,7–9, The New Jerusalem Bible).

[45] J. P. Migne, ed., *Patrologia Latina*. 221 vols. (Paris: Migne, 1844–1864), 14.385.

[46] Thomas Heywood, *The hierarchie of the blessed angels Their names orders and offices the fall of Lucifer with his angels* (London: Islip, 1635).

that, it becomes the *status quo* reading of the Genesis account for many centuries. Arnold Williams observes that in the early Church this view was "apparently popular" and "the 'sons of God' were understood to be angels, and the sin by which they fell was thus lust."[49]

Many modern commentators, translators, and Bible annotators have also understood Genesis 6:1–4 in this way. In his translation of the *Pentateuch,* Robert Alter retains the wording "Sons of God," and suggests that the narrative of divine beings comingling with humans deserves a wider and more spacious contextualization:

> The idea of male gods coupling with mortal women whose beauty ignites their desire is a commonplace of Greek myth, and E. A. Speiser has proposed that both the Greek and the Semitic stories may have a common source in the Hittite traditions of Asia Minor. The entourage of celestial beings obscurely implied in God's use of the first-person plural in the Garden story (compare 3:22) here produces, however fleetingly, active agents in the narrative. As with the prospect that man and woman might eat from the tree of life, God sees this intermingling of human and divine as the crossing of a necessary line of human limitation, and He responds by setting a new retracted limit [...] In any case, the notion of semidivine [...] touches on common ground with Greek and other mythologies.[50]

Alter makes it abundantly clear that he considers the "Sons of God" to be not of this earth and places them within a tradition of "gods" who seek out the company of women. It is not presumptuous to detect the prominent common threads linking Near Eastern and Grecian mythologies. The ancient Hebrews were not entirely isolated and immune to these religio-cultural influences.

---

[47]*Corpus Christianorum.* Series Latina. (Turnhout: Brepols, 1953), 3.204.

[48] J.P. Migne, ed., *Patrologia Graeca.* 166 vols. (Paris: Migne, 1857–1886), 7.1093.

[49] Arnold Williams, *The Common Expositor: An Account of the Commentaries on Genesis, 1527–1633* (Chapel Hill: University of North Carolina Press, 1948), 117.

[50] Robert Alter, 38–39.

The English Tanakh translation of the Hebrew scriptures also emphasizes that these "Sons of God" are not from the earth. Instead of "Sons of God," it curiously translates "the divine beings saw how beautiful the daughters of men were" and "the divine beings cohabited with the daughters of men."[51] "Divine beings" seem much less likely to be confused with humans, or at least the rendering underscores the degree of the gulf of difference between the two. Robert Davidson also favors the rendering "divine beings" and further argues for the disambiguation of the Genesis Text:

> This section is one of the strangest passages in the whole of the Old Testament [...] From the time of the Aramaic Targums onwards, misplaced piety has led commentators to side-step the plain meaning of the text. Attempts have been made to explain the sons of the gods as nobility or royalty or the true worshippers of God. By all Old Testament analogy the sons of the gods can only mean one thing, divine beings [...] Further, the daughters of men cannot mean anything other than mortal women. Such stories of sexual intercourse between gods and mortal women are common enough in religious mythology. In Canaanite mythology, as it is known to us from the Ugaritic texts, El, the supreme god, seduces two women and begets the twin gods Dawn and Evening.[52]

Charles Laymon similarly suggests that the "Sons of God" must of linguistic necessity be "gods" of sorts, and he also produces an explanation for why the children generated with the "daughters of men" were described as "giants."

---

[51] *Tanakh, The Holy Scriptures: The New Jewish Publications Society Translation According to the Traditional Hebrew Text* (Philadelphia: Jewish Publications Society, 1985), 10.

[52] Robert Davidson, "Genesis 1–11." *The Cambridge Bible Commentary.* Ed. P. R. Ackroyd, A. R. C. Leaney, and J. W. Packer, 70 vols. (Cambridge: Cambridge University Press, 1973), 69.

> The J source now emphasizes the cosmic nature of man's fall: the heavenly beings [...] wantonly marry mortal women. The text of vs 4, the interpretation of which is not entirely clear, seems to imply that the gods married existing gigantic earthly women and that these marriages produced the mighty men (heroes) of saga and legend i.e. demigods of gigantic size and superhuman strength.[53]

The annotations in modern Catholic Bibles often reaffirm the cherubic reading of Genesis 6:1–4. Consider the New American Bible's commentary:

> This is an apparent fragment of an old legend that had borrowed much from ancient mythology. The sacred author incorporates it here, not only in order to account for the prehistoric giants of Palestine, whom the Israelites called the Nephilim, but also to introduce the story of the flood with a moral orientation—the constantly increasing wickedness of mankind. [...] The sons of heaven: literally "the sons of the gods" or "the sons of God," i.e., the celestial beings of mythology.[54]

The New Jerusalem Bible underscores the earnestness of the author's literal presentation of the narrative in the Genesis J-1 fragment and the subsequent influence of this passage in theological thought:

> An obscure passage (from the Yahwistic tradition). The author uses a popular story of a race of giants, in Hebr. Nephilim, the Titans of eastern legend, born of the union be-

---

53 Charles M. Laymon, ed., *The Interpreter's One-Volume Commentary on the Bible: Introduction and Commentary for Each Book of the Bible Including the Apocrypha with General Articles* (Nashville: Abingdon, 1971), 153.

54 *Saint Joseph Edition of the New American Bible Translated from the Original Languages with Critical Use of All the Ancient Sources Including the Revised New Testament Authorized by the Board of Trustees of the Confraternity of Christian Doctrine and Approved by the Administrative Committee Board of the National Conference of Catholic Bishops and the United States Catholic Conference* (New York: Catholic Book Publishing, 1970), 8.

> tween gods and mortals. The author does not present this episode as a myth nor, on the other hand, does he deliver judgment on its actual occurrence; he records the anecdote of a superhuman race simply to serve as an example of the increase in human wickedness which was to provoke the Flood. Later Judaism and almost all the earliest ecclesiastical writers identify the 'sons of God' with the fallen angels.[55]

In light of modern scholarship, Gerhard Von Rad considers the historic debate surrounding the identity of the "Sons of God" to be definitively resolved.

> The question, which has been asked from the time of the early church down to our own day, whether, namely, the "sons of God" are to be understood as angelic beings or as men, i.e., as members of "the superior human race of Seth," can be considered finally settled. The *bene ha 'elohim,* here, by the way clearly contrasted to the daughters of men, are beings of the upper heavenly world. The ben ("son") describes them, however as sons of God, not in the physical genealogical sense, i.e., mythologically, but generally as belonging to the world of the Elohim (cf. as *bene hannebi'im,* disciples of the prophets II Kings 2.3,5,7). These angelic beings let themselves be enticed by the beauty of human women to grievous sin; they fall from their ranks and mix with them in wild licentiousness [...] For these giants were, of course, the children of that marriage of heavenly beings with human women.[56]

The tradition of reading the "Sons of God" as angels is one with a long history and tradition. Rabbinical scholars examine the text with this lens; the majority of the Patristics put faith in this narrative; many respected modern scholars continue to endorse the reasonable-

---

[55] *The New Jerusalem Bible* (New York: Doubleday, 1985), 25.

[56] Gerhard Von Rad, *Genesis: A Commentary* (Philadelphia: Westminster, 1972). 114–15.

ness and validity of such a reading. However, if this is such an obvious reading, why and in what manner did the rival Sethite tradition of exegesis emerge?

Genesis 6.1-4: Sethites

In the Pirqe Rabbi Eliezer, one of the oldest formal non-Biblical histories of the nation of Israel, the story of the Sethites as "Sons of God" is vividly expounded. Although the work is attributed to Rabbi Eliezer ben Hyrcanos (c.90–130 CE), it most certainly belongs to a later age, perhaps the eighth or ninth century CE. In this midrash that focuses on God and his creation, the "Sons of God" are "pious descendants of Seth, and the daughters of Men sinful descendants of Cain." The Rabbi relates that "when Abel died childless, mankind soon divides into two tribes: namely the Cainites who, apart from Enoch, were wholly evil, and the Sethites who were wholly righteous."[57]

> These Sethites inhabited a sacred mountain in the far north, near the Cave of Treasure—some take it for Mount Hermon. The Cainites lived apart in a valley to the westward. Adam, on his deathbed, ordered Seth to separate his tribe from the Cainites; and each Sethite patriarch publicly repeated this order, generation after generation. The Sethites were extraordinarily tall, like their ancestor; and, by living so close to the Gate of Paradise, won the name "Children of God."[58]

This midrash seems to represent a minority viewpoint among Jewish scholars even in the Middle Ages, and certainly does not reflect the more popular angel reading that predominated during the lifetime of its first-century putative compiler Rabbi Eliezer ben Hyrcanos. As early as the second century CE, the author of the *Genesis Rabba*, Rabbi Shimon ben Yohai, "since he never married or consorted with any female whatsoever [...] felt obliged to curse all who read

---

[57] The geography of this account is significant when compared with *Paradise Lost* 11.575–76: "From the high neighboring hills, which was their seat, / down to the plain descended."

[58] Graves, 102.

'Sons of God' in the Ugaritic sense […] Josephus's view, that the Sons of God were angels, survived for several centuries despite Shimon ben Yohai's curse."[59] Many eighth-century Rabbis still clung to the angel reading, perhaps with some misgivings, despite the changing critical tide. For example, Rabbi Eliezer places in a midrash: "The angels who fell from Heaven saw the daughters of Cain perambulating and displaying their secret parts, their eyes painted with antimony in the manner of harlots; and, being seduced, took wives from among them."[60] Other Rabbis, such as Joshua ben Qorha who had a decidedly fundamentalist critical sensibility is concerned about the mechanical implications of a union between the ethereal and the physical. He worries: "Is it possible that angels, who are flaming fire, could have performed the sexual act without scorching their brides internally?" His solution: "When these angels fell from Heaven, their strength and stature were reduced to those of mortals, and their fire changed into flesh."[61]

Some among the Patristic Fathers adopt the view that the "Sons of God" are Sethites. Julius Africanus, mentioned earlier as a weak supporter of the angel reading, does not rule out the possibility of the Sethites being the "Sons of God." Just before settling on the angel reading, Julius claims:

> What the Spirit means, in my opinion, is that the descendents of Seth are called the sons of God, because of the righteous men and patriarchs who have sprung from him (even down to the Savior himself). However, the descendants of Cain are named the seed of men, as having nothing divine in them. Because of the wickedness of their race.[62]

Ephem the Syrian (306–373) was much surer of his Sethite understanding. In his *Commentary on Genesis*, he confidently declares:

---

[59] Graves, 104.

[60] Graves, 104.

[61] Graves, 105.

[62] *The Ante-Nicene Fathers*, 6.131.

> [Moses] called the sons of Seth "sons of God," those who, like the sons of Seth, had been called "the righteous people of God." The beautiful daughters of men whom they saw were the daughters of Cain who adorned themselves and became a snare to the eyes of the sons of Seth. Then Moses said, "they took to wife such of them as they chose," because when "they took" them, they acted over haughtily over those whom they chose. A poor one would exalt himself over the wife of a rich man, and an old man would sin with one who was young. The ugliest of all would act arrogantly over the most beautiful.[63]

Perhaps the strongest and furthest reaching voice that spoke in favor of the Sethites and effectively squashes the notion that the "Sons of God" could possibly be angels is Augustine (354–430 CE). In the *City of God,* he writes:

> All that we indubitably know, from the authentic Scripture in the Hebrew and Christian traditions, is the fact that in the period before the flood there were many giants, all of whom belonged to the earthly city in human society, and that there were sons of God descended from Seth who abandoned their holiness and sank down into this city of men. There is nothing surprising in the fact that giants could be from men like that. In any case, they were not all giants, even though there were more giants before the flood than in all subsequent ages. They served a divine purpose in that they reveal to anyone who is wise that mere bodily magnitude and might have no more value than bodily beauty.[64]

Yet Augustine concedes that he cannot fully discount the possibility that humans might be able to achieve a sexual union with incorporeal creatures on some level:

---

[63] *Fathers of the Church: A New Translation,* 91:134–35.

[64] *Fathers of the Church: A New Translation,* 14:475.

> However, the same trustworthy Scripture testifies that angels have appeared to men in such bodies as could not only be seen, but also touched. There is, too, a very general rumor, which many have verified by their own experience, or which trustworthy persons who have heard the experience of others corroborate, that sylvans and fauns, who are commonly called "incubi," had often made wicked assaults upon women and satisfied their lust upon them [...] I dare not determine whether there be some spirits embodied in an aerial substance for this element, even when agitated by a fan, is sensibly felt by the body, and who are capable of lust of mingling sensibly with women; but certainly I could by no means believe that God's holy angels could at that time have so fallen.[65]

Although Augustine lacks certainty about the feasibility of sexual union between spirits and humans, he is positively sure that the account in Genesis does not refer to such an incident. For Augustine, the "Sons of God" are indisputably the descendants of Seth. The impress of Augustine's remarks entirely transformed the reading of Genesis chapter 6 for subsequent commentators. The Sethite view became orthodoxy during the Middle Ages. Aquinas, Nicholas of Lyra, and Alphonso Tostado all accept the summary judgment of Augustine in this matter.[66]

During the Renaissance, most Reformation scholars seem to heartily embrace the position of Augustine. In an encompassing and definitive study of Renaissance era treatments and commentaries upon Genesis, Arnold Williams explains that in the early Church of the Patristics, "The Sons of God were understood to be angels, and the sin by they fell was lust." According to Williams, the Reformation expositors of Genesis are aware of this traditional reading, carefully

---

[65] Augustine, *The City of God*, trans. Marcus Dods (New York: Modern Library, 1993), 15.23.

[66] Don Cameron Allen, "Milton and the Sons of God," *Modern Language Notes* 61.2 (1946): 75.

weighed it, but ultimately rejected it. "Several of the commentators allude to this idea, but none accepts it seriously."[67]

In addition to upholding the Sethite reading of Genesis chapter 6, Luther provides some substantive justification for why humans might be called "Sons of God."

> But when Adam had died and the respect for the remaining patriarchs declined, the sons of God (that is, those who had the promise of the blessed Seed and belonged to the blessed Seed) also yearned for marriages and affinity with the ungodly race. Moses simply calls the sons of the patriarchs, to whom the promise of the Seed was given, "sons of God"; they were the true church. When they yielded to the seductions of the Cainite church, they also proceeded to gratify the desires of the flesh and to take wives from the Cainite race, likewise concubines, as many as they wanted and whomever they chose. Lamech and Noah observed this with grief; and for this reason, perhaps they married rather late.[68]

Luther, in typical form, reads this ancient incident in terms of what it might mean typologically for the Reformation church. In acknowledging that clerics of the past had at times read the "Sons of God" as angels, Luther launches into an anti-Semitic diatribe against the work of Jewish scholars of antiquity and the Middle Ages:

> Here, too, the Jews come up with a variety of foolish ideas. They describe the sons of God as incubi from which that notorious and ungodly race was begotten; they further maintain that the sons of God are given this name because of their nature. The less extreme among them, on the other

[67] Arnold Williams, 117.

[68] *Luther's Works*, "Lectures on Genesis Chapters 6-14," Vol.2 (Saint Louis: Concordia, 1960) 42.268.

> hand, prove these foolish ideas to be false and descrie the "sons of God" as the sons of the mighty.[69]

As much as he wants to dismiss the "foolish ideas" of the Jews and what he perceives as amounting to tales of "incubi," Luther is obviously reluctant to contradict Augustine.

> So far as incubi and succubi are concerned, I do not deny, but believe, that the devil may happen to be either a succubus or an incubus; for I have heard many relate their very own experiences. Augustine, too declares that he heard the same sort of story from trustworthy people whom he felt compelled to believe. It delights Satan if he can delude us by taking on the appearance either of a young man or of a woman. But that anything can be born from the union of a devil and a human being is simply untrue.[70]

The chief objections raised by Luther are that the tradition stems from rabbinical study, and that he rejects the notion that offspring could come from a union with a spirit creature. He does not, however, deny the ability of angels to materialize and take on human form of either "a young man or a young woman."

John Calvin similarly rejects the notion that the Genesis "Sons of God" could be angels in disguise as humans.

> Therefore it was filthie ingratitude, that the posteritie of Seth had mingled itself with the Cainites and with other prophane nations, because the same of his own free will deprived it selfe of the most pretious grace of God. This also was intolerable sacrilege, to pervert and confound the order appointed of God [...] But we must know that it is no light offence, to breake the difference and order which God hath appointed; and that it was a holy order and reverently to be imbraced, that the worshippers of God should be separated from wicked nations, that there might be a Church of God

---

69 *Luthers Works*, 42.270.

70 *Luther's Works*, 42.270.

> upon the earth. Thirdly, that the sicknesses were past cure, when men rejected the remedie which God had ordeyned [...] That old fable concerning the lying of angels with women, is sufficiently confuted with the absurditie thereof: and it is a marvell that learned men were bewitched in old time with such grosse and monstrous dreams [...] So that Moses doeth not therefore seclude the sonnes of God from the daughters of men, as though either nature or originall were not in either equall or alike: but bycause they were by adoption the sonnes of God whom he had chosen to himself.[71]

Calvin does not consider the physical improbabilities as a basis for his dismissal of the angel reading, but rather, he summarily dismisses the notion as "that old fable." He is also deeply concerned with the morality of separateness between the godly and the ungodly, and expands the application to "nations." It is clear that he has in mind "non-Calvinist" when he writes "ungodly."

The 1560 Geneva Bible marginal notes on Genesis 6.1–4 make clear the dominance of the Sethite reading. The main text of Genesis 6.2 reads "then the sonnes of God sawe the daughters of men that they were faire, & they tooke them wiues of all that they liked." The note on "sonnes of God" does not refer directly to Seth but it does clearly indicate human sons: "the children of the godly who began to degenerate." The "daughters of men" are noted as "Those that had wicked parents, as if from Cain." And the moral to be drawn from the behavior of "the godly who began to degenerate"? The Geneva notes indicate that the great misstep of "the godly" was in "having more respect for their beauty and worldly considerations than for their manners and godliness." The Calvinistic doctrine of separation from the "ungodly" is reaffirmed by this story.

---

[71] *A commentarie of Iohn Caluine, vpon the first booke of Moses called Genesis: translated out of Latine into English, by Thomas Tymme, minister* (London: Henry Middleton, 1578), 169.

Subsequent English reformers took other cues from Calvin's reading and made similar applications of the scripture. Gervase Babington Bishop of Llandaff (1550–1610) in his Genesis commentary of 1592 comments upon Genesis 6:2. "Wee see howe greeuous a thing vnequall marriages bee, when the godlye with the vngodly. All the beleeuing with the Infidels, the religious with the superstitious, are vnequally yoaked euen so greeuous to God, that for this cause especially the whole world was destroyed by the Flud."[72] Gervase calls this unequal yoking "a secret poison that destroyeth virtue more speedily then anye thing" and draws attention to the warning examples of righteous men who married unbelievers such as "Salomon," and "Iehosaphat's sonne."

Writing in 1602, Nicholas Gibbens asserts that the "Sons of God" could only refer to Sethites:

> Wherefore it remianeth onlie, by testimony of Scripture, and the authoritie and the iudgement of the most and chiefest fathers & interpreters, that these who are called the sons of God, were not other but the posteritie of the godly Patriarkes, of the line of Seth, who being brought vp in true religion, declined fro[m] the steps of their religious ancestors, and by ioyning in affinitie with the wicked, by taking the wiues of the familie of Cane, became to be partakers of their sins, and therefore shortly after of their punishment.

Like Calvin, Gibbens acknowledges that Church fathers saw matters differently, but he concludes that they were bamboozled.

> Certain it is, that diuers ancient writers, & the vulgar sort of the Church of Rome doe affirme, that these sons of God were Angels, vnto whom as faith Lactantius, God had committed the gouernment & defence of man, against the

[72] *Certain plaine, briefe, and comfortable notes vpon euerie chapter of Genesis gathered and laid downe for the food of them that are not able to vse better helps, and yet carefull to read the worde, and right heartily desirous to taste the sweete of it. By the Reuerend Father Geruase Babington, Bishop Landaph.* (London. 1592), 43.

> power & deceits of Sathan. But what proofe of scripture may be found to fauour this assertion[n]? What sufficient reason to confirme this exposition? It have ofte[n] bin reported that euill have had to doe with women, witches, and other notorious wicked persons; which with it be, but a false imagination onelie of a mind giuen up to Sathan, or whether it be done in deed, as it may seeme as possible, for a spirit to do, as to eate meat, whereof the Scripture faith, hee set before them and they did eate; it is not for us to handle this argument. But that spirits should take them wiues, and beget children in such wedlock, as the word importeth, or that the Elect Angels should sinne by lust, after they were confirmed by the Lord, is vtterlie against the truth of God, and to be expelled from the hearts of Christians.[73]

Gibbens, like his cautious English Reformation progenitors and contemporaries is careful not to deny too much. He will not assert that sexual union between a human and angel is an impossibility, but rather, his objection is grounded on the unshakeable belief that an angel in the manifest presence of God in heaven could not possible be drawn away into a carnal relationship with a mere human.

It is clear from the foregoing, the angelic interpretation of the "Sons of God" is part of a long-standing exegetical practice stemming from the earliest points of the Judeo-Christian critical tradition. It is also true that the Sethite reading became standard practice after Augustine and was strongly endorsed by the major figures of the Reformation and their English followers. Milton was aware of both strands of theology. Which of these theological underpinnings is in play in *Paradise Lost*?

---

[73] *Questions and disputations concerning the Holy Scripture wherein are contained, briefe, faithfull and sound expositions of the most difficult and hardest places: approued by the testimony of the Scriptures themselues; fully correspondent to the analogie of faith, and the consent of the Church of God; conferred with the iudgement of the fathers of the Church, and interpreters of God, is free from the errors and slanders of atheists, papists, philosophers, and all heretikes. The first part of the first tome. By Nicholas Gibbens, minister and preacher of the word of God.* (London: Felix Kyngston, 1602), 231.

The Sethite Reading of Paradise Lost Prevails (For Now…)

It is with good reason that Miltonists can confidently state that Milton was well versed in both the "angelic" and "Sethite" theological musings. In *Paradise Regained* (1671), the fallen angel Belial advises Satan to place the temptation of sex with women before Jesus as he fasts in the wilderness. Satan voices skepticism about the viability of success with such a temptation for Jesus. He suggests that Belial is too quick to assess the weaknesses of others by assuming that everyone possesses his own weaknesses. Satan brings up a time when Belial himself toyed with women:

> Belial, in much uneven scale thou weighst
> All others by thyself; because of old
> Thou thyself dot'st on womankind, admiring
> Thir shape, thir color, and attractive grace,
> None are, thou think'st, but taken with such toys.
> Before the Flood thou with thy lusty Crew,
> False titl'd Sons of God, roaming the Earth
> Cast wanton eyes on the daughters of men,
> And coupl'd with them, and begot a race.[74]

For centuries, it was commonly asserted in editions of *Paradise Lost* and commentaries, that Milton was again referring to the story of Genesis chapter 6.1–4. It was also noticed that Milton in *Paradise Regained* seems to indicate that that the "Sons of God" are to be understood to be rebel angels "False titl'd Sons of God, roaming the Earth / Cast wanton eyes on the daughters of men, / And coupled with them, and begot a race." Some Miltonists have expressed concern that Milton seems inconsistent if in *Paradise Lost* the Genesis "Sons of God" are Sethites but in *Paradise Regained* they are cast as angels. After emphasizing that both Calvin and Luther reject the angel reading, Allen argues that Milton must have favored the Sethite reading for *Paradise Lost*: "this was the state of the controversy in Milton's age, and we

[74] Merritt Y. Hughes, *Paradise Regained, John Milton: Complete Poems and Major Prose* (New York: Odyssey, 1957), 2.173–181.

can now understand why the unorthodox interpretation was placed in the mouth of Satan and the accepted interpretation made the basic motif of Adam's vision. Satan's remark is artistically suited to the greatest of heretics."[75] Note that Allen assumes that Milton must always be "orthodox." Allen accepts the earlier argument of McColley that Milton made use of both Genesis chapter 6 and the apocryphal fleshing out of the Biblical account in the *Book of Enoch* in crafting Satan's dialogue with Belial in *Paradise Regained*.[76]

In 1950, Robert H. West calls for a radical reassessment of *Paradise Regained* in which he argues that Milton is not at all referring to Genesis chapter 6 in *Paradise Regained*. Therefore, according to West, there is no inconsistency.

> But this is no contradiction of Milton's earlier orthodox "interpretation" of Genesis. On the contrary, it clearly says that the work of angels with women, though it took place, is wrongly connected with the Genesis passage. The angels who "begot a race" were not, as the Book of Enoch and the early Fathers have it, good angels who lost station in consequence but evil angels already fallen and not referred to in the Genesis passage at all.[77]

According to West, Belial and his crew have sex with women but are not "The Sons of God" mentioned in Genesis chapter 6. The crux of West's thesis of denial is that Satan calls Belial a "false titl'd son of God." So whereas he concedes that "in *Paradise Regained* Satan says flatly—and we have no reason in the logic of the story to doubt him—that Belial and his crew had both the will and the ability" to couple with women, "evidently 'Sons of God' is merely another name under which Belial and his crew have cloaked their amorous activi-

---

[75] Don Cameron Allen, "Milton and the Sons of God" *Modern Language Notes* 61.2 (1946), 76.

[76] See "The Book of Enoch and Paradise Lost," *The Harvard Theological Review* 31 (1938), 31–33.

[77] Robert H. West, "Milton's Sons of God" *Modern Language Notes* 65.3 (1950), 189.

ties."[78] West also maintains that by calling them "false tit'ld" Milton makes clear that he does not view them as such: "When Milton has Satan say that Belial is 'false titled' a son of God, he means that Belial is not a son of God and should not be confused with sons of God, though like those sons of God who were Seth's, he did couple with daughters of men."[79]

West's insistence that *Paradise Regained* does not refer in any way to Genesis chapter 6 and that *Paradise Lost* refers to Genesis chapter 6, but merely pertains to Sethites instead of angelic "Sons of God," has gone largely unchallenged. The broad acceptance of the West thesis is apparent in nearly all subsequent scholarship touching upon the matter. Writing in 1975, Walter MacKellar sums up what was considered the relevant scholarship of the time on *Paradise Regained* 2.178–81:

> Commentators have generally believed that in PL 11.574–92 Milton represents the Sons of God as the posterity of Seth, but that in the present passage he inconsistently makes them the fallen angels. About the meaning of the former passage there is no disagreement; but R. H. West [...] has convincingly shown that there is no conflict between the two passages, as Milton's deliberate qualification, "False titl'd" ought to have warned commentators. Belial and his associates have cloaked their amorous activities under the name of Sons of God, to which they have no right.[80]

Edward E. Ericson raises questions about West's and Allen's treatment of the "Sons of God" in *Paradise Regained.* Ericson accepts the current orthodoxy among Milton scholars that the "Sons of God" in *Paradise Lost* are Sethites, but he argues that the "Sons of God" in *Paradise Regained* are fallen angels from Genesis chapter 6. Ericson

---

[78] Robert H. West, 190–91.

[79] Robert H. West, *Milton and the Angels* (Athens: University of Georgia Press, 1955), 129.

[80] Walter MacKellar, *A Variorum Commentary on the Poems of John Milton, Paradise Regain*ed Vol 4 (New York: Columbia University Press, 1975), 117. West is the only scholar noted for these lines in the *Variorum.*

does not believe it is particularly important to address the fact that his reading suggests a Miltonic inconsistency. He offers, "One possibility is that Milton simply changed his mind. We know that he did so on certain other occasions."[81] Ericson's dissent about Belial's crew of angels in *Paradise Regained* did not make many influential waves. His essay is not at all mentioned in the most recent Milton *Variorum* on *Paradise Lost* Books 11–12.[82] Hughes edition of Milton's works provides this note on *Paradise Regained* 2.178–189: "The reference is not to the story in Gen. vi, 2 of the seduction of the sons of Seth by the daughters of Cain, which is told at length in PL XI, 573–627, but—as R. H. West shows [...] to the adventures of the fallen angels with fallen women."[83]

As to the precise timing when Belial and his "crew" must have engaged in sexual relations with women, West does not say and seems to ignore that Milton does say when:

> Before the Flood thou with thy lusty Crew,
> False tit'ld Sons of God, roaming the Earth
> Cast wanton eyes on the daughters of men,
> And coupled with them, and begot a race

Certainly, Belial's crew "before the Flood" proved unworthy to be known as "Sons of God" per their deeds, hence "false tit'ld" in the sense that they did not behave as true "Sons of God." At any rate, West does not provide a viable alternative for the when and where of Belial's deeds. If *Paradise Regained* is not referring to Genesis chapter 6, and the connections seem obvious, to what could Milton possibly be referring? Nonetheless, West insists that this incident is not connected with Genesis 6. In making this claim and through its wide acceptance, West effectively severs critics from the possible reading that both *Paradise Regained* and *Paradise Lost* refer to angelic "Sons of

---

[81] Edward E. Ericson, Jr., "The Sons of God in *Paradise Lost* and *Paradise Regained*" *Milton Quarterly* 25.3 (1991), 88.

[82] Jameela Lares, 135–138.

[83] Hughes, 498.

God." Taken in isolation without the Belial gloss in *Paradise Regained,* it is easy to conclude, and many scholars do, that reading the "Sons of God" episode as an angelic visitation is not a tenable position. I, however, would like to re-evaluate that stance and strongly assert that an angelic reading of *Paradise Lost* Book 11 is both defensible and sound.

The Case for an "Angelic Reading" of Paradise Lost 11.553–729

As indicated in the foregoing sections, there is a long-established tradition of reading the account at Genesis chapter 6 with an understanding that the "Sons of God" are angels or divine beings. That such a tradition was prevalent and dominant in centuries preceding the work of Augustine is not in dispute nor is it contestable that Milton knew these sources. Strong Miltonist advocates of the Sethite reading of *Paradise Lost* invariably acknowledge that when Milton was composing the narrative of Book 11 and arrived at the moment for the depiction of the "Sons of God," Milton had a choice: angels or Sethites.

Above all other considerations of textual influence in the poem, Milton is a Biblical poet. Ancient and Modern exegetes, as we have seen, read Genesis 6.1–4 as a story about angels. Knowing the profound influence that the Bible exerted upon Milton's thought and art, I argue that there is internal biblical support for the Sethite reading.

The account at Genesis 6.1–4 says nothing regarding the lines of Cain and Seth, and the Bible contains no information suggesting that God placed a prohibition upon the mixing of the families' bloodlines. There is also no corroborating evidence elsewhere in the Bible to make the case. Some exegetes have suggested that "daughters of men" contrast with "Sons of God" just as "sons of men" is sometimes used in the Bible to demonstrate an unfavorable contrast with Godly people. Although "sons of men" at times carries a negative connotation, this is not consistently the case.[84]

---

[84] See in nearly any consistent translation of the Bible Psalms 4.2; 57.4; Proverbs 8.22, 30,31; Jeremiah 32.18, 19; Daniel 10.16.

The very next occurrence in the traditional ordering of the books of the Bible of the expression "Sons of God" is in the book of Job. Here the phrase explicitly applies to angelic attendants in heaven and possibly even Satan. "Nowe on a day when the children of God came and stoode before the Lorde, Satan came also among them."[85] Another reference found in Job refers to the time when God created the Earth. No humans were present, to be sure, yet the account relates:

> Where wast thou when I layd the foundations of the earth? Declare, if thou hast
> vnderstanding. Who hath layd the measures thereof, if thou knowest? Or who
> hath stretched the line vpon it? Wherepuon are the foundations thereof fastened?
> Or who layd the corner stone thereof? When the morning starres sang together,
> and all the sonnes of God shouted for ioy.[86]

The Bible contains several examples of angels taking on human form and assuming the normal functions of humans including even eating and drinking.[87] At Matthew 22.30, Jesus indicates that in the resurrection, elevated humans would be like the angels who do not marry. This distinction clearly applies to the angels in their spirit forms, and also may explain why angels might be curious about human sexuality due to their not having biologically sexed spirit bodies. Jesus words in no way preclude the possibility that angels possess the capacity to assume human bodies and engage in sexual activity. In the book of Jude, a warning is given:

> The Angels also which kept not their first estate, but left their owne habitation, hee hath reserued in euerlasting

[85] Job 1.6, Geneva Bible 1560. See also Job 2.1. Milton references this event in *Paradise Regained* 1.368.
[86] Job 38.4–1, *Authorized Version* 1611
[87] See Genesis 18:1–22; 19:1–3.

> chaines vnder darkenesse vnto the iudgement of the great day. As Sodom and Gomorrhe, and the cities about them, which in like maner as they did, committed fornication, and followed strange flesh, are set foorth for an ensample, and suffer the vengeance of eternall fire.[88]

Jude indicates that the "Angels who left their first estate," which is to say heaven were under judgment. Why? Because like the humans of Sodom and Gomorrah "they committed fornication and followed strange flesh." This seems to be a reasonable reference to the activities of the angelic "Sons of God" who "fornicated" and pursued very "strange flesh" indeed prior to the Flood.

Clearly, Biblical contexts give weighty support to Milton's possible use of the trope of the "Sons of God" as angels. Given the strong Biblical possibility of this meaning, it would seem rather odd if Milton did not follow it in his depiction of Genesis in *Paradise Lost* Book 11. To not do so, would simply be un-Miltonlike. Milton consistently yields to the Bible's authority in such matters, and it would be a great deviation if he were to ignore it in this instance.

In addition to the strong biblical precedent, the context of the poem itself lends support to an angelic reading. As the "Sons of God" are described as a "different sort"[89] compared to the human "daughters of men." Being angels, would certainly make them "different." Michael relates that "by their guise / just men they seem'd."[90] Both "guise" and "just" may be taken in two different senses. "Guise" can refer to any "manner of bearing," "expression," or "acoutra," but it could also suggest "dissemblance," "the putting on of airs," or outright "disguise." "Just" can indicate "righteousness" but it can also carry the sense of "merely."[91] Likewise, "seem'd" does not denote what they are but only what they seem to be. These lines brim with

---

[88] Jude 6,7, Geneva Bible 1560.

[89] *Paradise Lost* 11.574.

[90] *Paradise Lost* 11.577.

[91] OED "Guise 1.a 'manner, method, way; fashion, style' [...] Wycliffe c.1380 *Works* (1880) 186 [...] *Romance of the Rose* c. 1440 line 4292 [...] Milton 1644 *Areopagitica* 6." OED "Just 5.a 'merely' [...] Robert Hooke 1665 *Micrographia,* viii.38."

caveats and qualifiers. That is to say, the above expression very possibly means "by their looks they appeared to be merely men." This is also consistent with the tone of Michael's presentation: first he shows then he tells. They are called men, because that is what they look like to Adam. Adam observes them at "all their study bent / to worship God aright." Yes, they appear righteous, but so does Satan throughout the narrative of the poem who transforms himself into an angel of light and "for neither Man nor Angel can discern / Hypocrisy, the only evil that walks / Invisible, except to God alone."[92] Certainly, these angels who appear to be good men seem benign and even righteous to Adam, but Adam is at times a *mis*-reader. Adam also thinks that the marriage alliances that are formed with the women are fine and beneficial, but Michael sternly corrects him. It is in the midst of this correction that we find the first occurrence of "Sons of God."

> Judge not what is best
> By pleasure, though to Nature and seeming meet
> Created as thou art, to nobler end
> Holy and pure, conformity divine.[93]

Fallen Adam perceives the pleasure and wants to equate it with good. Michael reminds him that God is the measuring stick of what is good for humans. Some have argued that since the "Daughters of Men" are clearly Cainites then the "Sons of God" must be Sethites, otherwise why specify that the women are descendants of Cain? Who better to attract fallen angels? As Michael shows and the Genesis account relates, the descendants of Cain are the originators of the arts. Surely, wicked angels would not be drawn to cohabitate with righteous humans but rather would gravitate toward the impious. Michael goes on to explain how that these marriages between the "Daughters of Men" or Cainites would result in woe and suffering:

---

[92] *Paradise Lost* 3.681–83.

[93] *Paradise Lost* 11.603–06.

To these that sober race of men, whose lives
Religious titl'd them the Sons of God,
Shall yield up all their virtue, all their fame
Ignobly, to the trains and to the smiles
Of these fair Atheists and now swim in joy,
(Erelong to swim at large) and laugh; for which
The world erelong a world of tears must weep.[94]

If these are angels, is it not peculiar that they should be called a "sober race of men"? As indicated earlier, Michael presents the vision and then explains it to Adam the student. Just as Raphael refuses to provide all the information that Adam wants to know in Book 8, so likewise Michael refrains from total disclosure. Both Raphael and Michael explain what Adam needs to know but not all he wants to know. What the Angels do reveal is often in the form of theological accommodation or explaining spiritual things as if they were earthly things with which Adam is familiar.[95] To call these angels men, is just such an example of accommodation. These angels had "lives religious that titled them Sons of God." Once they began to live in a way that God disapproved, they were no longer true "Sons of God."

Another direct reference to Genesis 6.1–4 and the expression "Sons of God" occurs in *Paradise Lost* Book 5. Raphael comes to pass the time with Adam and Eve and to warn them that Satan is intent upon breaking their integrity to God. Raphael, the affable Angel is not overwhelmed by the beauty of nude Eve.

Meanwhile at table Eve
Minister'd naked, and their flowing cups
With pleasant liquors crown'd: O innocence
Deserving Paradise. If ever, then,
Then had the Sons of God excuse to have been
Enamour'd at that sight; but in those hearts
Love unlibidnious reign'd, nor jealousy

---

[94] *Paradise Lost* 11.622–27.

[95] Compare with the angels that visited Abraham in Genesis 18.1–8.

> Was understood, the injur'd Lover's Hell.[96]

How beautiful was Eve? So lovely that had she "enamour'd" the "Sons of God," it would have been excusable. This comment would make no sense if it merely referred to Sethites. The angels were by nature "unlibidinious" or possessed no sex drive, yet angels do have sex.[97] To seek a union with a human would require a deliberate motion of the will in such creatures. Just as Raphael was able to eat food and digest it, he could just as easily have determined to make love to Eve and accomplish it with ease.

Clearly, there is strong textual evidence to support the view that the "Sons of God" are angels who choose to debase themselves by cohabitating with humans. Some critics, however, object to this idea by clinging to Milton's apparent contempt for Justin Martyr who was among the ancient authorities who espoused a belief that the "Sons of God" of Genesis were angelic beings.[98] Milton writes in *Of Reformation* (1641):

> Who would think him fit to write an Apology for Christian Faith to the Roman Senate, that would tell them of how the Angels, which he needs must mean those in Gen. call'd he Sons of God, mixing with women were begotten the Devills, as good Justin Martyr in his Apology told them.[99]

Milton is not objecting to the fact that Justin Martyr accepts that the "Sons of God" are angels. He is objecting to Justin Martyr's view that by mixing with the women they then become the fallen angels. Milton, by contrast, contends that the fall of the angels occurs before the fall of Adam and Eve. Therefore, it is on that basis alone that Milton seeks to discredit the views of Justin Martyr.

---

96 *Paradise Lost* 11.443–50.

97 See Raphael's description of angelic sexuality in *Paradise Lost* 8.618–643.

98 See Robert H. West, *Milton and the Angels*, 129.

99 John Milton, *The Works of John Milton*, Gen. ed. Frank Allen Patterson. 18 vols. (New York: Columbia University Press, 1931–38), 3.21.

The Freedom of the Sons of God

If it is established that the "Sons of God" in *Paradise Lost* Book 11 are angels, does it really matter? Does it affect how one might read and think about *Paradise Lost* and *Paradise Regained* as a pair? What are the interpretative ramifications?

In many ways, the angel reading is a better fit with the stated objectives of the visionary Genesis "slideshow" presented by Michael. After the eye drops have begun to have effect by removing the "film [...] which that false fruit that promised clearer sight had bred," Michael directs God's first human creation:

> Adam, now ope thine eyes, and first behold
> The effects, which thy original crime hath wrought
> In some to spring from thee; who never touched
> The excepted tree; nor with the snake conspired;
> Nor sinned thy sin; yet from that sin derive
> Corruption, to bring forth more violent deeds.[100]

Michael wants to impress upon Adam that his negative actions will have sweeping consequences for many. Obviously, the notion of Augustinian "Original Sin" is at work here on the descendants of Adam, yet an additional layer of meaning may be operative here. Michael refers to the "effects [..] in some to spring from thee." Why not "all"? Apparently, in the Pauline biblical sense of Romans chapter 5 and most definitely in Augustine's reading of it, "all" human descendants are involved, but it would seem that Michael is pointing to yet further reaching ramifications that spring from Adam's revolt. Is Michael perhaps suggesting to Adam that his selfish action of eating from the tree of the knowledge of good and evil bears consequences upon the angels, not in terms of Augustinian sin, but in terms of profound cause and effect? Put another way, is it plausible that even the angels in the spirit realm must deal with the fallout from Adam's actions, which call directly into question the righteousness and right-

[100] *Paradise Lost* 11.423–428.

fulness of God's manner of exercising sovereignty over his universal creation?

From the moment that Adam and Eve disobey the divine injunction to abstain from the fruit of the tree in the middle of the garden, all of creation, angels included must deal with the unsought aftermath. When the angels who guarded Eden return to heaven, all of the angels in heaven "in multitudes, the ethereal people ran, to hear and know / how all befell: they towards the throne supreme, / accountable, made haste to appear."[101] The angels have deep concern here and are trying to make sense of a bad situation. This is due to the fact the disobedience and opprobrious conduct of any creature in God's universal family sews discord. What is performed by one must matter to all. That what Satan as a Son of God disrupted must be restored by Jesus as a Son of God so that all might once again be Sons of God is made clear in *Paradise Regained.*

In books 5–8 of *Paradise Lost,* Raphael strongly conveys to Adam the connection between angels and humans. Just as humans have interest in the spirit realm, angels too are fascinated by the material world. Both humans and angels serve God in assigned respective ways. Just as the rebellion of Satan and his angelic followers wreaks havoc upon the earth, the rebellion of Adam and Eve sends similar shockwaves through out what once was a tightly knit and cooperative creation.

The "Sons of God" as angels reading of *Paradise Lost* Book 11 brings into focus that not only is an earthly Paradise lost, but all of God's creation, both spiritual and material, is reeling from the blow. Michael essentially warns Adam that the channels of communication with angels and the sprit realm are now contaminated. Both fallen angels who forsake their heavenly position and humans share the blame equally. The very idea that angels could have sex with humans underscores a significant commonality between the two. More importantly, both humans and angels will benefit when the effects of Adam's sin are erased.

[101] *Paradise Lost* 10.26–28.

This thematic thread of redemption is sown early in the poem. The opening line provides a thesis statement of sorts:

Of Man's first disobedience, and the fruit
Of that forbidden tree, whose mortal taste
Brought death into the World, and all our woe,
With loss of Eden, till one greater Man
Restore us, and regain the blissful seat.[102]

The restoring of humans via the ransom sacrifice of the Son, or "one greater man" will not only heal humans but restore the connection between all of God's creation including the angels. When the full benefits of this restoration occur, then the speculations of Raphael will once again be a possibility:

Your bodies may at last turn all to spirit,
Improv'd by tract of time, and wing'd ascend
Ethereal, as we, or may at choice
Here or in Heav'nly Paradises dwell[103]

According to Raphael, humans might then be able to achieve the same pre-lapsarian freedom of angels. Understanding the "Sons of God" to be angelic creatures raises the stakes for Adam and his progeny. All creation, spiritual and earthly, is invested in the outcome of what Paul describes:

> For I count that the afflictions of this present time are not worthy of the glory, which shalbe shewed vnto vs. For the feruent desire of the creature waiteth when the sonnes of God shalbe reueiled.[104]

---

102 *Paradise Lost*, 1.1–5.

103 *Paradise Lost*, 5.497–500.

104 Romans 8.18, 19, Geneva Bible 1560.

Appendix A

The verses at Genesis 6:1–4 appear in the traditional Masoretic Text as:

ויהי כי־החל האדם לרב על־פני האדמה ובנות ילדו להם:

ויראו בני־האלהים[105] את־בנות האדם כי טבת הנה ויקחו להם נשים מכל אשר בחרו:

ויאמר יהוה לא־ידון רוחי באדם לעלם בשגם הוא בשר והיו ימיו מאה ועשרים שנה:

הנפלים היו בארץ בימים ההם וגם אחרי־כן אשר יבאו בני האלהים אל־בנות האדם וילדו להם המה הגברים אשר מעולם אנשי השם:[106]

[105] Or "Sons of God."

[106] Jay P. Green, ed., *The Pocket Interlinear Old Testament* Vol.1 (Grand Rapids: Baker, 1987). The highlighted portion is the expression generally rendered as "Sons of God."

Appendix B

The Septuagint renders Genesis 6:1–4 as the following:

Καὶ ἐγένετο ἡνίκα ἤρξαντο οἱ ἄνθρωποι πολλοὶ γίνεσθαι ἐπὶ τῆς γῆς, καὶ θυγατέρες ἐγενήθησαν αὐτοῖς. ἰδόντες δὲ οἱ υἱοὶ τοῦ θεοῦ[107] τὰς θυγατέρας τῶν ἀνθρώπων ὅτι καλαί εἰσιν, ἔλαβον ἑαυτοῖς γυναῖκας ἀπὸ πασῶν, ὧν ἐξελέξαντο . καὶ εἶπεν κύριος ὁ θεός Οὐ μὴ καταμείνῃ τὸ πνεῦμά μου ἐν τοῖς ἀνθρώποις τούτοις εἰς τὸν αἰῶνα διὰ τὸ εἶναι αὐτοὺς σάρκας, ἔσονται δὲ αἱ ἡμέραι αὐτῶν ἑκατὸν εἴκοσι ἔτη. οἱ δὲ γίγαντες ἦσαν ἐπὶ τῆς γῆς ἐν ταῖς ἡμέραις ἐκείναις καὶ μετ᾽ ἐκεῖνο, ὡς ἂν εἰσεπορεύοντο οἱ υἱοὶ τοῦ θεοῦ πρὸς τὰς[108]

---

[107] Or "Sons of God."

[108] *The Septuagint Version of the Old Testament with an English Translation and with Various Readings and Critical Notes* (Grand Rapids: Zondervan, 1970).

APPENDIX C

Jerome in the Latin Vulgate provides Genesis 6:1–4 as:

Cumque coepissent homines multiplicari super terram et filias procreassent, videntes filii Dei filias eorum quod essent pulchrae, acceperunt uxores sibi ex omnibus quas elegerant. Dixitque Deus, "Non permanebit spiritus meus in homine in aeternum, quia caro est, eruntque dies illius centum viginti annorum." Gigantes autem erant super terram in diebus illis, postquam enim ingressi sunt filii Dei[109] ad filias hominum illaeque genuerunt; isti sunt potentes a saeculo, viri famosi.[110]

---

[109] Or "Sons of God."

[110] Edgar Swift, ed., *The Vulgate Bible* "The Pentateuch" Vol. 1 (Cambridge: Harvard University Press, 2010).

APPENDIX D

Paradise Lost, 11.553-729

"Nor love thy life, nor hate; but what thou liv'st
Live well; how long, or short, permit to Heaven:
And now prepare thee for another sight."
He looked, and saw a spacious plain, whereon
Were tents[111] of various hue; by some, were herds
Of cattle grazing; others, whence the sound
Of instruments, that made melodious chime,
Was heard, of harp and organ; and, who moved
Their stops and chords, was seen; his volant touch,
Instinct through all proportions, low and high,
Fled and pursued transverse the resonant fugue.[112]
In other part stood one who, at the forge
Laboring, two massy clods of iron and brass
Had melted, (whether found where casual fire
Had wasted woods on mountain or in vale,
Down to the veins of earth; thence gliding hot
To some cave's mouth; or whether washed by stream
From underground;) the liquid ore he drained
Into fit moulds prepared; from which he formed
First his own tools; then, what might else be wrought
Fusil or graven in metal.[113] After these,
But on the hither side, a different sort

---

[111] Jabal, "the father of those who dwells in tents," is a descendant of Cain by six generations. "And Adah bare Jabal, who was the father of such as dwell in the tents, and of such as have cattle" (Genesis 4.20).

[112] [lines 559–63] Jubal, a descendant of Cain by six generations and the brother of Jabal. "And his brothers name was Jubal, who was the father of all that play on the harp and organs" (Genesis 4.21).

[113] [lines 564–73] Tubal-cain, a descendant of Cain by six generations. "And Zillah also bare Tubal-kain, who wrought cunningly every craft of brass and of iron: and the sister of Tubal-kain was Naamah.(Gen. 4:22)

From the high neighboring hills, which was their seat,
Down to the plain[114] descended; by their guise
Just men they seemed, and all their study bent
To worship God aright,[115] and know his works
Not hid;[116] nor those things last, which might preserve
Freedom and peace to Men;[117] they on the plain
Long had not walked, when from the tents, behold!
A bevy of fair women, richly gay
In gems and wanton dress;[118] to the harp they sung
Soft amorous ditties, and in dance came on:
The men, though grave, eyed them; and let their eyes
Rove without rein; till, in the amorous net

---

[114] [lines 575–76] Then land of Nod inhabited by the descendents of Cain. "And Cain went out from the presence of the LORD, and dwelt in the land of Nod, on the East of Eden" (Genesis 4.16).

[115] [lines 577–78] The righteous descendents of Seth, the third son of Adam and Eve. "And to ye same Sheth also there was borne a son, and he called his name Enosh. Then began men to call upon the name of the Lord" (Genesis 4.26). Geneva note: "In these days God began to move the hearts of the godly to restore religion, which had been suppressed by the wicked for a long time."

[116] [lines 578–79] "know his works not hid." "The secret things belong to the Lord our God, but the things revealed belong unto us, and to our children for ever, that we may doe all the words of this Law" (Deuteronomy 29.29).

[117] [lines 573–80] "And it came to pass, when men began to multiply on the face of the earth, and daughters were borne unto them" (Genesis 6.1).

[118] [lines 582–83] Contrast with Paul's admonition to Christian women. "Likewise also the women, that they array themselves in comely apparel, with shamefastness and modesty, not with braided hair, or gold, or pearls, or costly apparel" (1 Timothy 2.9). Geneva note: "Thirdly, he appoints women to learn in the public assemblies with silence and modesty, being dressed pleasantly, without any overindulgence or excess in their clothing."
"Whose appareling, let it not be that outward, with braided hear, and gold put about, or in putting on of apparel: But let it be the hid man of the heart, which consisteth in the incorruption of a meek and quiet spirit, which is before God a thing much set by" (1 Peter 3.3, 4). Geneva note: "He condemns the unrestrained indulgences and excesses of women, and sets forth their true apparel, such as is precious before God, that is, the inward and incorruptible, which consists in a meek and quiet spirit."

Fast caught, they liked; and each his liking chose;[119]
And now of love they treat, till the evening-star,
Love's harbinger, appeared; then, all in heat
They light the nuptial torch, and bid invoke
Hymen, then first to marriage rites invoked:
With feast and music all the tents resound.
Such happy interview, and fair event
Of love and youth not lost, songs, garlands, flowers,
And charming symphonies, attached the heart
Of Adam, soon inclined to admit delight,
The bent of nature; which he thus expressed.
"True opener of mine eyes, prime Angel blest;
Much better seems this vision, and more hope
Of peaceful days portends, than those two past;
Those were of hate and death, or pain much worse;
Here Nature seems fulfilled in all her ends."
To whom thus Michael. Judge not what is best
By pleasure, though to nature seeming meet;
Created, as thou art, to nobler end
Holy and pure, conformity divine.
Those tents thou saw'st so pleasant, were the tents
Of wickedness,[120] wherein shall dwell his race
Who slew his brother; studious they appear
Of arts that polish life, inventors rare;
Unmindful of their Maker, though his Spirit
Taught them; but they his gifts acknowledged none.[121]

---

[119] [lines 582–87] *Douay-Rheims*: "The sons of God seeing the daughters of men, that they were fair, took to themselves wives of all which they chose" (Genesis 6.2). See also *AV* and *GT*. *GE* "they took them wives of all that they liked." *BB* "they toke them wives, such as they liked, from among them all."

[120] [lines 607–08] "Tents of wickedness." *Authorized Version*: "For a day in thy courts, is better than a thousand: I had rather be a door keeper in the house of my God, then to dwell in the tents of wickedness" (Psalm 84.10). *GE* "Tabernacles of wickedness." *DR* "the tabernacles of sinners." *BB* "in [large] tabernacles of ungodliness." *GT* "tents of ungodliness."

Yet they a beauteous offspring shall beget;
For that fair female troop thou saw's't, that seemed
Of Goddesses, so blithe, so smooth, so gay,
Yet empty of all good wherein consists
Woman's domestic honor and chief praise;
Bred only and completed to the taste
Of lustful appetence, to sing, to dance,
To dress, and troll the tongue, and roll the eye:
To these that sober race of men, whose lives
Religious titled them the sons of God,
Shall yield up all their virtue, all their fame
Ignobly, to the trains and to the smiles
Of these fair atheists,[122] and now swim in joy,
Erelong to swim at large; and laugh, for which
The world erelong a world of tears must weep."
To whom thus Adam, of short joy bereft.
"O pity and shame, that they, who to live well
Entered so fair, should turn aside to tread
Paths indirect, or in the mid way faint!
But still I see the tenor of Man's woe
Holds on the same, from Woman to begin."
"From Man's effeminate slackness it begins,"
Said the Angel, "who should better hold his place
By wisdom, and superior gifts received.
But now prepare thee for another scene."

---

[121] [lines 609–12] The artistic descendents of Cain. "And Adah bare Jabal, who was the father of such as dwell in the tents, and of such as have cattle. And his brothers name was Jubal, who was the father of all that play on the harp and organs. And Zillah also bare Tubal-kain, who wrought cunningly every craft of brass and of iron: and the sister of Tubal-kain was Naamah" (Genesis 4.21–22).

[122] [lines 619–25] The Sons of God and the daughters of Cain. "So when men began to be multiplied upon the earth, and there were daughters borne unto them, Then the sons of God saw the daughters of men that they were faire, & they took them wives of all that they liked" (Genesis 6.1, 2). Geneva note on "Sons of God": "The children of the godly who began to degenerate." Geneva note on "daughters of men": "Those that had wicked parents, as if from Cain."

He looked, and saw wide territory spread
Before him, towns, and rural works between;
Cities of men with lofty gates and towers,
Concourse in arms, fierce faces threatening war,
Giants[123] of mighty bone and bold emprise;
Part wield their arms, part curb the foaming steed,
Single or in array of battle ranged
Both horse and foot, nor idly mustering stood;
One way a band select from forage drives
A herd of beeves, fair oxen and fair kine,
From a fat meadow ground; or fleecy flock,
Ewes and their bleating lambs over the plain,
Their booty; scarce with life the shepherds fly,
But call in aid, which makes a bloody fray;
With cruel tournament the squadrons join;
Where cattle pastured late, now scattered lies
With carcasses and arms the ensanguined field,
Deserted: Others to a city strong
Lay siege, encamped; by battery, scale, and mine,
Assaulting; others from the wall defend
With dart and javelin, stones, and sulphurous fire;
On each hand slaughter, and gigantic deeds.
In other part the scattered heralds call
To council, in the city-gates;[124] anon

---

[123] The offspring of the "daughters of men" and the "Sons of God" were "giants." "There were giants in the earth in those days: yea, and after that the sons of God came unto the daughters of men, and they had borne them children, these were mighty men, which in old time were men of renown" (Genesis 6.4). Geneva note: "Who usurped authority over others, and degenerated from that simplicity, in which their father's lived."

[124] The older men sit in council and judged cases at the city gates in the ancient Orient. "Then Hamor and Shechem his Son went unto the gate of their city, and communed with the men of their city, saying" (Genesis 34.20). Geneva note: "For the people used to assemble there, and justice was administered."
The provision of judges under the Mosaic Law. "Judges and officers shalt thou make thee in all thy cities, which the Lord thy God giveth thee, throughout thy

Gray-headed men and grave, with warriors mixed,
Assemble, and harangues are heard; but soon,
In factious opposition; till at last,
Of middle age one rising, eminent
In wise deport, spake much of right and wrong,
Of justice, or religion, truth, and peace,
And judgment from above:[125] him old and young
Exploded, and had seized with violent hands,
Had not a cloud descending snatched him thence
Unseen amid the throng:[126] so violence

---

tribes: and they shall judge the people with righteous judgment" (Deuteronomy 16.18). Geneva note: "He gave temporary authority to the people to choose magistrates for themselves."

Rebellious children are judged at the city gate. "Then shall his father and his mother take him, & bring him out unto the Elders of his city, & unto the gate of the place where he dwelleth" (Deuteronomy 16.18). *DR* "the gate of judgment." Geneva Bible: "These are ye things that ye shall doe. Speak ye every man the truth unto his neighbor: execute judgment truly & uprightly in your gates" (Zechariah 8.16). See also *AV* and *DR*. *BB* and *GT* "execute judgment truly and peaceably within your ports."

Absalom usurps the kingship of his father David and holds court at the gates. "Then the King arose, and sate in the gate: and they told unto all the people, saying, Behold, the King doeth sit in the gate: and all the people came before the King: for Israel had fled every man to his tent" (2 Samuel 19.8).

King Zedekiah holds court at the city gates. "Now when Ebed-melech ye black More one of ye Eunuchs, which was in the kings house, heard that they had put Jeremiah in the dungeon (then the King sate in the gate of Benjamin)" (Jeremiah 38.7).

125 [lines 666–68] Enoch condemns the wickedness of his day. "And Enoch also the seventh from Adam, prophesied of such, saying, Behold, the Lord commeth with thousands of his Saints, To give judgment against al men, and to rebuke all the ungodly among them of all their wicked deeds, which they have ungodly committed, and of all their cruel speakings, which wicked sinners have spoken against him" (Jude 14, 15).

126 [lines 664–71] God removes righteous Enoch from the violent Ante-Diluvian world. "Also Henoch lived sixty & five years, and begat Methushelah. And Henoch walked with God, after he begat Methushelah, three hundredth years, and begat sons and daughters. So all the days of Henoch were three hundredth

Proceeded, and oppression, and sword-law,
Through all the plain, and refuge none was found.
Adam was all in tears, and to his guide
Lamenting turned full sad; "O what are these,
Death's ministers, not men? who thus deal death
Inhumanly to men, and multiply
Ten-thousand-fold the sin of him who slew
His brother:[127] for of whom such massacre
Make they, but of their brethren; men of men?
But who was that just man, whom had not Heaven
Rescued, had in his righteousness been lost?"
To whom thus Michael. These are the product
Of those ill-mated marriages thou saw'st;
Where good with bad were matched, who of themselves
Abhor to join; and, by imprudence mixed,
Produce prodigious births of body or mind.
Such were these giants, men of high renown;[128]
For in those days might only shall be admired,
And valor and heroic virtue called;
To overcome in battle, and subdue

---

sixty and five years. And Henoch walked with God, and he was no more seen: for God took him away" (Genesis 5.21–24). Geneva note on "God took him": "To show that there was a better life prepared and to be a testimony of the immortality of souls and bodies. To inquire where he went is mere curiosity."
The translation of Enoch. "By faith was Enoch translated, that he should not see death: neither was he found: for God had translated him: for before he was translated, he was reported of, that he had pleased God" (Hebrews 11.5).

[127] [lines 674–79] The ten thousand slaughtered saints presumed to be contemporaries with Enoch. *Authorized Version*: "And Enoch also, the seventh from Adam, prophesied of these, saying, Behold, the Lord commeth with ten thousands of his Saints" (Jude 14). *GE* and *DR* "thousands of his saints." *GT* and *BB* "thousands of saints."

[128] [line 688] "There were giants in the earth in those days: yea, and after that the sons of God came unto the daughters of men, and they had borne them children, these were mighty men, which in old time were men of renown" (Genesis 6.4). Geneva note: "Who usurped authority over others, and degenerated from that simplicity, in which their father's lived."

Nations, and bring home spoils with infinite
Man-slaughter, shall be held the highest pitch
Of human glory; and for glory done
Of triumph, to be styled great conquerors
Patrons of mankind, Gods, and sons of Gods;[129]
Destroyers rightlier called, and plagues of men.
Thus fame shall be achieved, renown on earth;
And what most merits fame, in silence hid.
But he, the sev'nth from thee,[130] whom thou beheld'st
The only righteous in a world perverse,
And therefore hated, therefore so beset
With foes, for daring single to be just,
And utter odious truth, that God would come
To judge them with his Saints; him the Most High
Rapt in a balmy cloud with winged steeds[131]
Did, as thou saw'st, receive, to walk with God[132]
High in salvation and the climes of bliss,
Exempt from death; to show thee what reward
Awaits the good; the rest what punishment;
Which now direct thine eyes and soon behold."
He looked, and saw the face of things quite changed;
The brazen throat of war had ceased to roar;
All now was turned to jollity and game,

---

[129] "That the sons of God saw the daughters of men, that they were faire, and they took them wives, of all which they chose" (Genesis 6.2). Geneva note: "The children of the godly who began to degenerate."

[130] See note on 11.674–79.

[131] Compare with the similar deliverance of Elijah that was accomplished via "steeds." "And as they went walking and talking, behold, there appeared a chariot of fire, and horses of fire, and did separate them twain. So Elijah went up by a whirl wind into heaven" (2 Kings 2.11).

[132] Enoch walks with God. "And Henoch walked with God, after he begat Methushelah, three hundredth years, and begat sons and daughters" (Jude 14). Geneva note: "That is, he led an upright and godly life."
"And Henoch walked with God, and he was no more seen: for God took him away" (Genesis 5.24).

To luxury and riot, feast and dance;
Marrying or prostituting, as befell,
Rape or adultery, where passing fair
Allured them; thence from cups to civil broils.[133]
At length a reverend[134] sire[135] among them came,
And of their doings great dislike declared,
And testified against their ways; he oft
Frequented their assemblies, whereso met,
Triumphs or festivals; and to them preached
Conversion and repentance,[136] as to souls
In prison, under judgments imminent:[137]

---

[133] [lines 714–18] Jesus compares "days of Noah" to the "days of the son of man." "And as it was in the days of Noe, so shall it be in the days of the Son of man. They ate, they drank, they married wives, and gave in marriage unto the day that Noe went into the Ark: and the flood came, and destroyed them all" (Luke 17.26, 27). Geneva note: "The world will be taken by surprise with the sudden judgment of God, and therefore the faithful ought to continually watch."

[134] Noah "moved with reverence." Bishop's Bible: "By faith Noe being warned of God of things not seen as yet, moved with reverence, prepared the ark to the saving of his house, through the which [ark] he condemned the world, and became heir of the righteousness which is by faith" (Hebrews 11.7). See also *GE*. *AV* and *DR* "moved with fear." *GT* omits the phrase.

[135] "And Noah was six hundredth years old, when the flood of waters was upon the earth" (Genesis 7.6).

[136] [lines 720–24] Noah is a "preacher of righteousness." "Neither hath spared the old world, but saved Noe the eight person a preacher of righteousness, and brought in the flood upon the world of the ungodly" (2Peter 2.5). *DR* "the preacher of justice." Geneva note: "For one hundred and twenty years, he did not cease to warn the wicked both by word and deed, of the wrath of God hanging over their heads."

[137] [lines 723–25] The resurrected Jesus preaches to the spirits "in prison" who had not responded to Noah prior to the Flood. The *Geneva* note suggests a conflation of Jesus and Noah. Geneva Bible: "By the which he also went, and preached unto the spirits that are in prison. Which were in time passed disobedient, when once the long suffering of God abode in the days of Noe, while the Ark was preparing, wherein few, that is, eight souls were saved in the water" (1 Peter 3.19, 20). Geneva note: "A secret objection: Christ indeed might do this, but what is that to us? Indeed (faith the apostle) for Christ has showed his power in all ages

But all in vain: which when he saw, he ceased
Contending, and removed his tents far off;
Then, from the mountain hewing timber tall,
Began to build a vessel of huge bulk;

---

both in the preservation of the godly, were they never so few and miserable, and in avenging the rebellion of his enemies, as it appears by the history of the flood: for Christ is he who in those days (when God through his patience appointed a time of repentance to the world) was present, not in corporal presence, but by his divine power, preaching repentance, even by the mouth of Noah himself who then prepared the ark, to those disobedient spirits who are now in prison, waiting for the full recompense of their rebellion, and saved those few, (that is, only eight people) in the water."

LIST OF BIBLICAL ABBREVIATIONS

AV – 1612 Authorized Version

BB – 1568 Bishop's Bible

Coverdale – 1535 Coverdale's Bible

DR – 1610 Douay-Rheims Bible

GE – 1560 Geneva Bible

GT – 1539 Great Bible

LXX – Greek Septuagint

PL – Paradise Lost

Tyndale – 1526 Tyndale's Bible

Vg – Latin Vulgate

PARADISE REGAINED

BOOK ONE

I who erewhile the happy Garden sung
By one man's disobedience[1] lost, now sing
Recovered Paradise to all mankind,[2]
By one man's firm obedience fully tried
Through all temptation,[3] and the Tempter[4] foiled
In all his wiles,[5] defeated[6] and repulsed,

---

[1][Lines 1–4] A reference to Adamic sin. "For as by one man's disobedience many were made sinners, so by that obedience of that one shall many also be made righteous" (Romans 5:19). (Note: My default translation, unless otherwise noted, is the Geneva Bible.)

[2] The Son as the agent for restoring Paradise. "For as in Adam all die, even so in Christ shall all be made alive" (1 Corinthians 15:22). Compare with Jesus's words to the malefactor hanging next to him at Golgotha: "Then Jesus said unto him, Verily I say unto thee, today shalt thou be with me in Paradise" (Luke 23:43).

[3] "Through all temptation." The comprehensive nature of the "temptations" offered by Satan, "the tempter": "And was there forty days tempted of the devil, and in those days he did eat nothing: but when they were ended, he afterward was hungry" (Luke 4:2). Geneva note: "Christ, being tempted by Satan, first to distrust in God, secondly to the desire of riches and honor, and lastly to a vain confidence in himself, overcomes him three times by the word of God."

[4] "Then came to him the tempter, and said, If thou be the Son of God, command that these stones be made bread" (Matthew 4:3). "The Tempter" is consistently used of Satan in the writings of Paul: "Even for this cause, when I could no longer forbear, I sent him that I might know of your faith, lest the tempter had tempted you in any sort, and that our labor had been in vain" (1 Thessalonians 3:5). The Son prevails over temptation: "For in that he suffered, and was tempted, he is able to succor them that are tempted" (Hebrews 2:18).

[5] The wiles of the devil: "Put on the whole armor of God, that ye may be able to stand against the wiles of the devil" (Ephesians 6:11, AV). GE, BB, GT "assaults of the devil." DR "deceits of the devil."

[6] The ultimate defeat of Satan immediately foretold after the Edenic fall: "I will also put enmity between thee and the woman, and between thy seed and her

And Eden[7] raised in the waste Wilderness.[8]
Thou Spirit, who led'st this glorious Eremite
Into the desert,[9] his victorious field
Against the spiritual foe, and brought'st him thence
By proof the undoubted Son of God, inspire,
As thou art wont, my prompted song, else mute,
And bear through highth or depth of Nature's bounds,
With prosperous wing full summed, to tell of deeds
Above heroic, though in secret done,
And unrecorded left through many an age:

---

seed. He shall break thine head, and thou shalt bruise his heel" (Genesis 3:15). Geneva note identifies the "serpent" with Satan: "He chiefly means Satan, by whose action and deceit the serpent deceived the woman."

[7] The "wilderness" comes to be like "Eden." "For the Lord shall comfort Zion: he will comfort all her waste places, and he will make her wilderness like Eden, and her desert like the garden of the Lord: joy and gladness shall be found therein, thanksgiving, and the voice of melody" (Isaiah 51:3, AV and GE). BB and GT "Making her desert as a paradise." DR "he will make her desert as a place of pleasure."

[8] Compare the Son's forty day trek in the "waste wilderness" with the forty year wanderings of Israel following the Exodus from Egypt: "He found him in the land of the wilderness, in a waste, and roaring wilderness: he led him about, he taught him, and kept him as the apple of his eye" (Deuteronomy 32:10, GE and AV) Not BB GT "in a void ground and in a roaring wilderness" nor DR "in a place of horror, and of vast wilderness." Eden raised once again out of the post-lapsarian wilderness: "Also to Adam he said, Because thou hast obeyed the voice of thy wife, and hast eaten of the tree, (whereof I commanded thee, saying, Thou shalt not eat of it) cursed is the earth for thy sake: in sorrow shalt thou eat of it all the days of thy life. Thorns also, and thistles shall it bring forth to thee, and thou shalt eat the herb of the field" (Genesis 3:17, 18). Geneva note: "These are not the natural fruit of the earth, but proceed from the corruption of sin."

[9] [Lines 8–9] The Spirit leads the Son into the desert: "Then Jesus was led by the spirit into the desert, to be tempted by the devil" (Matthew 4:1, DR). AV, GE, BB, GT "into the wilderness." "And Jesus being full of the Holy Ghost, returned from the Jordan and was led the by the spirit into the desert, For the space of forty days, and was tempted by the devil. And he ate nothing in those days. And when they were ended, he was hungry" (Luke 4:1,2, DR; "led by that Spirit into the wilderness" AV, GE, BB, GT).

Worthy to have not remained so long unsung.
Now had the great Proclaimer, with a voice
More awful than the sound of trumpet, cried[10]
Repentance, and Heaven's kingdom nigh at hand
To all baptized.[11] To his great baptism[12] flocked

---

[10] [Lines 17–18] The voice that crieth in the wilderness. Draws from the prophetic book of Isaiah. Milton makes an antitypical connection with John the Baptist: "A voice crieth in wilderness: Prepare the way of the Lord, make straight the path of our God in the desert" (Isaiah 40:3); "For this is he, of whom it is spoken by the prophet Isaiah, saying. The voice of one crying in the wilderness: prepare ye the way of the Lord, make his paths straight" (Matthew 3:3); "The voice of one crying in the wilderness, Prepare ye the way of the Lord, make his paths straight" (Mark 1:3). "Running head in Great Bible: "The coming of St. John the Baptist." A voice like a trumpet. "Cry aloud, spare not: lift up thy voice like a trumpet, and show my people their transgression, and to the house of Jacob, their sins" (Isaiah 58:1). Geneva note: "The Lord thus speaks to the prophet willing him to use all diligence and severity to rebuke the hypocrites." Compare with the author of Hebrews' description of the trumpetlike voice of God heard when the Israelites were gathered before Mount Sinai to receive the law that they failed to keep: "For ye are not come unto the mount that is touched, & unto burning fire, and unto storm and darkness, and tempests of weather, And sound of a trumpet, & the voice of words: which [voice] they that heard it, wished away, that the word should not be spoken to them: (For they did not abide that which was commanded)" (Hebrews 12:18–20). A celestial trumpet voice of judgment: "And I was ravished in spirit on the Lords day, and heard behind me a great voice, as it had been of a trumpet" (Revelation 1:10); "After this I looked, and behold, a door was open in heaven, and the first voice which I heard, was as it were of a trumpet talking with me, saying, Come up hither, and I will show thee things which must be done hereafter" (Revelation 4:1).

[11] [Lines 19–20] John the Baptist calls for "baptism" in symbol of "repentance" due to the nearness of the "Heaven's Kingdom" and fulfills the prophesy of Isaiah: "In those days, came John the Baptist, preaching in the wilderness of Judea, and saying, 'Repent, for the kingdom of heaven is at hand'" (Matthew 3:1,2); "John did baptize in the wilderness, and preach the baptism of repentance, for the remission of sins" (Mark 1:4, AV, BB, GT). GE "baptism of amendment of life." DR "baptism of penance." "And he came into all the coasts about Jordan, preaching the baptism of repentance for the remission of sins" (Luke 3;3). Compare the principle of baptism to the words of Isaiah to ancient Israel: "Wash you, make you clean: take away the evil of your works from before mine eyes:

With awe the regions round,[13] and with them came
From Nazareth[14] the son of Joseph deemed[15]
To the flood Jordan,[16] came as then obscure,
Unmarked, unknown.[17] But him the Baptist soon
Descried, divinely warned, and witness bore
As to his worthier,[18] and would have resigned

---

cease to do evil. Learn to do well: seek judgment, relieve the oppressed: judge the fatherless and defend the widow. Come now, and let us reason together, saith the Lord: though your sins were as crimson, they shall be made white as snow: though they were red like scarlet, they shall be as wool" (Isaiah 1:16–18).

[12] John's is a "great baptism," but the Christ's is greater: "Indeed I [John] baptize you with water to amendment of life, but he that cometh after me, is mightier then I, whose shoes I am not worthy to bear: he will baptize you with the holy Ghost, and with fire" (Matthew 3:11).

[13] With awe the regions round. ("Awe" may be a pun upon "all.") "Then went out to him Jerusalem and all Judea, and all the region round about Jordan. And they were baptized of him in Jordan, confessing their sins" (Matthew 3:5,6; not DR "all the country about).

[14] From Nazareth to be baptized: "And it came to pass in those days, that Jesus came from Nazareth, a city of Galilee, and was baptized of John in Jordan" (Mark 1:9).

[15] Jesus is considered by others to be the son of Joseph or "son of Joseph deemed": "And Jesus himself began to be about thirty years of age, being as men supposed the son of Joseph, which was the son of Eli" (Luke 3:29).

[16] Jesus goes to the Jordan: "Then came Jesus from Galilee to Jordan unto John, to be baptized of him" (Matthew 3:13).

[17] Jesus "unknown" by others at the time of his baptism: "John answered them, saying, I baptize with water: but there is one among you, whom ye know not" (John 1:26).

[18] [Lines 25–26] John the Baptist "witness bore" "to his worthier" Jesus. "The next day John, seeth Jesus coming unto him, and saith, Behold that Lamb of God, which taketh away the sin of the world […] And I knew him not: but he that sent me to baptize with water, he said unto me, Upon whom thou shalt see that Spirit come down, and tarry still on him, that is he which baptizeth with the holy Ghost" (John 1:29,33). John did not feel worthy to baptize Jesus but rather felt that Jesus should be baptizing him: "Then came Jesus from Galilee to Jordan unto John, to be baptized of him. But John earnestly put him back, saying, I have need to be baptized of thee, and comest thou to me? Then Jesus answering, said to him, Let be now: for thus it becometh us to fulfill all righteousness. So he

To him his heavenly office. Nor was long
His witness unconfirmed: on him baptized
Heaven opened, and in likeness of a Dove
The Spirit descended, while the Father's voice
From Heaven pronounced him his beloved Son.[19]
That heard the Adversary, who, roving still
About the world,[20] at that assembly famed

---

suffered him" (Matthew 3:13–15); "John bare witness of him, and cried, saying, This was he of whom I said, He that cometh after me, was before me: for he was better then I" (John 1:15); "Indeed I baptize you with water to amendment of life, but he that cometh after me, is mightier then I, whose shoes I am not worthy to bear: he will baptize you with the holy Ghost, and with fire [...] But John earnestly put him back, saying, I have need to be baptized of thee, and comest thou to me?" (Matthew 3:11,14); "And preached, saying, A stronger than I cometh after me, whose shoes latchet I am not worthy to stoop down, and unloose (Mark 1:7); "John answered, and said to them all, Indeed I baptize you with water, but one stronger then I, cometh, whose shoes latchet I am not worthy to unloose: he will baptize you with the holy Ghost, and with fire" (Luke 3:16); "He it is that cometh after me, which was before me, whose shoe latchet I am not worthy to unloose" (John 1:27).

[19] [Lines 27–31] "And Jesus when he was baptized, came straight out of the water; lo, the heavens were opened unto him, & John saw the Spirit of God descending like a dove, and lighting upon him" (Matthew 3:16); "And straightway coming up out of the water, he saw the heavens opened, and the Spirit like a dove descending upon him. And there came a voice from heaven, saying, Thou art my beloved Son, in whom I am well pleased" (Mark 1:10,11, AV). AV "heavens opened," GE "heavens cloven in twain," BB and GT "heaven open," DR "heavens open;" "Now it came to pass, as all the people were baptized, and that Jesus was baptized and did pray, that the heaven was opened: And the holy Ghost came down in a bodily shape like a dove, upon him, and there was a voice from heaven, saying, Thou art my beloved Son: in thee I am well pleased" (Luke 3:21,22); "So John bare record, saying, I beheld that Spirit come down from heaven, like a dove, and it abode upon him, And I knew him not: but he that sent me to baptize with water, he said unto me, Upon whom thou shalt see that Spirit come down, and tarry still on him, that is he which baptizeth with the holy Ghost. And I saw, and bare record that this is that Son of God" (John 1:32–34).

[20] Satan continuously roves about the earth. "Now on a day when the children of God came and stood before the Lord, Satan came also among them. Then the

Would not be last, and, with the voice divine
Nigh thunder-struck, the exalted man to whom
Such high attest was given a while surveyed
With wonder; then, with envy fraught and rage,
Flies to his place,[21] nor rests,[22] but in mid air[23]
To council summons all his mighty Peers,
Within thick clouds and dark tenfold involved,
A gloomy consistory; and them amidst,
With looks aghast and sad, he thus bespake:
"O ancient Powers of Air[24] and this wide World
(For much more willingly I mention Air,
This our old conquest, than remember Hell,
Our hated habitation), well ye know
How many ages, as the years of men,
This Universe we have possessed, and ruled
In manner at our will the affairs of Earth,
Since Adam and his facile consort Eve

Lord said unto Satan, 'Whence comest thou?' And Satan answered the Lord, saying, 'From compassing the earth to and from, and from walking in it'" (Job 1:6,7); "Be sober, and watch: for your adversary the devil as a roaring lion walketh about, seeking whom he may devour" (1 Peter 5:8); compare DR "goeth about."

[21] Compare that Judas too sought his own place. "That he may take the room of this ministration and Apostleship, from which Judas hath gone astray, to go to his own place" (Acts 1:25).

[22] The unclean spirt finds no rest. "Now when the unclean spirit is gone out of a man, he walketh throughout dry places, seeking rest, and findeth none" (Matthew 12:43).

[23] Satan rules in the air. "Wherein, in times past ye walked, according to the course of this world, and after the prince that ruleth in the air, even the spirit, that now worketh in the children of disobedience" (Ephesians 2:2), compare GT and BB "the governor that ruleth in the air," DR "the prince of the power of this air."

[24] Rebel angels are "powers of air." "For we wrestle not against flesh and blood, but against principalities, against powers, and against the worldly governors, the princes of the darkness of this world, against spiritual wickedness, which are in the high places" (Ephesians 6:12).

Lost Paradise, deceived by me, though since
With dread attending when that fatal wound
Shall be inflicted by the seed of Eve
Upon my head.[25] Long the decrees of Heaven
Delay, for longest time to Him is short;[26]
And now, too soon for us, the circling hours
This dreaded time have compassed, wherein we
Must bide the stroke of that long-threatened wound[27]
(At least, if so we can, and by the head
Broken be not intended all our power
To be infringed, our freedom and our being
In this fair empire won of Earth and Air);
For this ill news I bring: The Woman's Seed,[28]
Destined to this, is late of woman born.
His birth to our just fear gave no small cause;

---

[25] Prophecy regarding the seed of the woman and the serpent. "I will also put enmity between thee and the woman, and between thy seed & her seed. He shall break thine head, and thou shalt bruise his heel" (Genesis 3:15) GE genders the seed "he." Compare AV and BB "it" with DR "she."

[26] God's perception and experience of time is "short." "For a thousand years in thy sight are as yesterday when it is past, & as a watch in the night" (Psalms 90:4, GE). Geneva note: "Though man thinks his life is long, which is indeed most short, yet though it were a thousand years, yet in God's sight it is as nothing, and as the watch that lasts only three hours." "Dearly beloved, be not ignorant of this one thing, that one day is with the Lord, as a thousand years, and a thousand years as one day" (2 Peter 3:8, GE). Geneva note: "The taking away of an objection: in that he seems to desire this judgment for a long time, in respect of us it is true, but not before God, which whom there is no time either long or short."

[27] [Lines 57–58] The presence of Jesus presages that time has expired for the rebel angels and that God will find replacement sons among faithful humans. "But when the fullness of time was come, God sent forth his Son made of a woman, and made under the Law, That he might redeem them which were under the Law, that we might receive the adoption of the sons" (Galatians 4:4,5). Compare with the fear of unclean spirits who called out to Jesus: "And behold, they cried out, saying, Jesus the son of God, what have we to do with thee? Art thou come hither to torment us before the time" (Matthew 8:29).

[28] See note for 1.57–58.

But his growth now to youth's full flower, displaying
All virtue, grace[29] and wisdom to achieve
Things highest, greatest, multiplies my fear.
Before him a great Prophet,[30] to proclaim
His coming, is sent harbinger, who all
Invites, and in the consecrated stream[31]

---

[29] [Lines 66–67]. The young Jesus achieved "grace" as he grew to maturity. "And Jesus advanced in wisdom and age and grace with God and men" (Luke 2:52, DR). See also Vg "et Iesus proficiebat sapientia aetate et *gratia* apud Deum et hominess." Not AV, GE, BB "increased in wisdom and stature, and in favor with God and man."

[30] John the Baptist. "As it is written in the Prophets, Behold, I send my messenger before thy face, which shall prepare thy way before thee. The voice of him that crieth in the wilderness is, Prepare the way of the Lord: make his paths straight" (Mark 1:2,3). Contrast with DR and Vg which literally render the Greek *angelon* as "angel" rather than human "messenger" as found in AV, GE, BB, GT.

[31] The consecrated stream of the Jordan River. "And they were baptized of him in Jordan, confessing their sins" (Matthew 3:6). "And all the country of Judea, & they of Jerusalem went out unto him, and were all baptized of him in the river Jordan, confessing their sins" (Mark 1:5). The Jordan River held sacred associations for Israel dating back to the Exodus and wandering in the wilderness before possessing the "land of promise." Consider the miraculous crossing: "And as they that bare the Ark came unto Jordan, and the feet of the Priests that bare the Ark were dipped in the brink of the water, (for Jordan useth to fill all his banks all the time of harvest). Then the waters that came down from above, stayed and rose upon an heap and departed far from the city of Adam, that was beside Zaretan: but the waters that came down toward the Sea of the wilderness, even the salt Sea, failed, and were cut off: so the people went right over against Jericho. But the Priests that bare the Ark of the covenant of the Lord, stood dry within Jordan ready prepared, and all the Israelites went over dry, until all the people were gone clean over through Jordan" (Joshua 3:15–17); "And when they came unto the borders of Jordan (which are in the land of Canaan) then the children of Reuben, and the children of Gad, and the half tribe of Manasseh, built there an altar by Jordan, a great altar to see to" (Joshua 22:10). Elijah crosses the Jordan: "And fifty men of the sons of the Prophets went and stood on the other side a far off, and they two stood by Jordan… After, he took the cloak of Elijah, that fell from him, and smote the waters, and said, Where is the Lord God of Elijah? And so he also, after he had stricken the waters, so that they were divided this way and that way, went over, even Elisha (2 Kings 2:7,14).

Pretends to wash off sin,[32] and fit them so
Purified to receive him pure,[33] or rather
To do him honour as their King. All come,[34]
And he himself among them was baptized,[35]
Not thence to be more pure, but to receive
The testimony of Heaven, that who he is
Thenceforth the nations may not doubt.[36] I saw
The Prophet do him reverence; on him,[37] rising
Out of the water, Heaven above the clouds
Unfold her crystal doors;[38] thence on his head

"What ailed thee, O Sea, that thou fledst? O Jordan, why wast thou turned back?" (Psalm 114:5). In his Greek poetic rendering of the Psalm, Milton uses the phrase *hiros iordanes* or "holy Jordan."

[32] "John did baptize in the wilderness, and preach the baptism of amendment of life, for remission of sins" (Mark 1.4). "And he came into all the coasts about Jordan, preaching the baptism of repentance for the remission of sins" (Luke 3:3).

[33] Purified to receive him pure. "And every man that hath this hope in him, purifieth himself, even as he is pure" (1 John 3:3, AV). Not GE, BB, GT "purgeth himself." DR. "sanctifieth himself."

[34] All come. "Then went out to him Jerusalem and all Judea, and all the region round about Jordan" (Matthew 3:5).

[35] Among them was baptized. "And it came to pass in those days, that Jesus came from Nazareth, a city of Galilee, and was baptized of John in Jordan" (Mark 1:9).

[36] Jesus was not yet widely known in generally and certainly not generally known as the Christ. "And I knew him not: but because he should be declared to Israel, therefore am I come, baptizing with water" (John 1:31).

[37] John reveres Jesus. "And I knew him not: but because he should be declared to Israel, therefore am I come, baptizing with water. Then Jesus answering, said to him, Let be now: for thus it becometh us to fulfill all righteousness. So he suffered him" (Matthew 3:14,15).

[38] [Lines 80–81] Heaven's crystal doors. "And as soon as he was come out of the water, John saw the heavens cloven in twain" (Mark 1:10a, GE). "And Jesus when he was baptized, came straight out of the water; lo, the heavens were opened unto him, & John saw the Spirit of God descending like a dove, and lighting upon him" (Matthew 3:16). "Yet he had commanded the clouds above, and had opened the doors of heaven" (Psalms 78:23). "After this I looked, and behold, a door was open in heaven, and the first voice which I heard, was as it

A perfect Dove[39] descend (whate'er it meant);[40]
And out of Heaven the sovereign voice I heard,
'This is my Son beloved, —in him am pleased.'[41]
His mother, than, is mortal, but his Sire
He who obtains the monarchy of Heaven;
And what will He not do to advance his Son?
His first–begot we know, and sore have felt,
When his fierce thunder drove us to the Deep;
Who this is we must learn,[42] for Man he seems[43]

---

were of a trumpet talking with me, saying, 'Come up hither, and I will show thee things which must be done hereafter'" (Revelation 4:1).

[39] "And the holy Ghost descending upon him like a dove" (Mark 1:10b). "And the holy Ghost came down in a bodily shape like a dove, upon him" (Luke 3:22a). "So John bare record, saying, I beheld that Spirit come down from heaven, like a dove, and it abode upon him" (John 1:32).

[40] Whate'er it meant. The empiricist Satan cannot perceive things pertaining to the spirit. Compare with Paul's description of the "sensual man" which stands in contrast to the "spiritual man." "But the natural man perceiveth not the things of the Spirit of God: for they are foolishness unto him: neither can he know them, because they are spiritually discerned" (1 Corinthians 2:14, DR). *Douay-Rheims* note: "The sensual man is either he who is taken up with sensual pleasures, with carnal and worldly affections; or he who measureth divine mysteries by natural reason, sense, and human wisdom only. Now such a man has little or no notion of the things of God." AV, GT, GE, BB "natural man."

[41] "Then there was a voice from heaven, saying, Thou art my beloved Son, in whom I am well pleased" (Mark 1:11). "And lo, a voice came from heaven, saying, This is my beloved Son, in whom I am well pleased" (Matthew 3:17). "And there was a voice from heaven, saying, Thou art my beloved Son: in thee I am well pleased" (Luke 3:22b).

[42] Satan must verify that this is "the Son of God." "Then came to him the tempter, and said, 'If thou be the Son of God, command that these stones be made bread' [...] And said unto him, 'If thou be the Son of God, cast thy self down: for it is written, that he will give his Angels charge over thee, and with their hands they shall lift thee up, lest at any time thou shouldest dash thy foot against a stone'" (Matthew 4:3, 6). "Then the devil said unto him, 'If thou be the Son of God, command this stone that it be made bread' [...] And the devil said unto him, 'All this power will I give thee, and the glory of those kingdoms: for that is delivered to me: and to whomsoever I will, I give it'" (Luke 4:3, 6).

In all his lineaments, though in his face[44]
The glimpses of his Father's glory shine.[45]
Ye see our danger on the utmost edge
Of hazard, which admits no long debate,
But must with something sudden be opposed
(Not force, but well-couched fraud, well-woven snares),[46]
Ere in the head of nations he appear,
Their king,[47] their leader, and supreme on Earth.

---

[43] For Man he seems. "But he made himself of no reputation, & took on him the form of a servant, & was made like unto men, and was found in shape as a man" (Philippians 2:7). Compare GE "shape as a man" with AV "in the likeness of men," Bishops "found in figure as a man," DR "in habit found as a man," Coverdale "like another man," GT and Tyndale "like unto men." "For there is one God, and one Mediator between God and man, which is the man Christ Jesus" (1 Timothy 2:5). "For (that that was impossible to the Law, in as much as it was weak, because of the flesh) God sending his own Son, in the similitude of sinful flesh, & for sin, condemned sin in the flesh" (Romans 8:3). Compare GE, Bishops, Coverdale, GT, Tyndale "similitude of sinful flesh" with AV & DR "likeness of sinful flesh."

[44] Contrast that Moses sees God's glory without seeing his face: "Again he said, I beseech thee, show me thy glory [...] Furthermore he said, Thou canst not see my face, for there shall no man see me, and live" (Exodus 33:17, 19). Satan is familiar with the face of God: "Now on a day when the children of God came and stood before the Lord, Satan came also among them" (Job 1:6).

[45] [Lines 91–92] In his face the glimpses of his Father's glory shine. "For God that commanded the light to shine out of darkness, is he which hath shined in our hearts, to give the light of the knowledge of the glory of God in the face of Jesus Christ" (2 Corinthians 4:6).

[46] Satan's snares. Paul warns that an *episcopos* (bishop) "must also be well reported of, even of them which are without, lest he fall into rebuke, and the snare of the devil" (1 Timothy 3:7). Not Coverdale, GT or Tyndale "snare of the evil speaker." "And come to amendment out of that snare of the devil, of whom they are taken prisoners, to doe his will" (2 Timothy 2:26).

[47] [Lines 97–98] Jesus as a future king: "Jesus answered, "My kingdom is not of this world: if my kingdom were of this world, my servants would surely fight, that I should not be delivered to the Jews: but now is my kingdom not from hence" (John 8:36). Geneva Note: "Christ affirms his spiritual kingdom but rejects a worldly one." "For unto us a child is born, and unto us a Son is given: and the government is upon his shoulder, and he shall call his name Wonderful,

I, when no other durst, sole undertook
The dismal expedition to find out
And ruin Adam,[48] and the exploit performed
Successfully: a calmer voyage now
Will waft me; and the way found prosperous once
Induces best to hope of like success."
He ended, and his words impression left
Of much amazement to the infernal crew,[49]
Distracted and surprised with deep dismay
At these sad tidings. But no time was then
For long indulgence to their fears or grief:
Unanimous they all commit the care
And management of this man enterprise
To him, their great Dictator, whose attempt
At first against mankind so well had thrived
In Adam's overthrow, and led their march
From Hell's deep-vaulted den[50] to dwell in light,
Regents, and potentates,[51] and kings, yea gods,[52]

Counselor, The mighty God, The everlasting Father, The prince of peace, The increase of his government & peace shall have none end: he shall sit upon the throne of David, and upon his kingdom, to order it, and to stablish it with judgment and with justice, from henceforth, even for ever: the zeal of the Lord of hosts will perform this" (Isaiah 9:6,7).

[48] Ruined Adam. "Wherefore, as by one man sin entered into the world, & death by sin, and so death went over all men: in who all men have sinned" (Romans 5:12).

[49] [Lines 104–105] His words impression left of much amazement. Compare the effect of Satan's rhetoric upon his followers with the effect of Jesus upon his disciples: "And the men marveled, saying, 'What man is this, that both the winds and the sea obey him!" (Matthew 8:27).

[50] Den (metonymically "darkness" contrasted with light). "The Angels also which kept not their first estate, but left their own habitation, he hath reserved in everlasting chains under darkness unto the judgment of the great day" (Jude 6). "For if God spared not the Angels that had sinned, but cast them down into hell, and delivered them into chains of darkness, to be kept unto damnation" (2 Peter 2:4)

Of many a pleasant realm and province wide.
So to the coast of Jordan[53] he directs
His easy steps, girded with snaky wiles,[54]

---

[51] Satan and the fallen angels usurp the exclusive right of the Christ to the title "potentate": "Which in his times he shall show, who is the blessed, and only Potentate, the King of kings, and Lord of lords" (1 Timothy 6:15, AV). Not GE and Bishops "prince" nor DV, GT, Coverdale, Tyndale "mighty."

[52] Gods. "But God doth know, that when ye shall eat thereof, your eyes shall be opened, and ye shall be as gods, knowing good and evil" (Genesis 3:5). Not Coverdale and Tyndale "God" singular. "For though there be that are called gods, whether in heaven, or in earth (as there be many gods, and many lords)" (1 Corinthians 8:5). "God standeth in the assembly of gods: he judgeth among gods [...] I have said, Ye are gods, and ye all are children of the most High" (Psalm 82:1, 6). The gods of the nations are fallen angels: "Nay, but that these things which the Gentiles sacrifice, they sacrifice to devils, and not unto God: and I would not that ye should have fellowship with the devils" (1 Corinthians 10:20). "For all the gods of the Gentiles are devils: but the Lord made the heavens" (Psalm 95:5 DR). The Greek Septuagint renders the Hebrew as *daimonia* (devil or god) as does The Latin Vulgate. Not GE, AV, GT, Coverdale, or Tyndale "idols" instead of "devils" (Psalm 96:5).

[53] The coast of Jordan. "And Jesus full of the holy Ghost returned from Jordan, and was led by that Spirit into the wilderness, And was there forty days tempted of the devil, & in those days he did eat nothing: but when they were ended, he afterward was hungry" (Luke 4:1, 2). "The Amalekites dwell in the South country, and the Hittites, and the Jebusites, & the Amorites dwell in the mountains, & the Canaanites dwell by the sea, & by the coast of Jordan" (Numbers 13:29). Not DR "near the streams of the Jordan." Not Coverdale "and about Jordan." "The plain also, and Jordan, and the coast thereof, from Chinnereth, even unto the sea of the plain, even the salt sea, under Ashdoth Pisgah Eastward" (Deuteronomy 3:17, AV). Not GE "Jordan, and the borders." Not DR merely "the Jordan."

[54] [Lines 118–119] Trans-Jordan will continue to be a center of demonic activity or "snaky wiles" throughout the ministry of Jesus. "And cried with a loud voice, and said, 'What have I to do with thee, Jesus the Son of the most high God? I will that thou swear to me by God, that thou torment me not.' (For he said unto him, 'Come out of the man, thou unclean spirit.') And he asked him, 'What is thy name?' and he answered, saying, 'My name is Legion: for we are many' [...] Then they began to pray him, that he would depart from their coasts" (Mark 5:7–9, 17). The morally ambiguous and monstrous Behemoth associated with the

Where he might likeliest find this new-declared,
This man of men, attested Son of God,
Temptation[55] and all guile[56] on him to try;
So to subvert whom he suspected raised
To end his reign on Earth so long enjoyed:[57]
But, contrary, unweeting he fulfilled
The purposed counsel, pre-ordained[58] and fixed,[59]

Jordan River: "Behold, he spoileth the river, and hasteth not: he trusteth that he can draw up Jordan into his mouth" (Job 40:23). Contrast "girded with snaky wiles with the Messianic prophecy: "And justice shall be the girdle of his loins, and faithfulness the girdle of his reins" (Isaiah 11:5). Contrast also with the Christian armor described by Paul that is girded to oppose the "snaky wiles": "Put on the whole armor of God, that ye may be able to stand against the wiles of the devil [...] Stand therefore, having your loins girt about with truth, and having on the breast-plate of righteousness" (Ephesians 6:11, 14, AV). Not DR "deceits of the devil." Not GE, GT, Bishops, Coverdale, or Tyndale "assaults of the devil." Geneva Note: "Against men, who are of a frail and brittle nature, against whom are set spiritual wiles, a thousand times more mighty than the flesh."

[55] "Then was Jesus led aside of the Spirit into the wilderness, to be tempted of the devil" (Matthew 4:1). "And Jesus full of the holy Ghost returned from Jordan, and was led by that Spirit into the wilderness, And was there forty days tempted of the devil, & in those days he did eat nothing: but when they were ended, he afterward was hungry [...] And when the devil had ended all the temptation, he departed from him for a little season" (Luke 4:1, 2, 13).

[56] Contrast guile with Christian discourse: "For our exhortation was not by deceit, nor by uncleanness, nor by guile" (1 Thessalonians 2:3).

[57] Satan as the ruler of the earth. "We know that we are of God, and this whole world lieth in wickedness" (1 John 5:19). "Now is the judgment of this world: now shall the prince of this world be cast out" (John 12:31). "Of judgment, because the prince of this world is judged" (John 16:11).

[58] Purposed counsel, pre-ordained: "In whom also we are chosen when we were predestinate according to the purpose of him, which worketh all things after the counsel of his own will" Ephesians 1:11). "According to the eternal purpose, which he wrought in Christ Jesus our Lord" (Ephesians 3:11). Geneva note: "Which was before all things."

[59] The "purposed counsel" or judgment cast against Satan after the Fall: "I will also put enmity between thee and the woman, and between thy seed & her seed. He shall break thine head, and thou shalt bruise his heel" (Genesis 3:15).

Of the Most High,[60] who, in full frequence bright
Of Angels, thus to Gabriel smiling spake:
"Gabriel, this day, by proof, thou shalt behold,
Thou and all Angels conversant on Earth
With Man or men's affairs,[61] how I begin
To verify that solemn message late,
On which I sent thee to the Virgin pure
In Galilee, that she should bear a son,
Great in renown, and called the Son of God.
Then told'st her, doubting how these things could be
To her a virgin, that on her should come
The Holy Ghost, and the power of the Highest
O'ershadow her.[62] This Man, born and now upgrown,[63]

---

60 "That they may know that thou, which art called Jehovah, art alone, even the most High over all the earth" (Psalm 83:18).

61 Gabriel's pattern of being conversant with Man: "And I heard a man's voice between the banks of Ulai, which called, and said, "Gabriel, make this man to understand the vision" (Daniel 8:16). "Yea, while I was speaking in prayer, even the man Gabriel, whom I had seen before in the vision, came flying, and touched me about the time of the evening oblation. And he informed me, and talked with me, and said, "O Daniel, I am now come forth to give thee knowledge and understanding" (Daniel 9:21, 22). "And the Angel answered, and said unto him, I am Gabriel that stand in the presence of God, and am sent to speak unto thee, & to show thee these good tidings [...] And in the sixth month, the Angel Gabriel was sent from God unto a city of Galilee, named Nazareth to a virgin affianced to a man whose name was Joseph, of the house of David, & the virgin's name was Marie" (Luke 1:19, 26, 27).

62 [Lines 132–139] "And the Angel went in unto her, and said, "Hail thou that art freely beloved: the Lord is with thee: blessed art thou among women." And when she saw him, she was troubled at his saying, and thought what manner of salutation that should be. Then the Angel said unto her, "Fear not, Mary: for thou hast found favor with God. For lo, thou shalt conceive in thy womb, and bear a son, and shalt call his name Jesus. He shall be great, and shall be called the Son of the Most High, and the Lord God shall give unto him the throne of his father David. And he shall reign over the house of Jacob for ever, and of his kingdom shall be none end." Then said Mary unto the Angel, "How shall this be, seeing I know not man?" And the Angel answered, & said unto her, "The holy Ghost shall come upon thee, and the power of the most High shall overshadow thee:

To shew him worthy of his birth divine
And high prediction, henceforth I expose
To Satan;[64] let him tempt, and now assay
His utmost subtlety,[65] because he boasts
And vaunts of his great cunning to the throng
Of his Apostasy. He might have learnt
Less overweening, since he failed in Job,[66]
Whose constant perseverance[67] overcame
Whate'er his cruel malice could invent.
He now shall know I can produce a man,[68]
Of female seed,[69] far abler to resist[70]
All his solicitations, and at length

---

therefore also that holy thing which shall be born of thee, shall be called the Son of God" (Luke 1:28–37).

[63] Now upgrown. "And Jesus increased in wisdom, and stature, and in favor with God and men" (Luke 2:52). DR, GT, Coverdale, and Tyndale "wisdom and age."

[64] Henceforth I expose to Satan. Compare with God's response to Satan's challenge of the integrity of Job: "Then the Lord said unto Satan, Lo, he is in thine hand, but save his life" (Job 2:6). GT & Tyndale "there hast thou him in thy power."

[65] The subtlety of Satan: "Now the serpent was more subtle then any beast of the field, which the Lord God had made: and he said to the woman, 'Yea, hath God indeed said, Ye shall not eat of every tree of the garden?'" (Genesis 3:1).

[66] He failed in Job. "In all this did not Job sin with his lips" (Job 2:10).

[67] "Behold, we count them blessed which endure. Ye have heard of the patience of Job, and have known what end the Lord made. For the Lord is very pitiful and merciful" (James 5:11).

[68] "For as by one man's disobedience many were made sinners, so by that obedience of that one shall many also be made righteous" (Romans 5:19).

[69] The seed of the woman. "I will also put enmity between thee and the woman, and between thy seed & her seed. He shall break thine head, and thou shalt bruise his heel" (Genesis 3:15). "But when the fullness of time was come, God sent forth his Son made of a woman, and made under the Law" (Galatians 4:4).

[70] Far abler to resist. The author of Hebrews refers to Jesus's role as High Priest: "For we have not an high Priest, which cannot be touched with the feeling of our infirmities, but was in all things tempted in like sort, yet without sin" (Hebrews 4:15).

All his vast force, and drive him back to Hell[71]
Winning by conquest[72] what the first man[73] lost
By fallacy[74] surprised. But first I mean
To exercise him in the Wilderness;[75]
There he shall first lay down the rudiments
Of his great warfare, ere I send him forth
To conquer Sin and Death,[76] the two grand foes.

---

[71] "For if God spared not the Angels that had sinned, but cast them down into hell, and delivered them into chains of darkness, to be kept unto damnation" (2 Peter 2:4). "And am alive, but I was dead: and behold, I am alive for evermore, Amen: and I have the keys of hell and of death" (Revelation 1:18).

[72] Jesus conquers sin and death. "These things have I spoken unto you, that in me ye might have peace: in the world ye shall have affliction, but be of good comfort: I have overcome the world" (John 16:33). "To him that overcommeth, will I grant to sit with me in my throne, even as I overcame, and sit with my Father in his throne" (Revelation 3:21). "And putting out the hand writing of ordinances that was against us, which was contrary to us, he even took it out of the way, and fastened it upon the cross, And hath spoiled the Principalities, and Powers, & hath made a shew of them openly, and hath triumphed over them in the same cross" (Colossians 2:14, 15).

[73] The first man Adam. "As it is also written, The first man Adam was made a living soul: and the last Adam was made a quickening Spirit" (1 Corinthians 15:45).

[74] By fallacy surprised. Satan invented lying: "Ye are of your father the devil, and the lusts of your father ye will do: he hath been a murderer from the beginning, and abode not in the truth, because there is no truth in him. When he speaketh a lie, then speaketh he of his own: for he is a liar, and the father thereof" (John 8:44).

[75] Wilderness testing. "Then was Jesus led aside of the Spirit into the wilderness, to be tempted of the devil" (Matthew 4:1). Not DR "desert." "And thou shalt remember all the way which the Lord thy God led the this forty year in the wilderness, for to humble thee and to prove thee, to know what was in thine heart, whether thou wouldst keep his commandments or no" (Deuteronomy 8:2). "And all the children of Israel murmured against Moses and Aaron: and the whole assembly said unto them, 'Would God we had died in the land of Egypt, or in this wilderness: would God we were dead'" (Numbers 14:2).

[76] The defeat of Sin and Death. "For the wages of sin is death: but the gift of God is eternal life, through Jesus Christ our Lord" (Romans 6:23). "So when this corruptible hath put on incorruption, and this mortal hath put on immortality,

By humiliation and strong sufferance[77]
His weakness[78] shall o'ercome[79] Satanic strength,[80]
And all the world,[81] and mass of sinful flesh;[82]

---

then shall be brought to pass the saying that is written, 'Death is swallowed up into victory. O death where is thy sting? O grave where is thy victory?' The sting of death is sin: and the strength of sin is the Law. But thanks be unto God, which hath given us victory through our Lord Jesus Christ" (1 Corinthians 15:54–57). "And God shall wipe away all tears from their eyes: and there shall be no more death, neither sorrow, neither crying, neither shall there be any more pain: for the first things are passed" (Revelation 21:4).

[77] [Lines 159–160] By humiliation and strong sufferance. "For it became him, for whom are all things, and by whom are all things, in bringing many sons unto glory, to make the Captain of their salvation perfect through sufferings [...] Forasmuch then as the children are partakers of flesh and blood, he also himself likewise took part of the same, that through death he might destroy him that had the power of death, that is, the devil: And deliver them, who through fear of death were all their lifetime subject to bondage" (Hebrews 2:10, 14, 15, AV). Douay-Rheims Coverdale, Tyndale also "sufferings." Not GE and Bishops "afflictions."

[78] "He humbled himself, and became obedient unto the death, even the death of the Cross. here fore God hath also highly exalted him, and given him a Name above every name, That at the name of Iesus should every knee bow, both of things in heaven, and things in earth, and things under the earth, And that every tongue should confess that Jesus Christ is the Lord, unto the glory of God the Father" (Philippians 2:8–11).

[79] "These shall fight with the Lamb, and the Lamb shall overcome them: for he is Lord of Lords, and King of Kings: and they that are on his side, called, and chosen, and faithful (Revelation 17:14).

[80] Weakness overcomes strength. "But the foolish things of the world hath God chosen, that he may confound the wise: and the weak things of the world hath God chosen, that he may confound the strong" (1 Corinthians 1:27, DR). Not GE, AV, GT, Bishops, Coverdale "mighty." "Out of the mouth of babes & sucklings hast thou ordained strength, because of thine enemies, that thou mightiest still the enemy and the avenger" (Psalm 8:2). "And he said unto me, 'My grace is sufficient for thee: for my power is made perfect through weakness.' Very gladly therefore will I rejoice rather in mine infirmities, that the power of Christ may dwell in me" (1 Corinthians 12:9). "For the foolishness of God is wiser then men, and the weakness of God is stronger then men" (1 Corinthians 1:25).

That all the Angels and aethereal Powers.
They now, and men hereafter may discern
From what consummate[83] virtue I have chose
This perfect man,[84] by merit called my Son,
To earn salvation for the sons of men."
So spake the Eternal Father,[85] and all Heaven
Admiring stood a space; then into hymns
Burst forth, and in celestial measures moved,
Circling the throne and singing,[86] while the hand

---

[81] Christ overcomes. "These things have I spoken unto you, that in me ye might have peace: in the world ye shall have affliction, but be of good comfort: I have overcome the world" (John 16:33).
[82] Mass of sinful flesh. "In whom also ye are circumcised with circumcision made without hand, by putting off the sinful body of the flesh, through the circumcision of Christ" (Colossians 2:11). "For (that that was impossible to the Law, in as much as it was weak, because of the flesh) God sending his own Son, in the similitude of sinful flesh, & for sin, condemned sin in the flesh" (Romans 8:3).
[83] Consummate. "And being consummated, he became, to all that obey him, the cause of eternal salvation" (Hebrews 5:9 Douay-Rheims).
[84] [Lines 165–166] Christ a perfect man. "Though he were the son, yet learned he obedience, by these things which he suffered: And being perfect, was made the author of eternal salvation unto all them that obey him" (Hebrews 5:8, 9 Bishops). See also AV, Coverdale, GT, and Tyndale "perfect." GE "consecrate." DR "consummated."
[85] Eternal Father. "For unto us a child is born, and unto us a Son is given: and the government is upon his shoulder, and he shall call his name Wonderful, Counselor, The mighty God, The everlasting Father, The prince of peace" (Isaiah 9:6 GE). Geneva note: "The author of eternity, and by whom the Church and every member of it will be preserved forever and have immortal life."
[86] Heavenly creatures sing praises of the Son. "And when he had taken the Book, the four beasts and the four & twenty Elders fell down before the Lamb, having every one harps & golden vials full of odors, which are the prayers of the Saints, And they sung a new song, saying, 'Thou art worthy to take the Book, and to open the seals thereof, because thou wast killed, and hast redeemed us to God by thy blood out of every kindred, and tongue, and people, and nation" (Revelation 5:8, 9). "And I heard a voice from heaven, as the sound of many waters, and as the sound of a great thunder: and I heard the voice of harpers harping with their

Sung with the voice, and this the argument:
"Victory and triumph to the Son of God,
Now entering his great duel, not of arms,
But to vanquish by wisdom hellish wiles!
The Father knows the Son;[87] therefore secure
Ventures his filial virtue, though untried,
Against whate'er may tempt, whate'er seduce,
Allure, or terrify, or undermine.
Be frustrate, all ye stratagems of Hell,
And, devilish machinations,[88] come to nought!"
So they in Heaven their odes and vigils tuned.
Meanwhile the Son of God, who yet some days
Lodged in Bethabara, where John baptized,[89]
Musing and much revolving in his breast
How best the mighty work he might begin
Of Saviour to mankind, and which way first
Publish his godlike office now mature,

---

harps. And they sung as it were a new song before the throne, and before the four beasts, and the Elders: and no man could learn that song, but the hundredth, forty and four thousand, which were bought from the earth" (Revelation 14:2, 3). "And I saw as it were a glassy sea, mingled with fire, and them that had gotten victory of the beast, and of his image, and of his mark, and of the number of his name, stand at the glassy sea, having the harps of God, And they sung the song of Moses the servant of God, & the song of the Lamb, saying, Great and marvelous are thy works, Lord God almighty: just and true are thy ways, King of Saints" (Revelation 15:2, 3).

[87] The Father knows the Son. "As the Father knoweth me, so know I the Father: and I lay down my life for my sheep" (John 10:15). "All things are given unto me of my Father: and no man knoweth the Son, but the Father: neither knoweth any man the Father, but the Son, and he to whom the Son will reveal him" (Matthew 11:27). All things are given me of my Father: and no man knoweth who the Son is, but the Father: neither who the Father is, save the Son, and he to whom the Son will reveal him" (Luke 10:22).

[88] "Put on the whole armor of God, that ye may be able to stand against the assaults of the devil" (Ephesians 6:11).

[89] "These things were done in Bethabara beyond Jordan, where John did baptize" (John 1:28).

One day forth walked alone, the Spirit leading[90]
And his deep thoughts, the better to converse
With solitude,[91] till, far from track of men,
Thought following thought, and step by step led on,
He entered now the bordering Desert[92] wild,
And, with dark shades and rocks environed round,
His holy meditations thus pursued.
"O what a multitude of thoughts at once
Awakened in me swarm, while I consider
What from within I feel myself, and hear
What from without comes often to my ears,
Ill sorting with my present state compared!
When I was yet a child, no childish play[93]
To me was pleasing; all my mind was set[94]
Serious to learn and know,[95] and thence to do,

---

[90] Spirit Leading. "Then was Jesus led aside of the Spirit into the wilderness, to be tempted of the devil" (Matthew 4:1). "And Jesus full of the holy Ghost returned from Jordan, and was led by that Spirit into the wilderness" (Luke 4:1). Contrast with Mark's driving spirit. "And immediately the Spirit driveth him into the wilderness" (Mark 1:12).

[91] Solitude. "And in the morning very early before day, Iesus arose & went out into a solitary place, and there prayed" (Mark 1:35). Not DR nor Coverdale "desert place."

[92] Desert. "Then Jesus was led by the spirit into the desert, to be tempted by the devil" (Matthew 4:1 DR; see also Luke 4:1). Not AV, GE, Bishops, DR, Coverdale, GT, Tyndale "wilderness." Geneva Map before the New Testament describes this region as "Arabia the desert."

[93] No childish play. Contrast with Paul's words "When I was a child, I spoke as a child, I understood as a child, I thought as a child: but when I became a man, I put away childish things" (1 Corinthians 13:11).

[94] [Lines 200–201] "And the child grew, and waxed strong in Spirit, and was filled with wisdom, and the grace of God was with him" (Luke 2:40).

[95] Jesus as a child was driven to know Godly things. "Which things also we speak, not in the words which man's wisdom teacheth, but which the holy Ghost teacheth, comparing spiritual things with spiritual things. But the natural man perceiveth not the things of the Spirit of God: for they are foolishness unto him: neither can he know them, because they are spiritually discerned" (1 Corinthians 2:13, 14).

What might be public good; myself I thought
Born to that end, born to promote all truth,[96]
All righteous things. Therefore, above my years,
The Law of God I read, and found it sweet;[97]
Made it my whole delight,[98] and in it grew
To such perfection that, ere yet my age
Had measured twice six years,[99] at our great Feast
I went into the Temple, there to hear
The teachers of our Law, and to propose
What might improve my knowledge or their own,
And was admired by all.[100] Yet this not all
To which my spirit aspired. Victorious deeds
Flamed in my heart,[101] heroic acts—one while

---

[96] Born to that end, born to promote all truth. "Pilate therefore said unto him: 'Art thou a king then?' Jesus answered: 'Thou sayest that I am a king. For this cause am I born, & for this cause came I into the world, that I should bear witness unto the truth: And all that are of the truth, hear my voice" (John 18:37 Bishops, see also GT and Tyndale). Not AV, GE, DR "everyone." Not Coverdale "who so ever."

[97] The Law of God I read, and found it sweet. "How sweet are thy promises unto my mouth! Yea, more then honey unto my mouth" (Psalm 119:103). "When their judges shall be cast down in stony places, they shall hear my words, for they are sweet" (Psalm 141:6).

[98] Delight in the Law. "But his delight is in the Law of the Lord, and in his Law doth he meditate day and night" (Psalm 1:2). Not DR "his will is in the Law of the Lord."

[99] Jesus in Jerusalem at "twice six years" for "the feast." "And when he was twelve years old, and they were come up to Jerusalem, after the custom of the feast" (Luke 2:41). Not DR "solemn day."

[100] [Lines 210–13] Teachers of our law. "And it fortuned after three days, that they found him in the temple, sitting among the teachers, hearing them, and opposing them. And all they that heard him, wondered at his understanding and answers. And when they saw him, they were astonished. And his mother said unto him: 'My son, why hast thou done this unto us? Behold, thy father and I have sought thee sorrowing.' And he said unto them: 'What is it, that ye have sought me? Wyst ye not, that I must go about my father's business?' And they understood not the saying that he spake unto them" (Luke 2:46–50 Coverdale). Not AV, GE, Bishops, DR, GT or Tyndale "sitting in the midst of the doctors."

To rescue Israel from the Roman yoke;[102]
Then to subdue and quell, o'er all the earth,[103]
Brute violence and proud tyrannic power,
Till truth were freed,[104] and equity restored:
Yet held it more humane, more heavenly, first
By winning words[105] to conquer willing hearts,[106]
And make persuasion[107] do the work of fear;
At least to try, and teach the erring soul,[108]

---

[101] Flamed in my heart. Compare with the burning hearts in the disciples that heard Jesus speak: "And they said between themselves, 'Did not our hearts burn within us, while he talked with us by the way, and when he opened to us the Scriptures"? (Luke 24:32). Compare also with the internal burning of Jeremiah as he begins his work as a prophet: "Then I said, 'I will not make mention of him, nor speak any more in his Name. But his word was in mine heart as a burning fire shut up in my bones, and I was weary with forbearing, and I could not stay" (Jeremiah 20:9).

[102] Roman yoke. In Jesus saying "take MY yoke" he implies that there is another yoke option (Matthew 11:29).

[103] Subdue the earth. Compare with the command given to the first man Adam: "And God blessed them, and God said to them, 'Bring forth fruit and multiply, and fill the earth, and subdue it, and rule over the fish of the sea, and over the fowl of the heaven, & over every beast that moveth upon the earth'" (Genesis 1:28).

[104] Till truth were freed. Verbal echo of the words of Jesus: "Then said Jesus to the Jew which believed in him, 'If ye continue in my word, ye are verily my disciples, And shall know the truth, and the truth shall make you free'" (John 8:31, 32).

[105] Winning words. "Let your speech be gracious always, and powdered with salt, that ye may know how to answer every man" (Colossians 4:6).

[106] Willing hearted. Compare with the generous spirit of the Israelites: "And they came both men and women, as many as were willing hearted, and brought bracelets, and earrings, and rings, & tablets, all jewels of gold: and everyman that offered, offered an offering of gold unto the Lord" (Exodus 35:22 AV, see also Bishops, Coverdale, GT, Tyndale). Not GE "free hearted." DR omits the phrase altogether.

[107] Let persuasion continue its work. "But continue thou in the things which thou hast learned, and which are committed unto thee, knowing of who thou hast learned them" (2 Timothy 3:14).

Not wilfully misdoing, but unware[109][110]
Misled;[111] the stubborn only to subdue.[112]
These growing thoughts my mother soon perceiving,
By words at times cast forth,[113] inly rejoiced,
And said to me apart, 'High are thy thoughts,[114]

---

108 Teach the erring soul. "Gracious & righteous is the Lord: therefore will he teach sinners in the way" (Psalm 25:8). "'The son of man is not come to destroy men's souls, but to save them.' And they went into another town" (Luke 9:56 Coverdale, see also Douay-Rheims). Not AV, GE, Bishops, GT, Tyndale "destroy men's lives."

109 Not willfully misdoing, but unaware. Provisions for the unintentional sin under the Mosaic Law: "If any person transgress & sin through ignorance by taking away things consecrated unto the Lord, he shall then bring for his trespass offering unto the Lord a ram without blemish out of the flock, worth two shekels of silver by thy estimation after the shekel of the Sanctuary, for a trespass offering" (Leviticus 5:15). Compare with Jesus words: "Then said Jesus, Father, forgive them: for they know not what they do; they parted his raiment, and cast lots" (Luke 23:34).

110 [Lines 223–224] Secret erring. "Who can understand his errors? Cleanse thou me from secret faults" (Psalm 19:12 AV, see also Bishops). Not GE "faults." Coverdale, DR, Tyndale, GT "how oft he offendeth."

111 Compare with Satan's beguiling of Eve: "And the Lord God said to the woman, 'Why hast thou done this?' And the woman said, 'The serpent beguiled me, and I did eat'" (Genesis 3:13). DR, Coverdale, Tyndale "deceived." "And Adam was not deceived, but the woman was deceived, and was in the transgression" (1 Timothy 2:14). Not DR "seduced."

112 The subduing of sin: "He will turn again, and have compassion upon us: he will subdue our iniquities, and cast all their sins into the bottom of the sea" (Micah 7:19). "Who shall change our vile body, that it may be fashioned like unto his glorious body, according to the working, whereby he is able even to subdue all things unto him self" (Philippians 3:21).

113 Mary's words cast forth when finding him at the Temple after days of searching. "So when they saw him, they were amazed, and his mother said unto him, 'Son, why hast thou thus dealt with us? Behold, thy father and I have sought thee with very heavy hearts" (Luke 2:48).

114 High are thy thoughts. Compare with the high thoughts of God. "'For my thoughts are not your thoughts, neither are your ways my ways,' saith the Lord. 'For as the heavens are higher than the earth, so are my ways higher then your ways, and my thoughts above your thoughts" (Isaiah 55:8, 9).

O Son! but nourish them, and let them soar
To what highth sacred virtue and true worth
Can raise them, though above example high;
By matchless deeds express thy matchless Sire.[115]
For know,[116] thou art no son of mortal man;
Though men esteem thee low of parentage,[117]
Thy Father[118] is the Eternal King[119] who rules
All Heaven and Earth, Angels and sons of men.
A messenger from God foretold thy birth
Conceived in me a virgin; he foretold[120]

---

[115] By matchless deeds express thy matchless Sire. "Then answered Jesus, and said unto them, 'Verily, verily I say unto you, the Son can do nothing of himself, save that he seeth the Father do: for whatsoever things he doth, the same things doth the Son in like manner'" (John 5:19).

[116] Compare Mary's strongly expressed conviction here with Elizabeth's commendation for her strong faith in the promises given about her son. "And blessed is she that believed: for those things shall be performed, which were told her from the Lord" (Luke 1:45).

[117] Esteemed thee of low parentage. "And Jesus himself began to be about thirty year of age, being as men supposed the son of Joseph, which was the son of Eli" (Luke 3:23).

[118] "Then said he unto them, 'How is it that ye sought me? Knew ye not that I must go about my Father's business?'" (Luke 2:49).

[119] God the Eternal King. "But the Lord is the God of truth: he is the living God, and an everlasting King: at his anger the earth shall tremble, and the nations cannot abide his wrath" (Jeremiah 10:10). "Now unto the King everlasting, immortal, invisible, unto God only wise, be honor and glory, for ever, and ever, Amen" (1 Timothy 1:17). "Thy kingdom is an everlasting kingdom, and thy dominion endureth throughout all ages" (Psalm 145:13). "For the invisible things of him, that is, his eternal power & Godhead, are seen by the creation of the world, being considered in his works, to the intent that they should be without excuse" (Romans 1:20).

[120] [Lines 237–238] "And in the sixth month, the Angel Gabriel was sent from God unto a city of Galilee, named Nazareth, to a virgin affianced to a man whose name was Joseph, of the house of David, & the virgin's name was Mary. And the Angel went in unto her, and said, 'Hail thou that art freely beloved: the Lord is with thee: blessed art thou among women.' And when she saw him, she was troubled at his saying, and thought what manner of salutation that should be.

Thou shouldst be great, and sit on David's throne,[121]
And of thy kingdom there should be no end.[122]
At thy nativity a glorious quire
Of Angels, in the fields of Bethlehem, sung[123]
To shepherds, watching at their folds by night,[124]
And told them the Messiah now was born,[125]
Where they might see him; and to thee they came,
Directed to the manger where thou lay'st;[126]

Then the Angel said unto her, 'Fear not, Mary: for thou hast found favor with God. For loe, thou shalt conceive in thy womb, and bear a son, and shalt call his name Jesus'" (Luke 1:26–31). Compare with Gabriel's words to Joseph, "But whiles he thought these things, behold, the Angel of the Lord appeared unto him in a dream, saying, 'Joseph, the son of David, fear not to take Mary thy wife: for that which is conceived in her, is of the holy Ghost. And she shall bring forth a son, and thou shalt call his name Jesus: for he shall save his people from their sins. And all this was done that it might be fulfilled, which is spoken of the Lord by the Prophet, saying, 'Behold, a virgin shall be with child, and shall bear a son, & they shall call his name Emmanuel, which is by interpretation, God with us'" (Matthew 1:20–23).

121 Thou shouldst be great and sit on David's throne. "He shall be great, and shall be called the Son of the most High, and the Lord God shall give unto him the throne of his father David" (Luke 1:32).

122 And of thy kingdom there should be no end. "And he shall reign over the house of Jacob for ever, and of his kingdom shall be none end" (Luke 1:33). "But unto the Son he saith, 'O God, thy throne is for ever and ever: the scepter of thy kingdom is a scepter of righteousness" (Hebrews 1:8).

123 "And straightway there was with the Angel a multitude of heavenly soldiers, praising God, and saying, 'Glory be to God in the high heavens, and peace in earth, and towards men good will" (Luke 2:13, 14).

124 "And there were in the same country shepherds, abiding in the field, and keeping watch by night over their flock" (Luke 2:8).

125 "That is, that unto you is born this day in the city of David, a Savior, which is Christ the Lord" (Luke 2:11).

126 [Lines 245–246] Directed to the manger where thou lay'st. "And this shall be a sign unto you; ye shall find the babe wrapped in swaddling clothes lying in a manger […] And they came with haste, and found Mary and Joseph, and the babe lying in a manger. And when they had seen it, they made known abroad the saying, which was told them, concerning this child" (Luke 2:12, 16, 17, AV). Not GE "the babe laid in the cratch."

For in the inn was left no better room.[127]
A Star, not seen before, in heaven appearing,[128]
Guided the Wise Men thither from the East,[129]
To honor thee with incense, myrrh, and gold;[130]
By whose bright course led on they found the place,
Affirming it thy star, new-graven in heaven,
By which they knew thee King of Israel born.
Just Simeon[131] and prophetic Anna,[132] warned

---

127 For in the inn was left no better room. "And she brought forth her first begotten son, and wrapped him in swaddling clothes, and laid him in a cratch, because there was no room for them in the inn" (Luke 2:7).
128 A star, not seen before, in heaven appearing. God controls the heavens and what appears in them. "And, Thou, Lord, in the beginning hast established the earth, and the heavens are the works of thine hands" (Hebrews 1:10).
129 "When Jesus then was born at Bethlehem in Judea, in the days of Herod the King, behold, there came Wisemen from the East to Jerusalem, Saying, 'Where is that King of the Jews that is born? For we have seen his star in the East, and are come to worship him [...] So when they had heard the King, they departed: and lo, the star which they had seen in the East, went before them, till it came and stood over the place where the babe was. And when they saw the star, they rejoiced with an exceeding great joy" (Matthew 2:1, 2, 9, 10).
130 To honor thee with incense, myrrh, and gold. "And went into the house, and found the babe with Mary his mother, and fell down, and worshipped him, and opened their treasures, and presented unto him gifts, even gold, and frankincense, and myrrh" (Matthew 2:11).
131 "And behold, there was a man in Jerusalem, whose name was Simeon: this man was just, and feared God, and waited for the consolation of Israel, and the holy Ghost was upon him. And it was declared to him from God by the holy Ghost, that he should not see death, before he had seen that Anointed of the Lord. And he came by the motion of the spirit into the Temple, and when the parents brought in the babe Jesus, to do for him after the custom of the Law, then he took him in his arms, and praised God, and said, 'Lord, now lettest thou thy servant depart in peace, according to thy word, For mine eyes have seen thy salvation, Which thou hast prepared before the face of all people, A light to be revealed to the Gentiles, and the glory of thy people Israel.' And Joseph and his mother marveled at those things, which were spoken touching him. And Simeon blessed them, and said unto Mary his mother, 'Behold, this child is appointed for the fall and rising again of many in Israel, and for a sign which shall be spoken

By vision, found thee in the Temple, and spake,
Before the altar and the vested priest,[133]
Like things of thee to all that present stood.'
This having heart, straight I again revolved
The Law and Prophets,[134] searching what was writ
Concerning the Messiah,[135] to our scribes

---

against, (Yea and a sword shall pierce through thy soul) that the thoughts of many hearts may be opened'" (Luke 2:25–35).

[132] "And there was a Prophetess, one Anna the daughter of Phanuel, of the tribe of Asher, which was of a great age, after she had lived with an husband seven years from her virginity: And she was widow about four score and four years, and went not out of the Temple, but served God with fastings & prayers, night and day. She then coming at the same instant upon them, confessed likewise the Lord, & spake of him to all that looked for redemption in Jerusalem" (Luke 2:36–38).

[133] The vested priest. Milton is referring to the Jewish High Priest who wore a special and ornate ephod. "Also thou shalt take the garments, and put upon Aaron the tunicle, and the robe of the Ephod, and the Ephod, and the breast plate, and shalt close them to him with the broidered girdle of the Ephod" (Exodus 29:5).

[134] The "Law and the Prophets" refers to the writings of Moses and the books attributed to various prophets in the Old Testament. "Therefore, whatsoever ye would that men should do to you, even so do ye to them: for this is the Law and the Prophets" (Matthew 7:12). "Philip found Nathanael, and said unto him, 'We have found him of whom Moses did write in the Law, and the Prophets, Jesus that son of Joseph, that was of Nazareth" (John 1:45). "Think not that I am come to destroy the Law, or the Prophets. I am not come to destroy them, but to fulfill them" (Matthew 5:17).

[135] [Lines 259–260] What was writ concerning the Messiah. "The Lord thy God will raise up unto thee a Prophet like unto me, from among you, even of thy brethren: unto him ye shall hearken, According to all that thou desiredst of the Lord thy God in Horeb, in the day of the assembly, when thou saidest, 'Let me hear the voice of my Lord God no more, nor see this great fire any more, that I die not.' And the Lord said unto me, 'They have well spoken. I will raise them up a Prophet from among their brethren like unto thee, and will put my words in his mouth, and he shall speak unto them all that I shall command him. And whosoever will not hearken unto my words, which he shall speak in my Name, I will require it of him'" (Deuteronomy 18:15–19). "Therefore the Lord himself will give you a sign. Behold, the virgin shall conceive and bear a son, and she shall

Known partly, and soon found of whom they spake[136]
I am[137]—this chiefly, that my way[138] must lie

---

call his name Immanuel" (Isaiah 7:14). "For unto us a child is born, and unto us a Son is given: and the government is upon his shoulder, and he shall call his name Wonderful, Counselor, The mighty God, The everlasting Father, The prince of peace, The increase of his government & peace shall have none end: he shall sit upon the throne of David, and upon his kingdom, to order it, and to establish it with judgment and with justice, from henceforth, even forever: the zeal of the Lord of hosts will perform this (Isaiah 9:6,7). "Behold, the days come, saith the Lord, that I will perform that good thing, which I have promised unto the house of Israel, & to the house of Judah. In those days and at that time, will I cause the branch of righteousness to grow up unto David, & he shall execute judgment, and righteousness in the land. In those days shall Judah be saved, and Jerusalem shall dwell safely, and he that shall call her, is the Lord our righteousness. For thus saith the Lord, David shall never want a man to sit upon the throne of the house of Israel" (Jeremiah 33:14–17).

[136] [Lines 259–261] Of whom they [the Law and Prophets] spake. The disciples also identify Jesus as the Messiah or Christ based upon their reading of the Law and Prophets: "And Jesus went out, and his disciples into the towns of Caesarea Philippi; by the way he asked his disciples, saying unto them, 'Whom do men say that I am?' And they answered, 'Some say, John Baptist: and some, Elias: and some, one of the Prophets." And he said unto them, 'But whom say ye that I am?' Then Peter answered, and said unto him, 'Thou art that Christ'" (Mark 8:27–29). See also Luke 9:18–20.

[137] Jesus will later apply the words of Isaiah the prophet to himself. "And he came to Nazareth where he had been brought up, and (as his custom was) went into the Synagogue on the Sabbath day, and stood up to read. And there was delivered unto him the book of the Prophet Esaias: and when he had opened the book, he found the place, where it was written, 'The Spirit of the Lord is upon me, because he hath anointed me, that I should preach the Gospel to the poor: he hath sent me, that I should heal the broken hearted, that I should preach deliverance to the captives, and recovering of sight to the blind, that I should set at liberty them that are bruised: And that I should preach the acceptable year of the Lord.' And he closed the book, and gave it again to the minister, and sat down: and the eyes of all that were in the Synagogue were fastened on him. Then he began to say unto them, 'This day is the Scripture fulfilled in your ears'" (Luke 4:16–21). Compare with the description of God at Exodus 3:15: "And God answered Moses, 'I Am That I Am.' Also, he said, 'Thus shalt thou say unto the children of Israel, I Am hath sent me unto you" (Exodus 3:14). Not Coverdale and Tyndale "I will be what I will be." "Jesus said unto them, 'Verily, verily I say

Through many a hard assay, even to the death,[139]
Ere I the promised kingdom can attain,
Or work redemption for mankind, whose sins'
Full weight must be transferred upon my head.[140]

---

unto you, before Abraham was, I am" (John 8:58). "Then the high Priest stood up amongst them, and asked Jesus, saying, 'Answerest thou nothing? What is the matter that these bear witness against thee?' But he held his peace and answered nothing. Again, the high Priest asked him, and said unto him, 'Art thou that Christ the Son of the Blessed?' And Jesus said, 'I am he, and ye shall see the Son of man sit at the right hand of the power of God and come in the clouds of heaven'" (Mark 14:60–62).

[138] [Lines 262–264] John the Baptist as the prophesied "messenger" prepares "the way" for Jesus and the foretold Kingdom is oppressed: "For this is he of whom it is written, 'Behold, I send my messenger before thy face, which shall prepare thy way before thee.' Verily I say unto you, among them which are begotten of women, arose there not a greater than John Baptist: notwithstanding, he that is the least in the kingdom of heaven, is greater than he. And from the time of John Baptist hitherto, the kingdom of heaven suffereth violence, and the violent take it by force" (Matthew 11:10–12).

[139] Through many a hard assay, even to death. The suffering Messiah: "He is despised and rejected of men: he is a man full of sorrows and hath experience of infirmities: we hide as it were our faces from him: he was despised and we esteemed him not [...] He was oppressed and he was afflicted, yet did he not open his mouth: he is brought as a sheep to the slaughter, and as a sheep before her shearer is dumb, so he openeth not his mouth. He was taken out from prison, and from judgment: and who shall declare his age? For he was cut out of the land of the living: for the transgression of my people was he plagued" (Isaiah 53:3, 7, 8). Compare the verbal echo of "even to death" with Jesus words to his disciples on the night of this death while praying in Gethsemane: "Then said Jesus unto them, 'My soul is very heavy, even unto the death: tarry ye here, and watch with me'" (Matthew 6:38).

[140] [Lines 265–266] Whose sins full weight must be transferred upon my head. "As for us we are all gone astray like sheep, everyone hath turned his own way: but the Lord hath thrown upon him all our sins" (Isaiah 53:6, Bishops). Not GE or AV "laid…iniquity." Not GT "through him the Lord pardoneth as our sins." Not Tyndale "heaped together the iniquity of us all." "Therefore, will I give him a portion with the great, and he shall divide the spoil with the strong, because he hath poured out his soul unto death: and he was counted with the transgressors, & he bear the sin of many, and prayed for the trespassers" (Isaiah 53:12).

Yet, neither thus disheartened or dismayed,
The time prefixed I waited; when behold
The Baptist (of whose birth I oft had heard,
Not knew by sight[141]) now come,[142] who was to come
Before Messiah,[143] and his way prepare.[144]
I, as all others, to his baptism came,[145]
Which I believed was from above;[146] but he

---

[141] Not knew by sight. Likewise, John the Baptist did not know Jesus his first cousin. "And I knew him not: but because he should be declared to Israel, therefore am I come, baptizing with water [...] and I knew him not: but he that sent me to baptize with water, he said unto me, 'Upon whom thou shalt see that Spirit come down, and tarry still on him, that is he which baptizeth with the holy Ghost" (John 1:31, 33).

[142] Now come. As prophesied by John, Jesus was "cometh" as the Messiah. "John answered, and said to them all, 'Indeed I baptize you with water, but one stronger than I cometh whose shoes latchet I am not worthy to unloose: he will baptize you with the holy Ghost, and with fire'" (Luke 3:16).

[143] Many of Jesus' disciples were prepared by John Baptist to anticipate the Messiah. "Andrew, Simon Peter's brother, was one of the two which had heard it of John, and that followed him. The same found his brother Simon first, and said unto him, 'We have found that Messias, which is by interpretation, that Christ'" (John 1:40, 41). "The woman said unto him, 'I know well that Messias shall come which is called Christ: when he is come, he will tell us all things'" (John 4:25).

[144] Before Messiah, and his way prepare. John the Baptist's prophesied role as the Messianic forerunner to "prepare the way" for the Messiah. "A voice crieth in the wilderness, 'Prepare ye the way of the Lord: make straight in the desert a path for our God. Every valley shall be exalted, and every mountain and hill shall be made low: and the crooked shall be straight, & the rough places plain'" (Isaiah 40:3, 4). "As it is written in the book of the sayings of Esaias the Prophet, which saith, The voice of him that crieth in the wilderness is, 'Prepare ye the way of the Lord: make his paths straight. Every valley shall be filled, and every mountain and hill shall be brought low, and crooked things shall be made straight, and the rough ways shall be made smooth'" (Luke 3:4, 5).

[145] I, as all others, to his baptism came. Jesus presents himself to John the Baptist for baptism: "Then came Jesus from Galilee to Jordan unto John, to be baptized of him. But John earnestly put him back, saying, 'I have need to be baptized of thee, and comest thou to me?' Then Jesus answering, said to him, 'Let be now: for thus it becometh us to fulfill all righteousness. So he suffered him'" (Matthew 3:13–15).

Straight knew me, and with loudest voice proclaimed
Me him (for it was shewn him so from Heaven)[147]
Me him whose harbinger he was; and first
Refused on me his baptism to confer,
As much his greater,[148] and was hardly won.
But, as I rose out of the laving stream,
Heaven opened her eternal doors,[149] from whence
The Spirit descended on me like a Dove;
And last, the sum of all, my Father's voice,
Audibly heard from Heaven,[150] pronounced me his,

---

[146] Which I believed was from above. Jesus knows that John's baptism is from above. Compare with his questioning of those who attempt to lure him into blasphemy: "'The baptism of John, whence was it? From heaven, or of men?' Then they reasoned among themselves, saying, 'If we shall say, From heaven, he will say unto us, Why did ye not then believe him?'" (Matthew 21:25).

[147] John the Baptist recounts he words from heaven acknowledges that Jesus is the Messiah and the Son of God. "The next day John, seeth Jesus coming unto him, and saith, 'Behold that Lamb of God, which taketh away the sin of the world. This is he of whom I said, After me cometh a man, which was before me: for he was better then I. And I knew him not: but because he should be declared to Israel, therefore am I come, baptizing with water.' So John bear record, saying, 'I beheld that Spirit come down from heaven, like a dove, and it abode upon him, And I knew him not: but he that sent me to baptize with water, he said unto me, Upon whom thou shalt see that Spirit come down, and tarry still on him, that is he which baptizeth with the holy Ghost. And I saw, and bear record that this is that Son of God'" (John 1:29–34).

[148] [Lines 277–278] The greater baptism of the Christ. "Indeed, I baptize you with water to amendment of life, but he that cometh after me, is mightier then I, whose shoes I am not worthy to bear: he will baptize you with the holy Ghost, and with fire" (Matthew 3:11).

[149] The eternal doors of heaven. "Lift up your heads ye gates, and be ye lift up ye everlasting doors, and the King of glory shall come in. Who is this King of glory? the Lord, strong and mighty, even the Lord mighty in battle Lift up your heads, ye gates, and lift up yourselves, ye everlasting doors, and the King of glory shall come in" (Psalms 24:7–9).

[150] [Lines 281–283] "And Jesus when he was baptized, came straight out of the water; lo, the heavens were opened unto him, & John saw the Spirit of God descending like a dove, and lighting upon him" (Matthew 3:16).

Me his beloved Son, in whom alone
He was well pleased:[151] by which I knew the time
Now full,[152] that I no more should live obscure,
But openly begin, as best becomes
The authority which I derived from Heaven.[153]
And now by some strong motion I am led[154]
Into this wilderness; to what intent
I learn not yet. Perhaps I need not know;
For what concerns my knowledge God reveals."[155]
So spake our Morning Star,[156] then in his rise,

---

[151] [Lines 283–285] "And lo, a voice came from heaven, saying, 'This is my beloved Son, in whom I am well pleased'" (Matthew 3:17). "And the holy Ghost came down in a bodily shape like a dove, upon him, and there was a voice from heaven, saying, 'Thou art my beloved Son: in thee I am well pleased'" (Luke 3:22).

[152] The time now full. "But when the fullness of time was come, God sent forth his Son made of a woman, and made under the Law" (Galatians 4:4).

[153] The authority which I derived from heaven. "And Jesus came, and spake unto them, saying, 'All power is given unto me, in heaven, and in earth'" (Matthew 28:18). "And hath given him authority to execute judgment also, because he is the Son of man" (John 5:27, AV). Not GE, GT, Bishops, DR, Coverdale, Tyndale "power." Compare with the Priests and others demanding to know from where Jesus received his authority: "And when he was come into the Temple, the chief Priests, and the Elders of the people came unto him, as he was teaching, and said, 'By what authority dost thou these things? And who gave thee this authority? When Iesus answered and said unto them, I also will ask of you a certain thing, which if ye tell me, I likewise will tell you by what authority I do these things" (Matthew 21:23, 24).

[154] By some strong motion I am led into this wilderness. "Then was Jesus led aside of the Spirit into the wilderness, to be tempted of the devil" (Matthew 4:1). "And Jesus full of the holy Ghost returned from Jordan, and was led by that Spirit into the wilderness" (Luke 4:1).

[155] [Lines 290–292]. God dispenses knowledge on a need-to-know basis. Compare with Jesus words concerning himself and angels regarding what is revealed about the Judgment Day: "But of that day and hour knoweth no man, no not the Angels of heaven, but my father only" (Matthew 24:36). "But of that day and hour knoweth no man, no, not the Angels which are in heaven, neither the Son himself, but the Father" (Mark 13:32).

And, looking round, on every side beheld
A pathless desert, dusk with horrid shades.
The way he came, not having marked return,
Was difficult, by human steps untrod;
And he still on was led, but with such thoughts
Accompanied of things past and to come
Lodged in his breast as well might recommend
Such solitude before choicest society.
Full forty days he passed, whether on hill
Sometimes, anon in shady vale, each night
Under the covert of some ancient oak
Or cedar to defend him from the dew,
Or harboured in one cave, is not revealed;
Nor tasted human food, nor hunger felt,
Till those days ended; hungered then at last[157]
Among wild beasts.[158] They at his sight grew mild,

---

[156] Jesus as the Morning Star. "I Jesus have sent mine Angel, to testify unto you these things in the Churches: I am the root and the generation of David, and the bright morning star" (Revelation 22:16).

[157] [Lines 302–308] Jesus fasts for forty days in the wilderness but does not feel hunger until the forty day period elapses. "And when he had fasted forty days, and forty nights, he was afterward hungry" (Matthew 4:2). "And was there forty days tempted of the devil, & in those days he did eat nothing: but when they were ended, he afterward was hungry" (Luke 4:2). When performing God's will, Jesus does not hunger: "But he said unto them, I have meat to eat that ye know not of. Then said the disciples between themselves, 'Hath any man brought him meat?' Jesus said unto them, 'My meat is that I may do the will of him that sent me, and finish his work'" (John 4:32–34).

[158] That Jesus was accompanied by wild beasts in the wilderness is only recorded in Mark's gospel: "And he was there in the wilderness forty days, and was tempted of Satan: he was also with the wild beasts, and the Angels ministered unto him" (Mark 1:13). Compare with Isaiah's restoration prophecy regarding Israel's mastery of animals: "The wolf also shall dwell with the lamb, and the leopard shall lie with the kid, & the calf, and the lion, and the fat beast together, and a little child shall lead them. And the cow and the bear shall feed: their young ones shall lie together: and the lion shall eat straw like the bullock. And the sucking child shall play upon the hole of the asp, and the weaned child shall

Nor sleeping him nor waking harmed; his walk
The fiery serpent[159] fled and noxious worm;[160]
The lion and fierce tiger glared aloof.[161] [162]

---

put his hand upon the cockatrice hole. Then shall none hurt nor destroy in all the mountain of mine holiness: for the earth shall be full of the knowledge of the Lord, as the waters that cover the sea" (Isaiah 11:6–9). Compare also with Ezekiel's restoration prophecy: "And I will make with them a covenant of peace, and will cause the evil beasts to cease out of the land: and they shall dwell safely in the wilderness, and sleep in the woods" (Ezekiel 34:25).

159 Compare with the fiery serpents sent by Yahweh to plague Israel in the wilderness: "Wherefore the Lord sent fiery serpents among the people, which stung the people: so that many of the people of Israel died" (Numbers 21:6). "Who was thy guide in the great and terrible wilderness (wherein were fiery serpents, & scorpions, and drought, where was no water, who brought forth water for thee out of the rock of flint" (Deuteronomy 8:15). Not DR "there was the serpent burning with his breath." Not Coverdale "where were serpents that spouted fire." "Rejoice not, (thou whole Palestina) because the rod of him that did beat thee, is broken for out of the serpent's root shall come forth a cockatrice, & the fruit thereof shall be a fiery flying serpent" (Isaiah 14:29, Geneva and AV). Not DR "shall come forth a basilisk, and his seed shall swallow the bird." Compare also: "The burden of the beasts of the south. In a land of trouble & anguish, from whence shall come the young and old lion, the viper and fiery serpent that fleeth against them that upon colts bear their riches, and upon camels their treasures, to a people that can do them no good" (Isaiah 30:6, Bishops [see also GT]). Not Geneva and AV "fiery flying serpents." "flying basilisk" DR. "shooting dragon" Coverdale.

160 Compare Isaiah 14:29 (see Note 159) "noxious worm" with Bishops "fiery fleeing worm." Coverdale "there shall wax a cockatrice, & the fruit shall be a fiery worm." Compare GT "there shall come an adder, & the fruit shall be a fiery flying worm."

161 [Lines 309–312] "The wolf and the lamb shall feed together, and the lion shall eat straw like the bullock: and to the serpent dust shall be his meat. They shall no more hurt nor destroy in all mine holy Mountain, saith the Lord" (Isaiah 65:25).

162 [Lines 309–312] Likewise, pre-lapsarian Adam in the likeness of God held dominion over all animals. "Furthermore, God said, 'Let us make man in our image according to our likeness, and let them rule over the fish of the sea, and over the fowl of the heaven, and over the beasts, and over all the earth, and over everything that creepeth and moveth on the earth.' Thus God created the man in his image: in the image of God created he him: he created them male and female.

But now an aged man in rural weeds,[163]
Following, as seemed, the quest of some stray eye,[164]
Or withered sticks[165] to gather, which might serve
Against a winter's day, when winds blow keen,
To warm him wet returned from field at eve,
He saw approach; who first with curious eye
Perused him, then with words thus uttered spake.
"Sir, what ill chance hath brought thee to this place,
So far from path or road of men, who pass
In troop or caravan? for single none
Durst ever, who returned, and dropt not here
His carcass,[166] pined with hunger and with droughth.

And God blessed them, and God said to them, 'Bring forth fruit and multiply, and fill the earth, and subdue it, and rule over the fish of the sea, and over the fowl of the heaven, & over every beast that moveth upon the earth.' And God said, 'Behold, I have given unto you every herb bearing seed, which is upon all the earth, and every tree, wherein is the fruit of a tree bearing seed: that shall be to you for meat. Likewise to every beast of the earth, and to every fowl of the heaven, and to every thing that moveth upon the earth, which hath life in itself, every green herb shall be for meat;' it was so" (Genesis 1:26–30).

[163] Aged man in rural weeds. Satan can take the appearance of a guileless figure. Compare "And no marvel: for Satan himself is transformed into an angel of light" (2 Corinthians 11:14). Also Tyndale "changed into the fashion of an angel of light."

[164] Following, as seemed, the quest of some strayed eye. That is to say, the swain appears to be following after a strayed sheep. Compare with Jesus' parable: "'How think ye? If a man have an hundred sheep, and one of them be gone astray, doth he not leave ninety & nine, & go into the mountains, and seek that which is gone astray? And if so be that he find it, verily I say unto you, he rejoiceth more of that sheep, then of the ninety and nine which went not astray" (Matthew 18:12, 13). "What man of you having an hundred sheep, if he lose one of them, doth not leave ninety and nine in the wilderness, and go after that which is lost, until he find it?" (Luke 15:4). Perhaps, Satan mocks and mimics the self-sacrificing attitude of Jesus, as Jesus says of himself "I am that good shepherd: that good shepherd giveth his life for his sheep" (John 10:11).

[165] The wicked likened to "withered sticks." "If a man abide not in me, he is cast forth as a branch, and withered: and men gather them, and cast them into the fire, and they burn" (John 15:6).

I ask the rather, and the more admire,
For that to me thou seem'st the man whom late
Our new baptizing Prophet at the ford
Of Jordan honoured so, and called thee Son[167]
Of God. I saw and heard, for we sometimes
Who dwell this wild, constrained by want, come forth
To town or village nigh (nighest is far),
Where aught we hear, and curious are to hear,
What happens new; fame also finds us out."[168]
To whom the Son of God. "Who brought me hither
Will bring me hence; no other guide I seek."
"By miracle he may," replied the swain;
"What other way I see not; for we here
Live on tough roots and stubs, to thirst inured
More than the camel, and to drink go far
Men to much misery and hardship born.
But, if thou be the Son of God, command
That out of these hard stones be made thee bread;[169]
So shalt thou save thyself, and us[170] relieve

---

[166] [Lines 323–324] Dropped not here his carcass. Contrast with the group of unfaithful Israelites in the wilderness after the Exodus and before taking possession of the promised land. "Your carcasses shall fall in this wilderness, and all you that were counted through all your numbers, from twenty year old and above, which have murmured against me" (Numbers 14:29).

[167] [Lines 327–328] "And I saw, and bare record that this is that Son of God" (John 1:34).

[168] [Lines 332–333] Compare with the Athenian pagans of Paul's day who were curious about new things. "For all the Athenians, and strangers which dwelt there, gave them selves to nothing else, but either to tell, or to hear some news" (Acts 17:21).

[169] [Lines 341–342] "Then the devil said unto him, 'If thou be the Son of God, command this stone that it be made bread'" (Luke 4:3). "Then came to him the tempter, and said, 'If thou be the Sonne of God, command that these stones be made bread'" (Matthew 4:3). Satan is twisting and misapplying the words of the Psalmist: "Behold, he smote the rock, that the water gushed out, and the streams overflowed: can he give bread also?" (Psalm 78:20).

With food, whereof we wretched seldom taste."
He ended, and the Son of God replied:
"Think'st thou such force in bread? Is it not written
(For I discern thee other than thou seem'st),
Man lives not by bread only, but each word
Proceeding from the mouth of God,[171] who fed
Our fathers here with manna?[172] In the Mount
Moses was forty days,[173] nor eat nor drank;[174]
And forty days Eliah without food[175]

---

[170] So shalt thou save thyself, and us. Verbal echo of one the malefactor's words to Jesus at his execution: "And one of the evil doers, which were hanged, railed on him, saying, 'If thou be that Christ, save thy self and us'" (Luke 23:39).

[171] [Lines 346–349] Jesus responds to the temptation of bread by quoting scripture. "But he answering said, 'It is written, Man shall not live by bread only, but by every worde that proceedeth out of the mouth of God'" (Matthew 4:4). "But Jesus answered him, saying, 'It is written, That man shall not live by bread only, but by every word of God'" (Luke 4:4). "Therefore he humbled thee, and made thee hungry, and fed thee with manna, which thou knewest not, neither did thy fathers know it, that he might teach thee that man liveth not by bread only, but by every word that proceedeth out of the mouth of the Lord, doth a man live" (Deuteronomy 8:3).

[172] "And when the dew that was fallen was ascended, behold, a small round thing was upon the face of the wilderness, small as the hoarfrost on the earth. And when the children of Israel saw it, they said one to another, 'It is manna,' for they wist not what it was; Moses said unto them, 'This is the bread which the Lord hath given you to eat'" (Exodus 16:14, 15).

[173] "And Moses entered into the midst of the cloud, and went up to the mountain: and Moses was in the mount forty days and forty nights" (Exodus 24:18).

[174] "'When I was gone up into the mount, to receive the tables of stone, the tables, I say, of the covenant, which the Lord made with you: and I abode in the mount forty days & forty nights, and I neither ate bread nor yet drank water'" (Deuteronomy 9:9). "So he was there with the Lord forty days and forty nights, and did neither eat bread nor drink water: and he wrote in the Tables the words of the covenant, even the ten commandments" (Exodus 34:28).

[175] Forty days Eliah without food. While hiding from murderous King Ahab and Queen Jezabel of the ten-tribe kingdom of Israel, the prophet Elijah was sustained for forty days in the wilderness. "And the Angel of the Lord came again the second time, and touched him, and said, 'Up, and eat: for thou hast a

Wandered this barren waste; the same I now.
Why dost thou, then, suggest to me distrust
Knowing who I am,[176] as I know who thou art?"
Whom thus answered the Arch-Fiend, now undisguised:
"'Tis true, I am that Spirit unfortunate
Who, leagued with millions more in rash revolt,
Kept not my happy station, but was driven
With them from bliss to the bottomless Deep[177]
Yet to that hideous place not so confined[178]
By rigour unconniving but that oft,
Leaving my dolorous prison, I enjoy
Large liberty to round this globe of Earth,[179]

---

great journey.' Then he arose, and did eat and drink, and walked in the strength of that meat forty days and forty nights, unto Horeb the mount of God" (1 Kings 19:7, 8). Compare with Jesus assurance to his disciples about God's ability to provide sustaining food, "Therefore take no thought, saying, 'What shall we eat? Or what shall we drink? Or where with shall we be clothed' (For after all these things seek the Gentiles) for your heavenly Father knoweth, that ye have need of all these things" (Matthew 6:31, 32).

[176] [Lines 354–355] Suggest to me distrust knowing who I am. Before tempting him with bread, Satan questioned Jesus' divine sonship: "Then the devil said unto him, 'If thou be the Son of God, command this stone that it be made bread" (Luke 4:3, GE). Geneva note: "Christ, being tempted by Satan, first to distrust in God, secondly to the desire of riches and honor, and lastly to a vain confidence in himself, overcomes him three times by the word of God. "Then came to him the tempter, and said, 'If thou be the Son of God, command that these stones be made bread'" (Matthew 4:3).

[177] [Lines 359–360] "The Angels also which kept not their first estate, but left their own habitation, he hath reserved in everlasting chains vender darkness unto the judgement of the great day" (Jude 6).

[178] Although hurled into the abyss or the deep, Satan and his demons may come and go at will. Note the fear of the demons who addressed Jesus: "When Jesus asked him, saying, 'What is thy name?' And he said, 'Legion,' because many devils were entered into him. And they besought him, that he would not command them to go out into the deep" (Luke 8:30, 31).

[179] Large liberty to round this globe of Earth. "Be sober, and watch: for your adversary the devil as a roaring lion walketh about, seeking whom he may devour" (1 Peter 5:8). Satan's liberty on the Earth in the days of Job: "Then the

Or range in the Air;[180] nor from the Heaven of Heavens[181]
Hath he excluded my resort sometimes.
I came, among the Sons of God, when he
Gave up into my hands Uzzean Job,[182]
To prove him, and illustrate his high worth;
And, when to all his Angels he proposed
To draw the proud king Ahab into fraud,[183]

Lord said unto Satan, 'Whence comest thou?' And Satan answered the Lord, saying, 'From compassing the earth to and from, and from walking in it'" (Job 1:7; Job 2:2). "And there was a battle in heaven, Michael and his Angels fought against the dragon, and the dragon fought and his angels. But they prevailed not, neither was their place found any more in heaven. And the great dragon, that old serpent, called the devil and Satan, was cast out, which deceiveth all the world: he was even cast into the earth, and his angels were cast out with him" (Revelation 12:7–9).

[180] Satan as the ruler of the air is able to "range in the air." "Wherein, in times past ye walked, according to the course of this world, and after the prince that ruleth in the air, even the spirit, that now worketh in the children of disobedience" (Ephesians 2:2).

[181] Heavens of the heavens or the manifest presence of God. Consider the prayer of Solomon at the dedication of the temple: "Is it true in deed that God will dwell on the earth? Behold, the heavens, and the heavens of heavens are not able to contain thee: how much more unable is this house that I have built?" (1 Kings 8:27). Satan had access to the heavens in the days of Job: "And on a day the children of God came and stood before the Lord, and Satan came also among them, and stood before the Lord" (Job 2:1).

[182] Gave up into my hands Uzzean Job. "Now on a day when the children of God came and stood before the Lord, Satan came also among them [...] 'But stretch out now thine hand & touch all that he hath, to see if he will not blaspheme thee to thy face.' Then the Lord said unto Satan, 'Lo, all that he hath is in thine hand: only upon himself shalt thou not stretch out thine hand.' So Satan departed from the presence of the Lord" (Job 1:6, 11, 12). "'But stretch now out thine hand, and touch his bones and his flesh, to see if he will not blaspheme thee to thy face.' Then the Lord said unto Satan, 'Lo, he is in thine hand, but save his life'" (Job 2:5, 6).

[183] [Lines 370–371] Milton's Satan claims to be the unnamed Angel who suggests that King Ahab be deceived by fraud: "Again he said, 'Hear thou therefore the word of the Lord. I saw the Lord sit on his throne, and all the host of heaven stood about him on his right hand and on his left hand. And the Lord said, "Who

That he might fall in Ramoth, they demurring,
I undertook that office, and the tongues
Of all his flattering prophets glibbed with lies[184]
To his destruction, as I had in charge:
For what he bids I do. Though I have lost
Much lustre of my native brightness,[185] lost
To be beloved of God, I have not lost
To love, at least contemplate and admire,
What I see excellent in good, or fair,
Or virtuous;[186] I should so have lost all sense.

---

shall entice Ahab that he may go and fall at Ramoth Gilead?" And one said on this manner, and another said on that manner. Then there came forth a spirit, & stood before the Lord, and said, "I will entice him;" the Lord said unto him, "Wherewith?" And he said, "I will go out, and be a false spirit in the mouth of all his prophets." Then he said, "Thou shalt entice him, and shalt also prevail: go forth, and do so." Now therefore behold, the Lord hath put a lying spirit in the mouth of all these thy prophets, and the Lord hath appointed evil against thee" (1 Kings 22:19–23).

184 Satan as the originator of lies. "Ye are of your father the devil, and the lusts of your father ye will do: he hath been a murderer from the beginning, and abode not in the truth, because there is no truth in him. When he speaketh a lie, then speaketh he of his own: for he is a liar, and the father thereof" (John 8:44).

185 Satan's "native brightness." Compare with the cherub metaphor applied to the King of Babylon: "Thou hast been in Eden the garden of God: every precious stone was in thy garment, the ruby, the topaz and the diamond, the chrysolite, the onyx, and the jasper, the sapphire, emerald, and the carbuncle and gold: the workmanship of thy timbrels, & of thy pipes was prepared in thee in the day that thou wast created. Thou art the anointed Cherub, that covereth, and I have set thee in honor: thou wast upon the holy mountain of God: thou hast walked in the midst of the stones of fire. Thou wast perfect in thy ways from the day that thou wast created, till iniquity was found in thee. By the multitude of thy merchandise, they have filled the midst of thee with cruelty, and thou hast sinned: therefore I will cast thee as profane out of the mountain of God: and I will destroy thee, O covering Cherub from the midst of the stones of fire. Thine heart was lifted up because of thy beauty, and thou hast corrupted thy wisdom by reason of thy brightness: I will cast thee to the ground: I will lay thee before Kings that they may behold thee" (Ezekiel 28:13–17).

What can be then less in me than desire
To see thee and approach thee, whom I know
Declared the Son of God, to hear attent[187]
Thy wisdom, and behold thy godlike deeds?
Men generally think me much a foe[188]
To all mankind. Why should I? they to me
Never did wrong or violence. By them
I lost not what I lost; rather by them
I gained what I have gained, and with them dwell
Copartner in these regions of the World,[189]
If not disposer—lend them oft my aid,
Oft my advice by presages and signs,
And answers, oracles, portents, and dreams,
Whereby they may direct their future life.[190]

---

[186] [Lines 380–381] Hypocritical appropriation. "Furthermore, brethren, whatsoever things are true, whatsoever things are honest, whatsoever things are just, whatsoever things are pure, whatsoever things are worthy love, whatsoever things are of good report, if there be any virtue, or if there be any praise, think on these things" (Philippians 4:8).

[187] Hear attent. Verbal echo of the prayer of Solomon: "Now my God, I beseech thee, let thine eyes be open, & thine ears attent unto the prayer that is made in this place" (2 Chronicles 6:40).

[188] Satan as foe. "And the enemy that soweth them, is the devil, and the harvest is the end of the world, and the reapers be the Angels" (Matthew 13:39).

[189] [Lines 390–391] Satan as the "copartner in these regions of the world if not disposer." Jesus words: "Hereafter will I not speak many things unto you: for the prince of this world cometh, and hath nought in me" (John 14:30).

[190] [Lines 393–395] Satan claims to direct humans through uncanny power. "Ye shall not eat the flesh with the blood, ye shall not use witchcraft, nor observe times […] Ye shall not regard them that work with spirits, neither soothsayers: ye shall not seek to them to be defiled by them: I am the Lorde your God" (Leviticus 19:26, 31). "Let none be found among you that maketh his son or his daughter to go through the fire, or that useth witchcraft, or a regarder of times, or a marker of the flying of fowls, or a sorcerer, or a charmer, or that counseleth with spirits, or a soothsayer, or that asketh counsel at the dead" (Deuteronomy 18:10, 11). A possessed woman claims to advocate for Paul as a servant of God, just as Satan is claiming benevolence toward humans: "And it came to pass that as we went to prayer, a certain maid having a spirit of divination, met us, which got her

Envy, they say, excites me, thus to gain
Companions of my misery and woe!
At first it may be; but, long since with woe
Nearer acquainted, now I feel by proof
That fellowship in pain divides not smart,
Nor lightens aught each man's peculiar load;
Small consolation, then, were Man adjoined.
This wounds me most (what can it less?) that Man,
Man fallen, shall be restored, I never more."[191]
To whom our Saviour sternly thus replied:
"Deservedly thou griev'st, composed of lies
From the beginning,[192] and in lies wilt end,
Who boast'st release from Hell, and leave to come
Into the Heaven of Heavens. Thou com'st, indeed,
As a poor miserable captive thrall
Comes to the place where he before had sat
Among the prime in splendour, now deposed,
Ejected, emptied, gazed, unpitied, shunned,[193]

---

masters much vantage with divining. She followed Paul and us, and cried, saying, 'These men are the servants of the most high God, which show unto you the way of salvation.' And this did she many days: but Paul being grieved, turned about, and said to the spirit, 'I command thee in the Name of Jesus Christ, that thou come out of her; he came out the same hour" (Acts 16:16–18). "What say I then? That the idol is anything? Or that that which is sacrificed to idols, is any thing? Nay, but that these things which the Gentiles sacrifice, they sacrifice to devils, and not unto God: and I would not that ye should have fellowship with the devils" (1 Corinthians 10:19, 20).

[191] [Lines 403–404] Humans are redeemable. Satan and his demons are not. "Who will that all men shall be saved, and come unto the acknowledging of the truth" (1 Timothy 2:4). "And the devil that deceived them, was cast into a lake of fire and brimstone, where that beast and that false prophet are, and shall be tormented even day and night for evermore" (Revelation 20:10).

[192] Composed of lies from the beginning. Consider Jesus' stern condemnation of the Pharisees: "Ye are of your father the devil, and the lusts of your father ye will do: he hath been a murderer from the beginning, and abode not in the truth, because there is no truth in him. When he speaketh a lie, then speaketh he of his own: for he is a liar, and the father thereof" (John 8:44).

A spectacle of ruin, or of scorn,
To all the host of Heaven. The happy place
Imparts to thee no happiness, no joy
Rather inflames thy torment, representing
Lost bliss, to thee no more communicable;[194]
So never more in Hell than when in Heaven.
But thou art serviceable to Heaven's King!
Wilt thou impute to obedience what thy fear
Extorts, or pleasure to do ill excites?[195]
What but thy malice moved thee to misdeem
Of righteous Job,[196] then cruelly to afflict him

---

[193] [Lines 412–414] "And the great dragon, that old serpent, called the devil and Satan, was cast out, which deceiveth all the world: he was even cast into the earth, and his angels were cast out with him" (Revelation 12:9). "For if God spared not the Angels that had sinned, but cast them down into hell, and delivered them into chains of darkness, to be kept unto damnation" (2 Peter 2:4). "The Angels also which kept not their first estate, but left their own habitation, he hath reserved in everlasting chains under darkness unto the judgment of the great day" (Jude 6).

[194] To thee no more communicable. "Ye can not drink the cup of the Lord, and the cup of the devils. Ye can not be partakers of the Lord's table, and of the table of the devils" (1 Corinthians 10:21). "Be not unequally yoked with the infidels: for what fellowship hath righteousness with unrighteousness? and what communion hath light with darkness? And what concord hath Christ with Belial? or what part hath the believer with the infidel?" (2 Corinthians 6:14, 15) Geneva [see also AV and Bishops] Not Tyndale, Coverdale, GT, "company."

[195] [Lines 421–422] Contrast with true willing obedience. "Thy people shall come willingly at the time of assembling thine army in holy beauty: the youth of thy womb shall be as the morning dew" (Psalm 110:3). Contrast also the false obedience of Satan disguised as a shepherd to a true shepherd of God: "Feed the flock of God, which dependeth upon you, caring for it not by constraint, but willingly: not for filthy lucer, but of a ready mind" (1 Peter 5:2).

[196] Righteous Job. "There was a man in the land of Uz called Job, & this man was an upright and just man, one that feared God, and eschewed evil" (Job 1:1). "Behold, we count them blessed which endure. Ye have heard of the patience of Job, and have known what end the Lord made. For the Lord is very pitiful and merciful" (James 5:11). "This temptation did God suffer to happen unto him, that

With all inflictions? but his patience won.
The other service was thy chosen task,
To be a liar in four hundred mouths;[197]
For lying is thy sustenance, thy food.
Yet thou pretend'st to truth![198] all oracles
By thee are given, and what confessed more true
Among the nations? That hath been thy craft,[199]
By mixing somewhat true to vent more lies.
But what have been thy answers? what but dark,
Ambiguous, and with double sense deluding,
Which they who asked have seldom understood,
And, not well understood, as good not known?
Who ever, by consulting at thy shrine,
Returned the wiser, or the more instruct
To fly or follow what concerned him most,
And run not sooner to his fatal snare?[200]
For God hath justly given the nations up[201]

---

they which came after, might have an example of his patience, like as of holy Job" (Tobit 2:12, Bishops).

197 [Lines 426–427] Satan moves the 400 prophets of King Ahab to falsely prophesy resulting in the death of Ahab. "Then the King of Israel gathered the prophets upon a four hundred men, and said unto them, 'Shall I go against Ramoth Gilead to battle, or shall I let it alone?' And they said, 'Go up: for the Lord shall deliver it into the hands of the King' […] Then there came forth a spirit, & stood before the Lord, and said, 'I will entice him;' the Lord said unto him, 'Wherewith?' And he said, 'I will go out, and be a false spirit in the mouth of all his prophets.' Then he said, 'Thou shalt entice him, and shalt also prevail: go forth, and do so" (1 Kings 22:6, 21, 22).

198 Thou pretend'st to truth. "Having a show of godliness, but have denied the power thereof: turn away therefore from such" (2 Timothy 3:5).

199 Satan's craftiness: "Put on ye armor of God that ye may stand steadfast against the crafty assaults of the devil" (Ephesians 6:11 Tyndale [see also Coverdale]). Not GE, GT or Bishops "assaults." Not AV "wiles. Not DR "deceits."

200 Satan's snares. "He must also be well reported of, even of them which are without, lest he fall into rebuke, and the snare of the devil" (1 Timothy 3:7).

201 God hath justly given the nations up. "Wherefore also God gave them up to their hearts lusts, unto uncleanness, to defile their own bodies between

To thy delusions;[202] justly, since they fell
Idolatrous. But, when his purpose is
Among them to declare his providence,
To thee not known, whence hast thou then thy truth,
But from him, or his Angels president[203]
In every province, who, themselves disdaining
To approach thy temples, give thee in command
What, to the smallest tittle, thou shalt say
To thy adorers? Thou, with trembling fear,[204]
Or like a fawning parasite, obey'st;

---

themselves: Which turned the truth of God unto a lie, and worshipped and served the creature, forsaking the Creator, which is blessed for ever, Amen [...] Which men, though they knew the Law of God, how that they which commit such things are worthy of death, yet not only do the same, but also favor them that do them" (Romans 1:24, 25, 32).

[202] Satan's delusions: "Even him whose coming is by the effectual working of Satan, with all power, and signs, and lying wonders, And in all deceivableness of unrighteousness, among them that perish, because they received not the love of the truth, that they might be saved. And therefore God shall send them strong delusion, that they should believe lies" (2 Thessalonians 2:9–11, Not DR "who have not believed." "For many shall come in my name, saying, 'I am Christ,' and shall deceive many [...] And many false prophets shall arise, & shall deceive many" (Matthew 24:5, 11). "Now the Spirit speaketh evidently, that in the latter times some shall depart from the faith, and shall give heed unto spirits of error, and doctrines of devils" (1 Timothy 4:1).

[203] Angels president. "For on the first day He created the heavens which are above and the earth and the waters and all the spirits which serve before him the angels of the presence, and the angels of sanctification, and the angels [of the spirit of fire and the angels] of the spirit of the winds, and the angels of the spirit of the clouds, and of darkness, and of snow and of hail and of hoar frost, and the angels of the voices and of the thunder and of the lightning, and the angels of the spirits of cold and of heat, and of winter and of spring and of autumn and of summer and of all the spirits of his creatures which are in the heavens and on the earth, (He created) the abysses and the darkness, eventide <and night>, and the light, dawn and day, which He hath prepared in the knowledge of his heart (Jubilees 2:2).

[204] Trembling devils. "Thou believest that there is one God: thou dost well: the devils also believe it, and tremble" (James 2:19).

Then to thyself ascrib'st the truth foretold.
But this thy glory shall be soon retrenched;
No more shalt thou by oracling abuse
The Gentiles; henceforth oracles are ceased,[205]
And thou no more with pomp and sacrifice
Shalt be enquired at Delphos or elsewhere—
At least in vain, for they shall find thee mute.
God hath now sent his living Oracle
Into the world to teach his final will,
And sends his Spirit of Truth[206] henceforth to dwell
In pious hearts, an inward oracle
To all truth requisite for men to know."[207]

---

205 Uncanny power will cease. "Love doth never fall away, though that prophesyings be abolished, or the tongues cease, or knowledge vanish away" (1 Corinthians 13:8).

206 The Spirit of Truth (holy spirit): "Howbeit, when he is come which is the Spirit of truth, he will lead you into all truth: for he shall not speak of himself, but whatsoever he shall hear, shall he speak, and he will show you the things to come" (John 16:13).

207 [Lines 459–463] Jesus Christ as "his living Oracle." "And of his fullness have all we received, and grace for grace. For the Law was given by Moses, but grace, and truth came by Jesus Christ (John 1:16, 17). "The woman said unto him, 'I know well that Messiah shall come which is called Christ: when he is come, he will tell us all things'" (John 4:25). "Pilate then said unto him, 'Art thou a King then?' Jesus answered, 'Thou sayest that I am a King: for this cause am I born, and for this cause came I into the world, that I should bear witness unto the truth: every one that is of the truth, heareth my voice'" (John 18:37). No further need for prophets: "At sundry times and in divers manners God spake in the old time to our fathers by the Prophets: in these last days he hath spoken unto vs by his Son, Whom he hath made heir of all things, by whom also he made the worlds" (Hebrews 1:1, 2). "And that Word was made flesh, and dwelt among vs, (and we saw the glory thereof, as the glory of the only begotten Sonne of the Father) full of grace and truth" (John 1:14). Living Oracle: "This is he that was in the Congregation, in the wilderness with the Angel, which spake to him in mount Sinai, and with our fathers, who received the lively oracles to give unto us" (Acts 7:38, Geneva and AV). Not Bishops, Coverdale, GT, Tyndale "words of life." To all truth requisite for men to know. "For if he that cometh, preacheth another Jesus whom we have not preached: or if ye receive another spirit whom

So spake our Saviour; but the subtle Fiend,
Though inly stung with anger and disdain,
Dissembled, and this answer smooth returned:
"Sharply thou hast insisted on rebuke,
And urged me hard with doings which not will,
But misery, hath wrested from me. Where
Easily canst thou find one miserable,
And not inforced oft-times to part from truth,
If it may stand him more in stead to lie,
Say and unsay, feign, flatter, or abjure?
But thou art placed above me; thou art Lord;
From thee I can, and must, submiss, endure
Cheek or reproof, and glad to scape so quit.
Hard are the ways of truth, and rough to walk,[208]
Smooth on the tongue discoursed, pleasing to the ear,
And tunable as sylvan pipe or song;
What wonder, then, if I delight to hear
Her dictates from thy mouth? most men admire
Virtue who follow not her lore. Permit me
To hear thee when I come (since no man comes),
And talk at least, though I despair to attain.
Thy Father, who is holy, wise, and pure,
Suffers the hypocrite or atheous priest
To tread his sacred courts,[209] and minister

---

ye have not received: either another Gospel, which ye have not received, ye might well have suffered him" (1 Corinthians 11:4). "But though that we, or an Angel from heaven preach unto you otherwise, then that which we have preached unto you, let him be accursed" (Galatians 1:8).

[208] Hard are the ways of truth, and rough to walk. "Enter in at the straight gate: for it is the wide gate, and broad way that leadeth to destruction: & many there be which go in thereat, Because the gate is straight, and the way narrow that leadeth unto life, and few there be that find it" (Matthew 7:13, 14). Compare with Paul's words: "For I do not the good thing, which I would, but the evil, which I would not, that do I" (Romans 7:19).

[209] To tread his sacred courts. Compare with Isaiah's condemnation of faithless temple priests: "What have I to do with the multitude of your sacrifices, saith the

About his altar, handling holy things,[210]
Praying or vowing,[211] and voutsafed his voice
To Balaam reprobate,[212] a prophet yet
Inspired: disdain not such access to me."[213]

Lord? I am full of the burnt offerings of rams, & of the fat of fed beasts: and I desire not the blood of bullocks, nor of lambs, nor of goats. When ye come to appear before me, who required this of your hands to tread in my courts?" (Isaiah 1:11, 12, Geneva, AV, and Bishops). Not Coverdale and GT "tread in my porches." Not DR "walk in my courts."

[210] About his altar handling holy things. "Do ye not know, that they which minister about the holy things, eat of the things of the Temple? And they which wait at the altar, are partakers with the altar?" (1 Corinthians 9:13).

[211] [Lines 485–489] Satan claims that God rightly tolerated the hypocrisy, violence, and corruption of "atheist priests" and perhaps grants Satan similar consideration. Consider the priestly sons of High Priest Eli: "Now the sons of Eli were wicked men, and knew not the Lord. For the Priests custom toward the people was this: when any man offered sacrifice, the Priest's boy came, while the flesh was seething, and a fleshhook with three teeth, in his hand, and thrust it into the kettle, or into the cauldron, or into the pan, or into the pot: all that the fleshhook brought up, the Priest took for himself: thus they did unto all the Israelites, that came thither to Shiloh. Yea, before they burnt the fat, the priest's boy came and said to the man that offered, 'Give me flesh to roast for the priest: for he will not have sodden flesh of thee, but raw.' And if any man said unto him, 'Let them burn the fat according to the custom, then take as much as thine heart desireth': then he would answer, 'No, but thou shalt give it now: and if thou wilt not, I will take it by force.' Therefore the sin of the young men was very great before the Lord: for men abhorred the offering of the Lord" (1 Samuel 2:12–17).

[212] Balaam reprobate. Compare with Paul's rejection of reprobation. "But I beat down my body, & bring it into subjection, lest by any means after that I have preached to other, I myself should be reproved" AV and others "cast away." The Vulgate renders "*reprobas*" signifying "rejection."

[213] [Lines 490–491] Satan contrasts God's intolerance for Satan with God's apparent tolerance of the apostate prophet Balaam: "Behold, these caused the children of Israel through the counsel of Balaam to commit a trespass against the Lord, as concerning Peor, and there came a plague among the Congregation of the Lord" (Numbers 31:16). "Which forsaking the right way, have gone astray, following the way of Balaam, the son of Bosor, which loved the wages of unrighteousness" (2 Peter 2:15). Compare with the resurrected Jesus complaint

To whom our Saviour, with unaltered brow:—
"Thy coming hither, though I know thy scope,
I bid not, or forbid. Do as thou find'st
Permission from above; thou canst not more."[214]
He added not; and Satan, bowling low
His gray dissimulation, disappeared,
Into thin air diffused: for now began
Night with her sullen wing to double-shade
The desert; fowls in their clay nests were couched;
And now wild beasts came forth the woods to roam.[215]

---

about the first-century congregation of Pergamum's tolerance of the teaching of Balaam: "But I have a few things against thee, because thou hast there them that maintain the doctrine of Balaam, which taught Balac to put a stumbling block before the children of Israel, that they should eat of things sacrificed unto Idols, and commit" (Revelation 2:14).

[214] [Lines 493–495] Jesus refuses to consider going beyond whatever God permits or forbids and insists that Satan is also incapable of going beyond what God allows. Compare with Jesus words to Pontius Pilate while on trial: "Jesus answered, 'Thou couldest have no power at all against me, except it were given thee from above: therefore he that delivered me unto thee, hath the greater sin'" (John 19:11).

[215] [Lines 499–501] Compare: "Thou makest darkness, and it is night, wherein all the beasts of the forest creep forth" (Psalm 104:20).

Book Two

Meanwhile the new-baptized,[1] who yet remained
At Jordan with the Baptist, and had seen
Him [2]whom they heard[3] so late expressly called
Jesus Messiah,[4] Son of God,[5] declared,

---

[1] Simon Peter and Andrew were disciples of John the Baptist before John directed them to Jesus as the promised Messiah: "The next day, John stood again, and two of his disciples. And he beheld Jesus walking by, and said, 'Behold that Lamb of God. And the two disciples heard him speak, and followed Jesus. Then Jesus turned about, and saw them follow, and said unto them, 'What seek ye?' And they said unto him, 'Rabbi (which is to say by interpretation, Master) where dwellest thou?' He said unto them, 'Come, and see.' They came and saw where he dwelt, and abode with him that day: for it was about the tenth hour. Andrew, Simon Peter's brother, was one of the two which had heard it of John, and that followed him. The same found his brother Simon first, and said unto him, 'We have found that Messiah, which is by interpretation, that Christ" (John 1:35–42).

[2] [Lines 2–3] At Jordan with the Baptist, and had seen Him. "He it is that cometh after me, which was before me, whose shoe latchet I am not worthy to unloose. These things were done in Bethabara beyond Jordan, where John did baptize. The next day John, seeth Jesus coming unto him, and saith, 'Behold that Lamb of God, which taketh away the sin of the world'" (John 1:27–29).

[3] "And Jesus when he was baptized, came straight out of the water; lo, the heavens were opened unto him, & John saw the Spirit of God descending like a dove, and lighting upon him. And lo, a voice came from heaven, saying, 'This is my beloved Son, in whom I am well pleased'" (Matthew 3:16, 17). "Then there was a voice from heaven, saying, 'Thou art my beloved Son, in whom I am well pleased'" (Mark 1:11). "And the holy Ghost came down in a bodily shape like a dove, upon him, and there was a voice from heaven, saying, 'Thou art my beloved Son: in thee I am well pleased'" (Luke 3:22).

[4] So late expressly called Jesus Messiah. As foretold, Jesus did not frequently call himself the Messiah. "All we like sheep have gone astray: we have turned every one to his own way, and the Lord hath laid upon him the iniquity of us all. He was oppressed and he was afflicted, yet did he not open his mouth: he is brought as a sheep to the slaughter, and as a sheep before her shearer is dumb, so he openeth not his mouth (Isaiah 53:7). "And Jesus went out, and his disciples into the towns of Caesarea Philippi; by the way he asked his disciples, saying unto

And on that high authority had believed,
And with him talked, and with him lodged—I mean
Andrew and Simon, famous after known,
With others,[6] though in Holy Writ not named,
Now missing him, their joy so lately found,[7]
So lately found and so abruptly gone,
Began to doubt, and doubted many days,
And, as the days increased, increased their doubt.[8]
Sometimes they thought he might be only shewn,
And for a time caught up to God, as once
Moses was in the Mount and missing long,[9]

---

them, 'Whom do men say that I am?' And they answered, 'Some say, John Baptist: and some, Elias: and some, one of the Prophets.' And he said unto them, 'But whom say ye that I am?' Then Peter answered, and said unto him, 'Thou art that Christ.' And he sharply charged them, that concerning him they should tell no man" (Mark 8:27–30). "And it came to pass, as he was alone praying, his disciples were with him: and he asked them, saying, 'Whom say the people that I am?' They answered, and said, 'John Baptist: and others say, Elias: and some say, that one of the old Prophets is risen again.' And he said unto them, 'But whom say ye that I am?' Peter answered, and said, 'That Christ of God.' And he warned and commanded them, that they should tell that to no man" (Luke 9:18–21). The first person that Jesus directly told that he was the Messiah was the Samaritan woman at the well. It was not a conspicuous public announcement: "The woman said unto him, 'I know well that Messiah shall come which is called Christ: when he is come, he will tell us all things.' Jesus said unto her, 'I am he, that speak unto thee'" (John 4:25).

[5] Son of God. "Then Simon Peter answered, & said, 'Thou art that Christ, the Son of the living God'" (Matthew 16:16).

[6] "And as soon as they were come out of the Synagogue, they entered into the house of Simon and Andrew, with James and John" (Mark 1:29).

[7] Found. "The same found his brother Simon first, and said unto him, 'We have found that Messiah, which is by interpretation, that Christ" (John 1:41).

[8] Compare with Jesus' reception among the apostles even after his resurrection: "And when they saw him, they worshipped him: but some doubted" (Matthew 28:17).

[9] [Lines 14–15] "And Moses entered into the midst of the cloud, and went up to the mountain: and Moses was in the mount forty days and forty nights" (Exodus 24:18). "But when the people saw, that Moses tarried long or he came down from

And the great Thisbite,[10] who on fiery wheels
Rode up to Heaven,[11] yet once again to come.
Therefore, as those young prophets then with care
Sought lost Eliah, so in each place these
Nigh to Bethabara;[12] in Jericho
The city of palms,[13] Aenon, and Salem[14] old,
Machaerus, and each town or city walled
On this side the broad lake Genezaret,[15]

---

the mountain, the people gathered themselves together against Aaron, and said unto him, 'Up, make us gods to go before us: for of this Moses (the man that brought us out of the land of Egypt) we know not what is become of him'" (Exodus 32:1).

[10] The great Thisbite. Elijah the prophet: "And the word of the Lord came unto Elijah the Tishbite, saying" (1 Kings 21:17).

[11] [Lines 14–15] Who on fiery wheels rode up to heaven. The prophet Elijah: "And as they went walking and talking, behold, there appeared a chariot of fire, and horses of fire, and did separate them twain. So Elijah went up by a whirlwind into heaven [...] And said unto him, 'Behold now, there be with thy servants fifty strong men: let them go, we pray thee, and seek thy master, if so be the Spirit of the Lord hath taken him up, and cast him upon some mountain, or into some valley.' But he said, 'Ye shall not send.' Yet they were instant upon him, until he was ashamed: wherefore he said, 'Send.' So they sent fifty men, which sought three days, but found him not" (2 Kings 2:11, 16–17).

[12] "These things were done in Bethabara beyond Jordan, where John did baptize" (John 1:28).

[13] [Lines 20–21] Jericho the city of palms. "And the South, and the plain of the valley of Jericho, the city of palm trees, unto Zoar" (Deuteronomy 34:3). Not Tyndale "the city of date trees."

[14] Aenon and Salem. "And John also baptized in Enon besides Salim, because there was much water there: and they came, and were baptized" (John 3:23). "Salem old" was ruled by the King-Priest Melchizedek during the days of Abraham: "And Melchi-zedek King of Shalem brought forth bread and wine: and he was a Priest of the most high God (Genesis 14:18). "For this Melchi-sedec was King of Salem, the Priest of the most high God, who met Abraham, as he returned from the slaughter of the Kings, and blessed him: To whom also Abraham gave the tithe of all things: who first is by interpretation King of righteousness: after that, he is also King of Salem, that is, King of peace" (Hebrews 7:1, 2).

Or in Peraea, but returned in vain.[16]
Then on the bank of Jordan,[17] by a creek,
Where winds with reeds[18] and osiers whispering play,
Plain fishermen[19] (no greater men them call),
Close in a cottage low together got,
Their unexpected loss and plaints outbreathed:
"Alas, from what high hope to what relapse
Unlooked for are we fallen! Our eyes beheld
Messiah certainly now come, so long
Expected of our fathers; we have heard
His words, his wisdom full of grace and truth.[20]

---

[15] "Then it came to pass, as the people pressed upon him to hear the word of God, that he stood by the lake of Gennesaret" (Luke 5:1). "And when they were come over, they came into the land of Gennezaret" (Matthew 14:34). "And they came over, and went into the land of Gennesaret, and arrived" (Mark 6:53).

[16] [Lines 19–24] First century Jews were on the watch for the return of Elijah the prophet, just as Elijah's contemporaries sought for him when after he ascended in the whirlwind: "Behold, I will send you Elijah the Prophet before the coming of the great and fearful day of the Lord" (Malachi 4:5). "And they said, 'Some say, John Baptist: and some, Elias: and others, Jeremiah, or one of the Prophets" (Matthew 16:14). "And they answered, 'Some say, John Baptist: and some, Elias: and some, one of the Prophets'" (Mark 8:28). "They answered, and said, John Baptist: and others say, Elias: and some say, that one of the old Prophets is risen again'" (Luke 9:19). "And if ye will receive it, this is that Elias, which was to come" (Mark 11:14).

[17] "The land of Zabulon, and the land of Nephthalim by the way of the sea, beyond Jordan, Galilee of the Gentiles" (Matthew 4:15).

[18] "And as they departed, Jesus began to speak unto the multitude, of John, What went ye out into the wilderness to see? A reed shaken with the wind?" (Matthew 11:7).

[19] "And Jesus walking by the sea of Galilee, saw two brethren, Simon, which was called Peter, and Andrew his brother, casting a net into the sea (for they were fishers.) And he said unto them, 'Follow me, and I will make you fishers of men.' And they straightway leaving the nets, followed him. And when he was gone forth from thence, he saw other two brethren, James the son of Zebedee, and John his brother in a ship with Zebedee their father, mending their nets, & he called them. And they without tarrying, leaving the ship, and their father, followed him" (Matthew 4:18–22).

'Now, now, for sure, deliverance is at hand;
The kingdom shall to Israel be restored:'[21]
Thus we rejoiced, but soon our joy is turned
Into perplexity and new amaze.
For whither is he gone? what accident
Hath rapt him from us? will he now retire
After appearance, and again prolong
Our expectation? God of Israel,
Send thy Messiah forth; the time is come.
Behold the kings of the earth, how they oppress
Thy Chosen,[22] to what highth their power unjust
They have exalted, and behind them cast
All fear of Thee; arise, and vindicate
Thy glory; free thy people from their yoke!
But let us wait; thus far He hath performed,
Sent his Anointed, and to us revealed him
By his great Prophet[23] pointed at and shown
In public, and with him we have conversed.
Let us be glad of this, and all our fears

---

[20] [Lines 30–34] "The same found his brother Simon first, and said unto him, 'We have found that Messiah,' which is by interpretation, that Christ [...] Philippe found Nathanael, and said unto him, 'We have found him of whom Moses did write in the Law, and the Prophets, Jesus that son of Joseph, that was of Nazareth' [...] Nathanael answered, and said unto him, 'Rabbi, thou art that Son of God: thou art that King of Israel'" (John 1:41, 45, 49). Full of grace and truth. "And that Word was made flesh, and dwelt among us, (and we saw the glory thereof, as the glory of the only begotten Son of the Father) full of grace and truth" (John 1:14). Not Tyndale "full of grace and verity."

[21] The Kingdom shall to Israel be restored. "When they therefore were come together, they asked of him, saying, 'Lord, wilt thou at this time restore the kingdom to Israel?'" (Acts 1:6).

[22] [Lines 44–45] Behold the kings of the earth, how they oppress thy Chosen. "The Kings of the earth band themselves, and the princes are assembled together against the Lord, and against his Christ" (Psalms 2:2).

[23] John the Baptist the Prophet: "And he beheld Jesus walking by, and said, 'Behold that Lamb of God.' And the two disciples heard him speak, and followed Jesus" (John 1:36, 37).

Lay on his providence;[24] He will not fail,
Nor will withdraw him now,[25] nor will recall—
Mock us with his blest sight, then snatch him hence:
Soon we shall see our hope,[26] our joy, return."
Thus they out of their plaints new hope resume
To find whom at the first they found unsought.[27]
But to his mother Mary, when she saw
Others returned from baptism, not her Son,
Nor left at Jordan tidings of him none,
Within her breast though calm, her breast though pure,[28]
Motherly cares[29] and fears got head, and raised

---

[24] [Lines 53–54] All our fears lay on his providence. "Cast thy burden upon the Lord, and he shall nourish thee: he will not suffer the righteous to fall forever" (Psalm 55:22). "Cast all your care on him: for he careth for you" (1 Peter 5:7).

[25] Nor will withdraw him now. "There shall not a man be able to withstand thee all the days of thy life: as I was with Moses, so will I be with thee: I will not leave thee, nor forsake thee" (Joshua 1:5).

[26] Soon shall we see our hope. "For this cause therefore have I called for you, to see you, and to speak with you: for that hope of Israels sake, I am bound with this chain" (Acts 28:20). "Paul an Apostle of Jesus Christ, by the commandment of God our Savior, and of our Lord Jesus Christ our hope" (1 Timothy 1:1).

[27] To whom at first they found unsought. Messianic prophecy: "I have been sought of them that asked not: I was found of them that sought me not: I said, 'Behold me, behold me, unto a nation that called not upon my Name'" (Isaiah 65:1).

[28] "Then said Mary unto the Angel, 'How shall this be, seeing I know not man?' [...] 'For he hath looked on the poor degree of his servant: for behold, from henceforth shall all ages call me blessed'" (Luke 1:34, 48).

[29] Motherly cares of Mary. "And she brought forth her first begotten son, and wrapped him in swaddling clothes, and laid him in a cratch, because there was no room for them in the inn [...] And Simeon blessed them, and said unto Mary his mother, 'Behold, this child is appointed for the fall and rising again of many in Israel, and for a sign which shall be spoken against' [...] So when they saw him, they were amassed, and his mother said unto him, 'Sonne, why hast thou thus dealt with us? Behold, thy father and I have sought thee with very heavy hearts'" (Luke 2:7, 35, 48). "Then stood by the cross of Jesus his mother, and his mother's sister, Mary the wife of Cleopas, and Mary Magdalene. And when Jesus saw his mother, and the disciple standing by, whom he loved, he said unto his

Some troubled thoughts, which she in sighs thus clad:—
"Oh, what avails me now that honor high,
To have conceived of God, or that salute,
'Hail, highly favoured, among women blest!'[30]
While I to sorrows am no less advanced,
And fears as eminent above the lot
Of other women, by the birth I bore:
In such a season born, when scarce a shed
Could be obtained to shelter him or me
From the bleak air? A stable was our warmth,
A manger his[31]; yet soon enforced to fly
Thence into Egypt,[32] till the murderous king[33]
Were dead,[34] who sought his life, and, missing, filled
With infant blood the streets of Bethlehem.
From Egypt home returned,[35] in Nazareth[36]

---

mother, 'Woman, behold thy son.' Then said he to the disciple, 'Behold thy mother: and from that hour, the disciple took her home unto him" (John 19:25–27).

[30] "And the Angel went in unto her, and said, 'Hail thou that art freely beloved: the Lord is with thee: blessed art thou among women'" (Luke 1:28).

[31] Manger. "And they came with haste, and found Mary and Ioseph, and the babe lying in a manger" (Luke 2:16). Not GE "cratch."

[32] Thence into Egypt. "After their departure, behold, the Angel of the Lord appeareth to Ioseph in a dream, saying, Arise, and take the babe & his mother, and flee into Egypt, and be there til I bring thee word: for Herod will seek the babe, to destroy him. So he arose and took the babe and his mother by night, and departed into Egypt" (Luke 2:13, 14).

[33] The murderous king. "Then Herod, seeing that he was mocked of the Wisemen, was exceeding wroth, and sent forth, and slew all the male children that were in Beth-leem, and in all the coasts thereof, from two year old and under, according to the time which he had diligently searched out of the Wisemen. Then was that fulfilled which is spoken by the Prophet Jeremiah, saying, "In Rhama was a voice heard, mourning, and weeping, and great howling: 'Rachel weeping for her children, and would not be comforted, because they were not'" (Luke 2:16–18).

[34] Herod's death: "And was there unto the death of Herod, that that might be fulfilled, which is spoken of the Lord by the Prophet, saying, 'Out of Egypt have I called my son'" (Matthew 2:15).

Hath been our dwelling many years; his life
Private, unactive, calm, contemplative,
Little suspicious to any king.[37] But now,
Full grown to man, acknowledged, as I hear,
By John the Baptist, and in public shewn,
Son owned from Heaven by his Father's voice,[38]
I looked for some great change. To honor? no;
But trouble, as old Simeon plain foretold,
That to the fall and rising he should be
Of many in Israel, and to a sign
Spoken against[39]—that through my very soul
A sword shall pierce.[40] This is my favoured lot,
My exaltation to afflictions high![41]

---

[35] "And when Herod was dead, behold, an Angel of the Lord appeareth in a dream to Joseph in Egypt, Saying, 'Arise, and take the babe and his mother, and go into the land of Israel: for they are dead which sought the babes life.' Then he arose up and took the babe and his mother, and came into the land of Israel" (Matthew 2:19–21).

[36] "And went and dwelt in a city called Nazareth, that it might be fulfilled which was spoken by the Prophets, which was, That he should be called a Nazarite" (Matthew 2:23).

[37] Little suspicion to any king. The utterance of the disciple Nathaniel about Nazareth seems proverbial: "Then Nathanael said unto him, 'Can there any good thing come out of Nazareth?' Philip said to him, 'Come, and see' (John 1:46).

[38] "And lo, a voice came from heaven, saying, 'This is my beloved Son, in whom I am well pleased'" (Matthew 3:17).

[39] Spoken against. "And Simeon blessed them, and said unto Mary his mother, 'Behold, this child is appointed for the fall and rising again of many in Israel, and for a sign which shall be spoken against'" (Luke 2:34).

[40] A sword shall pierce. Simeon's prophecy regarding how the death of Jesus would afflict Mary: "(Yea and a sword shall pierce through thy soul) that the thoughts of many hearts may be opened" (Luke 2:35).

[41] The suffering Messiah. "But he was wounded for our transgressions, he was broken for our iniquities: the chastisement of our peace was upon him, and with his stripes we are healed. All we like sheep have gone astray: we have turned everyone to his own way, and the Lord hath laid upon him the iniquity of us all. He was oppressed and he was afflicted, yet did he not open his mouth: he is brought as a sheep to the slaughter, and as a sheep before her shearer is dumb, so

Afflicted I may be, it seems, and blest!
I will not argue that, nor will repine.
But where delays he now? Some great intent
Conceals him. When twelve years he scarce had seen,
I lost him, but so found as well I saw
He could not lose himself, but went about
His Father's business.[42] What he meant I mused,[43]
Since understand; much more his absence now
Thus long to some great purpose he obscures.
But I to wait with patience am inured;
My heart hath been a storehouse long of things
And sayings laid up, pretending strange events."
Thus Mary, pondering oft, and oft to mind
Recalling what remarkably had passed
Since first her Salutation heard,[44] with thoughts

---

he openeth not his mouth. He was taken out from prison, and from judgment: and who shall declare his age? For he was cut out of the land of the living: for the transgression of my people was he plagued" (Isaiah 53:5–8).

42 [Lines 96–99] "And when he was twelve year old, and they were come up to Jerusalem, after the custom of the feast, And had finished the days thereof, as they returned, the child Jesus remained in Jerusalem, and Joseph knew not, nor his mother, But they supposing, that he had been in the company, went a days journey, and sought him among their kinsfolk, and acquaintance. And when they found him not, they turned back to Jerusalem, and sought him. And it came to pass three days after, that they found him in the Temple, sitting in the midst of the doctors, both hearing them, and asking them questions: And all that heard him, were astonished at his understanding and answers. So when they saw him, they were amazed, and his mother said unto him, 'Son, why hast thou thus dealt with vs? Behold, thy father and I have sought thee with very heavy hearts.' Then said he unto them, 'How is it that ye sought me? Knew ye not that I must go about my Father's business? But they understood not the word that he spake to them'" (Luke 2:42–50).

43 What he meant I mused. "Then he went down with them, and came to Nazareth, and was subject to them: and his mother kept all these sayings in her heart" (Luke 2:51).

44 The angel Gabriel's greeting to Mary: "And the Angel went in unto her, and said, 'Haile thou that art freely beloved: the Lord is with thee: blessed art thou among women'" (Luke 1:28).

Meekly composed awaited the fulfilling:
The while her Son, tracing the desert wild,
Sole, but with holiest meditations fed,
Into himself descended, and at once
All his great work[45] to come before him set:[46]
How to begin, how to accomplish best
His end of being on Earth, and mission high.[47]
For Satan, with sly preface to return,
Had left him vacant, and with speed was gone
Up to the middle region of thick air,[48]
Where all his Potentates[49] in council sate.
There, without sign of boast, or sign of joy,
Solicitous and blank, he thus began:
"Princes, Heaven's ancient Sons,[50] Aethereal Thrones,
Daemonian Spirits now, from the element

---

[45] "Jesus said unto them, 'My meat is that I may do the will of him that sent me, and finish his work'" (John 4:34).

[46] [Lines 111–112] Into himself descended, and at once / All his great work to come before him set. "Believest thou not, that I am in the Father, and the Father is in me? The words that I speak unto you, I speak not of myself: but the Father that dwelleth in me, he doth the works" (John 14:10).

[47] Mission high. "Pilate then said unto him, 'Art thou a King then?' Jesus answered, 'Thou sayest that I am a King: for this cause am I born, and for this cause came I into the world, that I should bear witness unto the truth: every one that is of the truth, heareth my voice'" (John 18:37).

[48] Satan is the ruler of the air where he holds court. "Wherein, in times past ye walked, according to the course of this world, and after the prince that ruleth in the air, even the spirit, that now worketh in the children of disobedience" (Ephesians 2:2).

[49] His Potentates are the high-ranking angels that rebelled against God and fell with Satan. "For we wrestle not against flesh and blood, but against principalities, against powers, and against the worldly governors, the princes of the darkness of this world, against spiritual wickedness, which are in the high places" (Ephesians 6:12).

[50] All angels are considered Sons of God or Heaven: "Then the sons of God saw the daughters of men that they were fair, & they took them wives of all that they liked" (Genesis 6:2).

Each of his reign allotted, rightlier called
Powers of Fire, Air, Water, and Earth beneath
(So may we hold our place and these mild seats
Without new trouble!) such an enemy
Is risen to invade us, who no less
Threatens than our expulsion down to Hell.
I, as I undertook, and with the vote
Consenting in full frequence was impowered,
Have found him, viewed him, tasted him;[51] but find
Far other labor to be undergone
Than when I dealt with Adam, first of men,[52]
Though Adam by his wife's allurement fell,
However to this Man inferior far,
If he be Man by mother's side, at least[53]
With more than human gifts from Heaven adorned,
Perfections absolute, graces divine,
And amplitude of mind to greatest deeds.
Therefore I am returned, lest confidence
Of my success with Eve in Paradise
Deceive ye to persuasion over-sure
Of like succeeding here. I summon all
Rather to be in readiness with hand
Or counsel to assist, lest I, who erst
Thought none my equal, now be overmatched."
So spake the old Serpent,[54] doubting, and from all

---

[51] Taste in the sense of experience or testing out. "Taste ye and see, how gracious the Lord is: blessed is the man that trusteth in him" (Psalm 34:8).

[52] Adam, first of men. The correspondence of Jesus to Adam: "For as by one man's disobedience many were made sinners, so by that obedience of that one shall many also be made righteous" (Romans 5:19).

[53] If he be man by mother's side at least. "Concerning his Son Jesus Christ our Lord (which was made of the seed of David according to the flesh, And declared mightily to be the Son of God, touching the Spirit of sanctification by the resurrection from the dead)" (Romans 1:3, 4). "And Jesus himself began to be about thirty year of age, being as men supposed the son of Joseph, which was the son of Eli" (Luke 3:23).

With clamour was assured their utmost aid
At his command; when from amidst them rose
Belial,[55] the dissolutest Spirit that fell,
The sensualest, and, after Asmodai,[56]

---

[54] Satan as the old serpent: "And the great dragon, that old serpent, called the devil and Satan, was cast out, which deceiveth all the world: he was even cast into the earth, and his angels were cast out with him" (Revelation 12:9).

[55] Belial (in Hebrew literally "worthlessness" or "good for nothing") is linked with sexual violence in the scriptures. "Now as they were making their hearts merry, behold, the men of the city, certain sons of Belial, beset the house round about, and beat at the door, and spake to the master of the house, the old man, saying; 'Bring forth the man that came into thine house, that we may know him.' And the man, the master of the house, went out unto them, and said unto them, 'Nay my brethren, nay, I pray you do not so wickedly; seeing that this man is come into mine house, do not this folly. Behold, here is my daughter, a maiden, and his concubine, them I will bring out now, and humble ye them, and do with them what seemeth good unto you: but unto this man do not so vile a thing.' But the men would not hearken to him: so the man took his concubine, and brought her forth unto them, and they knew her, and abused her all the night until the morning: and when the day began to spring, they let her go. Then came the woman in the dawning of the day, and fell down at the door of the man's house, where her lord was, until it was light. And her lord rose up in the morning, & opened the doors of the house, and went out to go his way: and behold, the woman his concubine was fallen down at the door of the house, and her hands were upon the threshold. And he said unto her, 'Up, and let us be going.' But none answered: then the man took her up upon an ass, and the man rose up, and got him unto his place. And when he was come into his house, he took a knife, and laid hold on his concubine, and divided her, together with her bones, into twelve pieces, and sent her into all the coasts of Israel. And it was so that all that saw it, said, 'There was no such deed done nor seen, from the day that the children of Israel came up out of the land of Egypt, unto this day: consider of it, take advise, and speak your minds" (Judges 19:22–30 AV [See also Coverdale and DR]). Not GE "wicked men." Not GT and Bishops "men of the city which were wicked."

[56] "Because she had been married to seven husbands, whom Asmodeus the evil spirit had killed, before that they had lain with her. 'Dost thou not know,' said they, 'that thou hast strangled thine husbands? thou hast had now seven husbands, neither wast thou named after any of them" (Tobit 3:8). "And I am the only begotten son of my father, and I am afraid, least I go in to her, and die as the

The fleshliest Incubus, and thus advised:
"Set women in his eye and in his walk,
Among daughters of men[57] the fairest found.
Many are in each region passing fair
As the noon sky, more like to goddesses
Than mortal creatures, graceful and discreet,
Expert in amorous arts, enchanting tongues
Persuasive, virgin majesty with mild
And sweet allayed, yet terrible to approach,[58]
Skilled to retire, and in retiring draw
Hearts after them tangled in amorous nets.
Such object hath the power to soften and tame
Severest temper, smooth the rugged'st brow,
Enerve, and with voluptuous hope dissolve,
Draw out with credulous desire, and lead
At will the manliest, resolutest breast,
As the magnetic hardest iron draws.
Women, when nothing else, beguiled the heart
Of wisest Solomon, and made him build,
And made him bow, to the gods of his wives."[59]

---

other before: for a wicked spirit loveth her, which hurteth no body, but those which come in to her: wherefore I also fear least I die, and bring my fathers and my mothers life because of me to the grave with sorrow: for they have no other son to bury them" (Tobit 6:14).

[57] Daughters of men. Compare: "Then the sons of God saw the daughters of men that they were fair, & they took them wives of all that they liked" (Genesis 6:2).

[58] Terrible and unapproachable beauty. "Thou art beautiful, my love, as Tirzah, comely as Jerusalem, terrible as an army with banners" (Song of Solomon 6:4).

[59] [Lines 169–171] "But King Solomon loved many outlandish women: both the daughter of Pharaoh, and the women of Moab, Ammon, Edom, Zidon and Heth, Of the nations, whereof the Lord had said unto the children of Israel, 'Go not ye in to them, nor let them come in to you: for surely they will turn your hearts after their gods,' to them, I say, did Solomon join in love. And he had seven hundred wives, that were princesses, and three hundred concubines, and his wives turned away his heart. For when Solomon was old, his wives turned his heart after other gods, so that his heart was not perfect with the Lord his God, as was the heart of David his father. For Solomon followed Ashtaroth the god of the

To whom quick answer Satan thus returned:
"Belial, in much uneven scale thou weigh'st
All others by thyself. Because of old
Thou thyself doat'st on womankind, admiring
Their shape, their colour, and attractive grace,
None are, thou think'st, but taken with such toys.
Before the Flood, thou, with thy lusty crew,
False titled Sons of God, roaming the Earth,
Cast wanton eyes on the daughters of men,
And coupled with them, and begot a race.[60]
Have we not seen, or by relation heard,
In courts and regal chambers how thou lurk'st,
In wood or grove, by mossy fountain-side,
In valley or green meadow, to waylay
Some beauty rare, Calisto, Clymene,
Daphne, or Semele, Antiopa,
Or Amymone, Syrinx, many more
Too long—then lay'st thy scapes on names adored,
Apollo, Neptune, Jupiter, or Pan,
Satyr, or Faun, or Silvan? But these haunts

Zidonians, and Milcom the abomination of the Ammonites. So Solomon wrought wickedness in the sight of the Lord, but continued not to follow the Lord, as did David his father. Then did Solomon build an high place for Chemosh the abomination of Moab, in the mountain that is over against Jerusalem, and unto Molech the abomination of the children of Ammon. And so did he for all his outlandish wives, which burnt incense and offered unto their gods" (1 Kings 11:1–8).

[60] [Lines 178–181] Belial and other angelic sons of God took human form before the global flood and cohabitated with women, producing a race of giants. "So when men began to be multiplied upon the earth, and there were daughters born unto them, Then the sons of God saw the daughters of men that they were fair, & they took them wives of all that they liked. Therefore the Lord said, 'My Spirit shall not always strive with man, because he is but flesh, and his days shall be an hundred & twenty years.' There were giants in the earth in those days: yea, and after that the sons of God came unto the daughters of men, and they had born them children, these were mighty men, which in old time were men of renown" (Genesis 6:1–4).

Delight not all. Among the sons of men
How many have with a smile made small account
Of beauty and her lures, easily scorned
All her assaults, on worthier things intent!
Remember that Pellean conqueror,
A youth, how all the beauties of the East
He slightly viewed, and slightly overpassed;
How he surnamed of Africa dismissed,
In his prime youth, the fair Iberian maid.
For Solomon, he lived at ease[61], and, full
Of honor,[62] wealth,[63] high fare,[64] aimed not beyond

---

[61] For Solomon, he lived at ease. "For he ruled in all the region on the other side of the River, from Tiphsah even unto Azzah, over all the Kings on the other side the River: and he had peace round about him on every side. And Judah and Israel dwelt without fear, every man under his vine, and under his fig tree, from Dan, even to Beer-sheba, all the days of Solomon (1 Kings 4:24, 25).

[62] Solomon was "full of honor." "And God gave Solomon wisdom and understanding exceeding much, & a large heart, even as the sand that is on the sea shore, And Solomon's wisdom excelled the wisdom of all the children of the East and all the wisdom of Egypt. For he was wiser than any man: yea, then were Ethan the Ezrahite, the Heman, then Chalcol, then Darda the sons of Mahol: and he was famous throughout all nations round about. And Solomon spake three thousand proverbs: and his songs were a thousand and five. And he spake of trees, from the cedar tree that is in Lebanon, even unto the hyssop that springeth out of the wall: he spake also of beasts, and of fowls, and of creeping things, and of fishes. And there came of all people to hear the wisdom of Solomon, from all Kings of the earth, which had heard of his wisdom" (1 Kings 4:29–34).

[63] The wealth of Solomon: "So King Solomon exceeded all the kings of the earth both in riches and in wisdom" (1 Kings 10:23).

[64] Solomon's "high fare." "And Solomon had twelve officers over all Israel, which provided vittles for the King and his household: each man had a month in the year to provide vittles [...] And Solomon's vittles for one day were thirty measures of fine flour, and threescore measures of meal: Ten fat oxen, and twenty oxen of the pastures, and a hundred sheep, beside harts, and bucks, and bugles, and fat fowl [..] And Solomon had forty thousand stalls of horses for his chariots, and twelve thousand horsemen. And these officers provided vittles for king Solomon, and for all that came to King Solomons table, every man his month, and they suffered to lack nothing (1 Kings 4:7, 22, 23, 26, 27).

Higher design than to enjoy his state;[65]
Thence to the bait of women lay exposed.
But he whom we attempt is wiser far
Than Solomon,[66] of more exalted mind,
Made and set wholly on the accomplishment
Of greatest things. What woman will you find,
Though of this age the wonder and the fame,
On whom his leisure will voutsafe an eye
Of fond desire? Or should she, confident,
As sitting queen adored on Beauty's throne,
Descend with all her winning charms begirt
To enamour, as the zone of Venus once
Wrought that effect on Jove (so fables tell),
How would one look from his majestic brow,
Seated as on the top of Virtue's hill,
Discountenance her despised, and put to rout
All her array, her female pride deject,
Or turn to reverent awe! For Beauty stands
In the admiration only of weak minds
Led captive; cease to admire, and all her plumes
Fall flat, and shrink into a trivial toy,
At every sudden slighting quite abashed.
Therefore with manlier objects we must try
His constancy—with such as have more shew
Of worth, of honor, glory, and popular praise

---

[65] [Lines 201–203] Solomon, the putative author of Ecclesiastes and accepted by Milton as such, concludes his treatise after exploring many of the various pursuits of humanity: "Let us hear the end of all: fear God and keep his commandments: for this is the whole duty of man" (Ecclesiastes 12:13).

[66] [Lines 205–206] Jesus is "wiser far than Solomon." "The Queen of the South shall rise in judgment with this generation, and shall condemn it: for she came from the utmost parts of the earth to hear the wisdom of Solomon: and behold, a greater than Solomon is here" (Matthew 12:42). "The Queen of the South shall rise in judgment, with the men of this generation, and shall condemn them: for she came from the utmost parts of the earth to hear the wisdom of Solomon, and behold, a greater than Solomon is here" (Luke 11:31).

(Rocks whereon greatest men have oftest wrecked);
Or that which only seems to satisfy
Lawful desires of nature, not beyond.
And now I know he hungers, where no food
Is to be found,[67] in the wide Wilderness:
The rest commit to me; I shall let pass
No advantage, and his strength as oft assay."
He ceased, and heard their grant in loud acclaim;
Then forthwith to him takes a chosen band
Of Spirits likest to himself in guile,[68]
To be at hand and at his beck appear,
If cause were to unfold some active scene
Of various persons, each to know his part;
Then to the desert takes with these his flight,
Where still, from shade to shade, the Son of God,
After forty days' fasting, had remained,
Now hungering first, and to himself thus said:
"Where will this end? Four times ten days I have passed
Wandering this woody maze, and human food

---

[67] [Lines 231–232] And now I know he hungers, where not food is to be found. "And was there forty days tempted of the devil, & in those days he did eat nothing: but when they were ended, he afterward was hungry" (Luke 4:2). "And when he had fasted forty days, and forty nights, he was afterward hungry" (Matthew 4:2).

[68] [Lines 236–237] Then forthwith to him takes a chosen band / Of Spirits likest to himself in guile. Demons often work together in squads. Compare "Then he goeth, & taketh unto him seven other spirits worse than himself, and they enter in, and dwell there: and the end of that man is worse then the beginning. Even so shall it be with this wicked generation" (Matthew 12:45). "Then goeth he, and taketh to him seven other spirits worse then himself: and they enter in, and dwell there: so the last state of that man is worse than the first" (Luke 11:26). "Then Jesus asked him, saying, 'What is thy name?' And he said, 'Legion,' because many devils were entered into him" (Luke 8:30). "And he asked him, 'What is thy name?' and he answered, saying, 'My name is Legion: for we are many' […] And they came to Jesus, and saw him that had been possessed with the devil, and had the legion, sit both clothed, and in his right mind: and they were afraid" (Mark 5:9, 15).

Nor tasted, nor had appetite. That fast
To virtue I impute not, or count part
Of what I suffer here. If nature need not,
Or God support nature without repast,
Though needing, what praise is it to endure?
But now I feel I hunger; which declares
Nature hath need of what she asks. Yet God
Can satisfy that need some other way,
Though hunger still remain. So it remain
Without this body's wasting, I content me,
And from the sting of famine fear no harm;
Nor mind it, fed with better thoughts, that feed
Me hungering more to do my Father's will."[69]
It was the hour of night, when thus the Son
Communed in silent walk, then laid him down[70]
Under the hospitable covert nigh
Of trees thick interwoven. There he slept,
And dreamed, as appetite is wont to dream,
Of meats and drinks, nature's refreshment sweet.
Him thought he by the brook of Cherith stood,
And saw the ravens with their horny beaks
Food to Elijah bringing even and morn
Though ravenous, taught to abstain from what they brought;[71]
He saw the Prophet also, how he fled

---

[69] "Jesus said unto them, 'My meat is that I may do the will of him that sent me, and finish his work'" (John 4:34). "Blessed are they which hunger and thirst for righteousness: for they shall be filled" (Matthew 5:6). Compare with the attitude of Job: "Neither have I departed from the commandment of his lips, and I have esteemed the words of his mouth more then mine appointed food" (Job 23:12).

[70] "Tremble, and sin not: examine your own heart upon your bed, and be still. Selah" (Psalm 4:4).

[71] [Lines 266–269] Jesus dreams of how God miraculously fed Elijah. "So he went & did according unto the word of the Lord: for he went, and remained by the river Cherith that is over against Jordan. And the ravens brought him bread & flesh in the morning, and bread & flesh in the evening, and he drank of the river" (1 Kings 17:5, 6).

Into the desert, and how there he slept
Under a juniper—then how, awaked,
He found his supper on the coals prepared,
And by the Angel was bid rise and eat,
And eat the second time after repose,
The strength whereof sufficed him forty days:
Sometimes that with Elijah he partook,[72]
Or as a guest with Daniel at his pulse.[73]

---

[72] [Lines 270–277] God sustained Elijah for forty days. "But he went a day's journey into the wilderness, and came and sat down under a juniper tree, and desired that he might die, and said, 'It is now enough: O Lord, take my soul, for I am no better than my fathers.' And as he lay and slept under the juniper tree, behold now, an Angel touched him, and said unto him, 'Up, and eat.' And when he looked about, behold, there was a cake baked on the coals, and a pot of water at his head: so he did eat and drink, and returned and slept. And the Angel of the Lord came again the second time, and touched him, and said, 'Up, and eat: for thou hast a great journey.' Then he arose, and did eat and drink, and walked in the strength of that meat forty days and forty nights, unto Horeb the mount of God" (1 Kings 19:4–8).

[73] Or as a guest of Daniel at his pulse. "But Daniel had determined in his heart, that he would not defile him self with the portion of the King's meat, nor with the wine which he drank: therefore, he required the chief of the Eunuchs that he might not defile himself. (Now God had brought Daniel into favor, and tender love with the chief of the Eunuchs) And the chief of the Eunuchs said unto Daniel, 'I fear my lord the King, who hath appointed your meat and your drink: therefore if he see your faces worse liking then the other children, which are of your sort, then shall you make me lose mine head unto the King.' Then said Daniel to Melzar, whom the chief of the Eunuchs had set over Daniel, Hananiah, Mishael, and Azariah, 'Proue thy servants, I beseech thee, ten days, and let them give us pulse to eat, and water to drink. Then let our countenances be looked upon before thee, and the countenances of the children that eat of the portion of the King's meat: and as thou seest, deal with thy servants.' So he consented to them in this matter, an proved them ten days. And at the end of ten days, their countenances appeared fairer, and in better liking then all the children's, which did eat the portion of the King's meat. Thus, Melzar took away the portion of their meat, and the wine that they should drink, and gave them pulse. As for these four children, God gave them knowledge, & understanding in all learning and wisdom: also, he gave Daniel understanding of all visions and dreams. Now when the time was expired, that the King had appointed to bring them in, the

Thus wore out night; and now the harald Lark
Left his ground-nest, high towering to descry
The Morn's approach, and greet her with his song.
As lightly from his grassy couch up rose
Our Saviour, and found all was but a dream;
Fasting he went to sleep, and fasting waked.
Up to a hill anon his steps he reared,
From whose high top to ken the prospect round,
If cottage were in view, sheep-cote, or herd;
But cottage, herd, or sheep-cote, none he saw—
Only in a bottom saw a pleasant grove,
With chaunt of tuneful birds resounding loud.
Thither he bent his way, determined there
To rest at noon, and entered soon the shade
High-roofed, and walks beneath, and alleys brown,
That opened in the midst a woody scene;
Nature's own work it seemed (Nature taught Art),
And, to a superstitious eye, the haunt
Of wood-gods and wood-nymphs. He viewed it round;
When suddenly a man before him stood,
Not rustic as before, but seemlier clad,
As one in city or court or palace bred,
And with fair speech these words to him addressed:
"With granted leave officious I return,
But much more wonder that the Son of God
In this wild solitude so long should bide,
Of all things destitute, and, well I know,
Not without hunger. Others of some note,
As story tells, have trod this wilderness:

---

chief of the Eunuchs brought them before Nebuchadnezzar. And the King communed with them: and among them all was found none like Daniel, Hananiah, Mishael, and Azariah: therefore, stood they before the king." (Daniel 1:8–19). Nor GT or Coverdale "pottage" instead of "pulse."

The fugitive Bond-woman, with her son,[74]
Outcast Nebaioth,[75] yet found here relief
By a providing Angel; all the race
Of Israel here had famished, had not God
Rained from heaven manna;[76] and that Prophet bold,[77]

---

[74] The fugitive Bond-woman, with her son. Hagar the concubine of Abraham and their son Ishmael. "Wherefore she said unto Abraham, 'Cast out this bond woman and her son: for the son of this bond woman shall not be heir with my son Isaac' […] So Abraham arose up early in the morning, and took bread, and a bottle of water, and gave it unto Hagar, putting it on her shoulder, and the child also, and sent her away: who departing wandered in the wilderness of Beer-sheba […] Then God heard the voice of the child, and the Angel of God called to Hagar from heaven, and said unto her, 'What aileth thee, Hagar? fear not, for God hath heard the voice of the child where he is. Arise, take up the child, and hold him in thine hand: for I will make of him a great people.' And God opened her eyes, and she saw a well of water. so she went and filled the bottle with water, and gave the boy drink" (Genesis 21:10, 14, 17–19). Not Tyndale, Coverdale, GT: "bond maid."

[75] God named the child Ishmael, but Satan refers to Ishmael by the name of his son Naboth. "Also the Angel of the Lord said unto her, 'See, thou art with child, and shalt bear a son, and shalt call his name Ishmael: for the Lord hath heard thy tribulation" (Genesis 16:11). "And these are the names of the sons of Ishmael, name by name, according to their kindreds; the eldest son of Ishmael was Nebaioth, then Kedar, and Adbeel, and Mibsam" (Genesis 25:13).

[76] "Afterward all the Congregation of the children of Israel departed from Elim, and came to the wilderness of Sin, (which is between Elim and Sinai) the fifteenth day of the second month after their departing out of the land of Egypt […] Then said the Lord unto Moses, 'Behold, I will cause bread to rain from heaven to you, & the people shall go out, and gather that that is sufficient for every day, that I may prove them, whether they will walk in my Law or no […] And when the dew that was fallen was ascended, behold, a small round thing was upon the face of the wilderness, small as the hoare frost on the earth. And when the children of Israel saw it, they said one to another, 'It is manna, for they wist not what it was;' Moses said unto them, 'This is the bread which the Lord hath given you to eat […] And the children of Israel did eat manna forty years, until they came unto a land inhabited: they did eat manna until they came to the borders of the land of Canaan (Exodus 16:1, 4, 14–15, 35).

[77] The Prophet bold Elijah: "Elias, because he was zealous and fervent in the Law, was taken up even unto heaven" (1 Maccabees 2:58). "Consider Elijah's boldness

Native of Thebez, wandering here, was fed
Twice by a voice inviting him to eat.[78]
Of thee those forty days none hath regard,
Forty and more deserted here indeed."
To whom thus Jesus: "What conclud'st thou hence?
They all had need; I, as thou seest, have none."
"How hast thou hunger then?" Satan replied.
"Tell me, if food were now before thee set,
Wouldst thou not eat?" "Thereafter as I like
the giver," answered Jesus. "Why should that
Cause thy refusal?" said the subtle Fiend.
"Hast thou not right to all created things?[79]
Owe not all creatures, by just right, to thee
Duty and service, nor to stay till bid,
But tender all their power?[80] Nor mention I

---

before King Ahab: "And Elijah the Tishbite one of the inhabitants of Gilead said unto Ahab, "As the Lord God of Israel liveth, before whom I stand, there shall be neither dew nor rain these years, but according to my word" (1 Kings 17:1).

[78] Elijah "twice by voice invited to eat." "And as he lay and slept under the juniper tree, behold now, an Angel touched him, and said unto him, "Up, and eat." And when he looked about, behold, there was a cake baked on the coals, and a pot of water at his head: so he did eat and drink, and returned and slept. And the Angel of the Lord came again the second time, and touched him, and said, "Up, and eat: for thou hast a great journey" (1 Kings 19:5–7).

[79] Hast thou not right to all created things? Jesus is the heir to all things: "At sundry times and in divers manners God spoke in the old time to our fathers by the Prophets: in these last days he hath spoken unto us by his Son, whom he hath made heir of all things, by whom also he made the worlds," (Hebrews 1:1, 2). All things are for the Christ: "Who is the image of the invisible God, the first begotten of every creature. For by him were all things created, which are in heaven, and which are in earth, things visible and invisible: whether they be Thrones or Dominions, or Principalities, or Powers, all things were created by him, and for him" (Colossians 1:15, 16).

[80] [Lines 325–327] "That at the Name of Jesus should every knee bow, both of things in heaven, and things in earth, and things under the earth, And that every tongue should confess that Jesus Christ is the Lord, unto the glory of God the Father" (Philippians 2:10, 11).

Meats by the law unclean,[81] or offered first
To idols[82]—those young Daniel could refuse;[83]

---

[81] Meats by the law unclean. "But these ye shall not eat, of them that chew the cud, and of them that divide and cleave the hoof only: the camel, nor the hare, nor the cony: for they chew the cud, but divide not the hoof: therefore they shall be unclean unto you: Also the swine, because he divideth the hoof, and cheweth not the cud, shall be unclean unto you: ye shall not eat of their flesh, nor touch their dead carcasses [...] And whatsoever hath no fins nor scales, ye shall not eat: it shall be unclean unto you [...] But these are they, whereof ye shall not eat: the eagle, nor the goshawk, nor the osprey, Nor the glead nor the kite, nor the vulture, after their kind, Nor all kind of ravens, Nor the ostrich, nor the nightcrow, nor the semeaw, nor the hawke after her kind, Neither the little owl, nor the great owl, nor the redshank, Nor the pelican, nor the swan, nor the cormorant: The stork also, and the heron in his kind, nor the lapwing, nor the bat. And every creeping thing that flieth, shall be unclean unto you: it shall not be eaten [...] Ye shall eat of nothing that dieth alone, but thou shalt give it unto the stranger that is within thy gates, that he may eat it: or thou mayest sell it unto a stranger: for thou art an holy people unto the Lord thy God. Thou shalt not seeth a kid in his mother's milk" (Deuteronomy 14:7, 8, 10, 12–19, 21). "Every creeping thing therefore that creepeth upon the earth shall be an abomination, and not be eaten. Whatsoever goeth upon the breast, and whatsoever goeth upon all four, or that hath many feet among all creeping things that creep upon the earth, ye shall not eat of them, for they shall be abomination. Ye shall not pollute your selves with any thing that creepeth, neither make yourselves unclean with them, neither defile your selves thereby: ye shall not, I say, be defiled by them, For I am the Lord your God: be sanctified therefore, and be holy, for I am holy, and defile not your selves with any creeping thing, that creepeth upon the earth. This is the law of beasts, and of fowls, and of every living thing that moveth in the waters, and of everything that creepeth upon the earth: That there may be a difference between the uncleaned and clean, and between the beast that may be eaten, and the beast that ought not to be eaten" (Leviticus 11:42–47).

[82] [Lines 328–329] [Meats] offered first to idols. Paul discouraged eating flesh sacrificed to idols, not because of the Mosaic law, but out of consideration for the weak consciences of others who might be offended. "But if any man say unto you, 'This is sacrificed unto idols, eat it not, because of him that shewed it, and for the conscience (for the earth is the Lord's, and all that therein is)" (1 Corinthians 10:28). "For if any man see thee which hast knowledge, sit at table in the idols temple, shall not the conscience of him which is weak, be boldened to eat those things which are sacrificed to idols? And through thy knowledge shall the weak brother perish, for whom Christ died" (1 Corinthians 8:10, 11). "That

Nor proffered by an enemy—though who
Would scruple that, with want oppressed? Behold,
Nature ashamed, or, better to express,
Troubled, that thou shouldst hunger, hath purveyed
From all the elements her choicest store,
To treat thee as beseems, and as her Lord
With honor. Only deign to sit and eat."
He spake no dream; for, as his words had end,
Our Saviour, lifting up his eyes, beheld,
In ample space under the broadest shade,
A table richly spread in regal mode,
With dishes piled and meats of noblest sort
And savour—beasts of chase, or fowl of game,
In pastry built, or from the spit, or boiled,
Grisamber-steamed; all fish, from sea or shore,
Freshet or purling brook, of shell or fin,
And exquisitest name, for which was drained
Pontus, and Lucrine bay, and Afric coast.
Alas! how simple, to these cates compared,
Was that crude Apple that diverted Eve![84]

---

is, that ye abstain from things offered to idols, and blood, and that that is strangled, and from fornication: from which if ye keep yourselves, ye shall do well. Fare ye well" (Acts 15:29).

[83] Those young Daniel could refuse. "But Daniel had determined in his heart, that he would not defile him self with the portion of the King's meat, nor with the wine which he drank: therefore he required the chief of the Eunuchs that he might not defile himself" (Daniel 1:8).

[84] Was that crude Apple that diverted Eve. "Now the serpent was more subtle then any beast of the field, which the Lord God had made: and he said to the woman, 'Yea, hath God indeed said, 'Ye shall not eat of every tree of the garden?' And the woman said unto the serpent, 'We eat of the fruit of the trees of the garden, But of the fruit of the tree which is in the midst of the garden, God hath said, Ye shall not eat of it, neither shall ye touch it, lest ye die.' Then the serpent said to the woman, 'Ye shall not die at all, But God doth know, that when ye shall eat thereof, your eyes shall be opened, and ye shall be as gods, knowing good and evil.' So the woman (seeing that the tree was good for meat, and that it was pleasant to the eyes, and a tree to be desired to get knowledge) took of the

And at a stately sideboard, by the wine,
That fragrant smell diffused, in order stood
Tall stripling youths rich-clad, of fairer hue
Than Ganymed or Hylas; distant more,
Under the trees now tripped, now solemn stood,
Nymphs of Diana's train, and Naiades
With fruits and flowers from Amalthea's horn,
And ladies of the Hesperides, that seemed
Fairer than feigned of old, or fabled since
Of faery damsels met in forest wide
By knights of Logres, or of Lyones,
Lancelot, or Pelleas, or Pellenore.
And all the while harmonious airs were heard
Of chiming strings or charming pipes; and winds
Of gentlest gale Arabian odours fanned
From their soft wings, and Flora's earliest smells.
Such was the splendour; and the Tempter now
His invitation earnestly renewed:
"What doubts the Son of God to sit and eat?
These are not fruits forbidden; no interdict
Defends the touching of these viands pure;
Their taste no knowledge works, at least of evil,
But life preserves, destroys life's enemy,
Hunger, with sweet restorative delight.
All these are Spirits of air, and woods, and springs,
Thy gentle ministers, who come to pay
Thee homage, and acknowledge thee their Lord.
What doubt'st thou, Son of God? Sit down and eat."
To whom thus Jesus temperately replied:
"Said'st thou not that to all things I had right?
And who withholds my power that right to use?
Shall I receive by gift what of my own,

---

fruit thereof, and did eat, & gave also to her husband with her, and he did eat" (Genesis 3:1–6).

When and where likes me best, I can command?[85]
I can at will, doubt not, as soon as thou,

[85] [Lines 379–382] Jesus often responds with questions instead of direct answers. For example, this exchange with the Pharisees after they had accused his disciples of violating the Sabbath: "But he said unto them, 'Have ye not read what David did when he was an hungered, & they that were with him? How he entered into the house of God, and did eat the show bread, which was not lawful for him to eat, neither for them which were with him, but only for the Priests? Or have ye not read in the Law, how that on the Sabbath days the Priests in the Temple break the Sabbath, and are blameless? But I say unto you, that here is one greater then the Temple. Wherefore if ye knew what this is, I will have mercy, and not sacrifice, ye would not have condemned the innocents. For the son of man is Lord, even of the Sabbath'" (Matthew 12:3–8). A confrontation with the Pharisees regarding ritual handwashing: "But he answered & said unto them, 'Why do ye also transgress the commandment of God by your tradition? For God hath commanded, saying, Honor thy father and mother: and he that curseth father or mother, let him die the death. But ye say, Whosoever shall say to father or mother, By the gift that is offered by me, thou mayest have profit, Though he honor not his father, or his mother, shall be free: thus have ye made the commandment of God of no authority by your tradition. O hypocrites, Isaiah prophesied well of you, saying, This people draweth near unto me with their mouth, and honoreth me with the lips, but their heart is far off from me. But in vain they worship me, teaching for doctrines, men's precepts'" (Matthew 15:3–9). "'Tell us therefore, how thinkest thou? Is it lawful to give tribute unto Cesar, or not?' But Jesus perceived their wickedness, and said, 'Why tempt ye me, ye hypocrites? Show me the tribute money;' they brought him a penny. And he said unto them, 'Whose is this image and superscription?' They said unto him, 'Caesars.' Then said he unto them, 'Give therefore to Caesar, the things which are Caesar's, and give unto God, those things which are God's'" (Matthew 22:17–21). Jesus often responds to a question with a question: "And the disciples of John, and the Pharisees did fast, and came and said unto him, 'Why do the disciples of John, and of the Pharisees fast, and thy disciples fast not?' And Jesus said unto them, 'Can the children of the marriage chamber fast, while the bridegroom is with them? as long as they have the bridegroom with them, they cannot fast'" (Mark 2:18, 19). "Then the Scribes & the Pharisees began to reason, saying, 'Who is this that speaketh blasphemies? who can forgive sins, but God only?' But when Jesus perceived their reasoning, he answered, and said unto them, 'What reason ye in your hearts? Whether is easier to say, Thy sins are forgiven thee, or to say, Rise and walk?'" (Luke 5:21–23).

Command a table in this wilderness,[86]
And call swift flights of Angels ministrant,
Arrayed in glory, on my cup to attend:[87]
Why shouldst thou, then, obtrude this diligence
In vain, where no acceptance it can find?
And with my hunger what hast thou to do?
Thy pompous delicacies I contemn,
And count thy specious gifts no gifts, but guiles."
To whom thus answered Satan, male-content:
"That I have also power to give thou seest;
If of that power I bring thee voluntary
What I might have bestowed on whom I pleased,
And rather opportunely in this place
Chose to impart to thy apparent need,
Why shouldst thou not accept it? But I see
What I can do or offer is suspect.
Of these things others quickly will dispose,
Whose pains have earned the far-fet spoil." With that
Both table and provision vanished quite,

---

[86] Verbal echo: "They spake against God also, saying, 'Can God prepare a table in the wilderness?'" (Psalm 78:19).

[87] [Lines 385–386] Angels ministrant, / Arrayed in glory, on my cup to attend. Compare with the angel comforting Jesus as he mused a "cup" in the Garden of Gethsemane: "Saying, 'Father, if thou wilt, take away this cup from me: nevertheless, not my will, but thine be done.' And there appeared an Angel unto him from heaven, comforting him" (Luke 22:42–43). Alternatively, AV and DR "strengthened him." "So he went a little further, and fell on his face, and prayed, saying, 'O my Father, if it be possible, let this cup pass from me: nevertheless, not as I will, but as thou wilt' [...] Either thinkest thou, that I cannot now pray to my Father, and he will give me more then twelve legions of Angels? How then should the Scriptures be fulfilled, which say, that it must be so?' (Matthew 26:39, 53, 54). "For he shall give his Angels charge over thee to keep thee in all thy ways. They shall bear thee in their hands, that thou hurt not thy foot against a stone" (Psalm 91:11, 12). The cup of Jesus: "And Jesus answered and said, 'Ye know not what ye ask. Are ye able to drink of the cup that I shall drink of, and to be baptized with the baptism that I shall be baptized with?' They said to him, 'We are able'" (Matthew 20:22).

With sound of harpies' wings and talons heard;
Only the importune Tempter still remained,
And with these words his temptation pursued:
"By hunger, that each other creature tames,
Thou art not to be harmed, therefore not moved;
Thy temperance, invincible besides,
For no allurement yields to appetite;
And all thy heart is set on high designs,
High actions. But wherewith to be achieved?
Great acts require great means of enterprise;
Thou art unknown, unfriended, low of birth,
A carpenter thy father known,[88] thyself
Bred up in poverty and straits at home,
Lost in a desert here and hunger-bit.[89]
Which way, or from what hope, dost thou aspire
To greatness? whence authority deriv'st?[90]
What followers, what retinue canst thou gain,
Or at thy heels the dizzy multitude,
Longer than thou canst feed them on thy cost?[91]

---

[88] "Is not this the carpenter's son? Is not his mother called Mary, and his brethren James and Joseph, and Simon and Judas?" (Matthew 13:55).

[89] "His strength shall be hunger-bitten, and destruction shall be ready at his side" (Job 18:12, AV). GE and DR "famine." Coverdale and GT "hungry." "The lions shall be hunger-bit, and pined with famine much; But as for them that fear the Lord, no lack shall be to such" (Psalm 34:10, *The Whole Booke of Psalms Collected into Metre* by Thomas Sternhold, 1562). AV, Bishops, GE, DR, GT, Coverdale, Tyndale "hungry."

[90] Whence authority deriv'st? Compare with the Pharisaical interrogation of Jesus: "And when he was come into the Temple, the chief Priests, and the Elders of the people came unto him, as he was teaching, and said, 'By what authority dost thou these things? And who gave thee this authority?'" (Matthew 21:23).

[91] [Lines 420–421] "Now when the people saw that Jesus was not there, neither his disciples, they also took shipping, and came to Capernaum, seeking for Iesus. And when they had found him on the other side of the sea, they said unto him, 'Rabbi, when camest thou hither?' Jesus answered them; and said, 'Verily, verily I say unto you, ye seek me not because ye saw the miracles, but because ye ate of the loaves, and were filled'" (John 6:24–26).

Money brings honor, friends, conquest, and realms.
What raised Antipater the Edomite,
And his son Herod placed on Juda's throne,
Thy throne, but gold, that got him puissant friends?[92]
Therefore, if at great things thou wouldst arrive,[93]
Get riches first, get wealth, and treasure heap[94]
Not difficult, if thou hearken to me.
Riches are mine,[95] fortune is in my hand;
They whom I favour thrive in wealth amain,
While virtue, valour, wisdom, sit in want."
To whom thus Jesus patiently replied:
"Yet wealth without these three is impotent
To gain dominion, or to keep it gained

---

[92] The folly of human riches and puissance: "Beware least thou say in thine heart, 'My power, and the strength of mine own hand hath prepared me this abundance. But remember the Lord thy God: for it is he which giveth thee power to get substance to establish his covenant which he swore unto thy fathers, as appeareth this day" (Deuteronomy 8:17, 18).

[93] If at great things you would arrive. Contrast with God's counsel to Baruch the secretary of the prophet Jermiah: "And seekest thou great things for thyself? Seek them not: for behold, I will bring a plague upon all flesh, saith the Lord: but thy life will I give thee for a prey in all places, whither thou goest" (Jeremiah 45:5, GE [See also AV and DR]. Coverdale, Tyndale, Bishops "seekest thou promotion."

[94] Get riches first, get wealth, and treasure heap. Contrast Satan's confident trust in wealth with Paul's admonition: "Charge them that are rich in this world, that they be not high minded, & that they trust not in uncertain riches, but in the living God, (which giveth us abundantly, all things to enjoy)" (1 Timothy 6:17). Instead of riches, the Proverbs use similar language to encourage the acquisition of wisdom (personified as a woman) and understanding: "Get wisdom: get understanding: forget not, neither decline from the words of my mouth. Forsake her not, and she shall keep thee: love her and she shall preserve thee. Wisdom is the beginning: get wisdom therefore: and above all thy possession get understanding" (Proverbs 4:5–7).

[95] Satan lies when saying "Riches are mine." "'The silver is mine, and the gold is mine,' saith the Lord of hosts" (Haggai 2:8). "He that trusteth in his riches, shall fall: but the righteous shall flourish as a leaf" (Proverbs 11:28). "There is that maketh himself rich, and hath nothing, and that maketh himself poor, having great riches" (Proverbs 13:7).

Witness those ancient empires of the earth,
In highth of all their flowing wealth dissolved;
But men endued with these have oft attained,
In lowest poverty,[96] to highest deeds
Gideon,[97] and Jephtha,[98] and the shepherd lad[99]

---

[96] "For ye know the grace of our Lord Jesus Christ, that he being rich, for your sakes became poor, that ye through his poverty might be made rich" (2 Corinthians 8:9).

[97] The poverty of Gideon at the time of his calling: "And he answered him, 'Ah my Lord, whereby shall I save Israel? Behold, my father is poor in Manasseh, and I am the least in my father's house'" (Judges 6:15). Gideon successfully defeats the Midianite invaders: "And the three companies blew with trumpets and broke the pitchers, and held the lamps in their left hands, and the trumpets in their right. Hands to blow withal: and they cried, 'The sword of the Lord and of Gideon.' And they stood, every man in his place round about the host: and all the host ran, and cried and fled. And the three hundred blew with trumpets, and the Lord set every man's sword upon his neighbor, & upon all the host: so the host fled to Beth-hashittah in Zererah, & to the border of Abel-meholah, unto Tabbath" (Judges 7:20–21).

[98] Jephtha's humble beginnings an outcast orphan: "Then Gilead begat Jephtha, and Jephtha the Gileadite was a valiant man, but the son of an harlot. And Gilead's wife bore him sons, and when the woman's children were come to age, they thrust out Jephtha, and said unto him, 'Thou shalt not inherit in our fathers house: for thou art the son of a strange woman'" (Judges 11:1, 2).

[99] David the Shepherd Lad. "He chose David also his servant, and took him from the sheepfold. Even from behind the ewes with young brought he him to feed his people in Jacob, and his inheritance in Israel. So he fed them according to the simplicity of his heart, and guided them by the discretion of his hands" (Psalms 78:70–72). David was the youngest of his household and less physically impressive than his older brothers, as observed by the prophet Samuel: "Finally, Samuel said unto Jesse, 'Are there no more children but these?' And he said, 'There remaineth yet a little one behind, that keepeth the sheep.' Then Samuel said unto Jesse, 'Send and set him: for we will not sit down, until he be come hither" (1 Samuel 16:11). Despite his slight stature and young age, David bravely slays the Philistine giant Goliath: "So David was the least: and the three eldest went after Saul [...] For Israel & the Philistines had put themselves in array, army against army. And as he talked with them, behold, the man that was between the two armies, came up, (whose name was Goliath the Philistine of Gath) out of the army of the Philistines, and spake such words, and David heard them. And all

Whose offspring on the throne of Juda sate
So many ages,[100] and shall yet regain
That seat,[101] and reign in Israel without end.[102]

---

the men of Israel, when they saw the man, ran away from him, and were sore afraid [...] Then David spoke to the men that stood with him, and said, 'What shall be done to the man that killeth this Philistine, and taketh away the shame from Israel? for who is this uncircumcised Philistine, that he should revile the host of the living God? [...] And when the Philistine arose to come and draw near unto David, David hasted and ran to fight against the Philistine. And David put his hand in his baggage, and took out a stone, and slung it, & smote the Philistine in his forehead, that the stone stuck in his forehead, and he fell groveling to the earth. So David overcame the Philistine with a sling & with a stone, & smote the Philistine, and slew him, when David had no sword in his hand. (1 Samuel 17:14, 22–24, 48–50).

[100] [Lines 440–441] David's line sat unbroken on the throne of Israel around 400 years before Nebuchadnezzar the King of Babylon executed the songs of King Zedekiah of Judah and took him back to Babylon in chains in the seventh century BC. "Then the city was broken up, and all the men of war fled by night, by the way of the gate, which is between two walls that was by the King's garden: now the Chaldees were by the city round about: and the King went by the way of the wilderness. But the army of the Chaldees pursued after the King, and took him in the deserts of Jericho, and all his host was scattered from him. Then they took the King, and carried him up to the King of Babel to Riblah, where they gave Judgment upon him. And they slew the sons of Zedekiah before his eyes, and put out the eyes of Zedekiah, and bound him in chains, and carried him to Babel. And burnt the house of the Lord, and the King's house, and all the houses of Jerusalem, and all the great houses burnt he with fire" (2 Kings 25:4–9).

[101] Shall yet regain the seat. "And I will set up a shepherd over them, and he shall feed them, even my servant David, he shall feed them, and he shall be their shepherd. And I the Lord will be their God, and my servant David shall be the prince among them. I the Lord have spoken it" (Ezekiel 34:23, 24).

[102] [Lines 440–442] David's heir (Jesus) shall "reign in Israel without end." "For unto us a child is born, and unto us a Son is given: and the government is upon his shoulder, and he shall call his name Wonderful, Counselor, The mighty God, The everlasting Father, The prince of peace. The increase of his government & peace shall have none end: he shall sit upon the throne of Dauid, and upon his kingdom, to order it, and to establish it with judgment and with justice, from henceforth, even for ever: the zeal of the Lord of hosts will perform this" (Isaiah 9:6, 7). The angel Gabriel to Mary: "He shall be great, and shall be called the Son

Among the Heathen (for throughout the world
To me is not unknown what hath been done
Worthy of memorial) canst thou not remember
Quintius, Fabricius, Curius, Regulus?
For I esteem those names of men so poor,
Who could do mighty things, and could contemn
Riches, though offered from the hand of kings.
And what in me seems wanting but that I
May also in this poverty as soon
Accomplish what they did, perhaps and more?
Extol not riches, then, the toil of fools,
The wise man's cumbrance, if not snare;[103] more apt
To slacken virtue and abate her edge
Than prompt her to do aught may merit praise.
What if with like aversion I reject
Riches and realms! Yet not for that a crown,
Golden in shew, is but a wreath of thorns,[104]
Brings dangers, troubles, cares, and sleepless nights,

---

of the most High, and the Lord God shall give unto him the throne of his father David. And he shall reign over the house of Jacob for ever, and of his kingdom shall be none end" (Luke 1:32, 33). "And in mercy shall the throne be prepared, and he shall sit upon it in steadfastness, in the tabernacle of David, judging, and seeking judgment, and hasting justice" (Isaiah 16:5). "In that day will I raise up the tabernacle of David, that is fallen down, and close up the breaches thereof, and I will raise up his ruins, and I will build it, as in the days of old" (Amos 9:11).

[103] "And Jesus looked round about, & said unto his disciples, 'How hardly do they that have riches, enter into the kingdom of God'" (Mark 10:23).

[104] "And platted a crown of thorns, and put it upon his head, and a reed in his right hand, and bowed their knees before him, and mocked him, saying, 'God save thee King of the Jews'" (Matthew 27:29). "And clad him with purple, and platted a crown of thorns, and put it about his head" (Mark 15:17). "Then Pilate took Jesus & scourged him. And the soldiers platted a crown of thorns, and put it on his head, and they put on him a purple garment, And said, 'Hail, King of the Jews;' they smote him with their rods. Then Pilate went forth again, and said unto them, 'Behold, I bring him forth to you, that ye may know, that I find no fault in him at all.' Then came Jesus forth wearing a crown of thorns, and a purple garment; Pilate said unto them, 'Behold the man'" (John 19:1–5).

To him who wears the regal diadem,
When on his shoulders each man's burden lies;
For therein stands the office of a king,
His honor, virtue, merit, and chief praise,
That for the public all this weight he bears.
Yet he who reigns within himself, and rules
Passions, desires, and fears, is more a king
Which every wise and virtuous man attains;
And who attains not, ill aspires to rule
Cities of men, or headstrong multitudes,[105]
Subject himself to anarchy within,
Or lawless passions in him,[106] which he serves.
But to guide nations in the way of truth
By saving doctrine, and from error lead
To know, and, knowing, worship God aright,
Is yet more kingly. This attracts the soul,
Governs the inner man, the nobler part;
That other o'er the body only reigns,
And oft by force—which to a generous mind
So reigning can be no sincere delight.[107]
Besides, to give a kingdom[108] hath been thought

---

[105] [Lines 466–470] "A patient man is better the one strong: and he that can rule himself, is more worth then he that winneth a city." (Proverbs 16:32, Bishops [See also Coverdale and GT). AV and DR "ruleth his spirit." GE "ruleth his mind."

[106] Controlling the inner man with God's spirit. "That he might grant you according to the riches of his glory, that ye may be strengthened by his Spirit in the inner man" (Ephesians 3:16).

[107] [Lines 479–480] The generous mind finds delight as it supports the weak and does not tyrannize those in its care. "I have showed you all things, how that so laboring, ye ought to support the weak, and to remember the words of the Lord Jesus, how that he said, 'It is a blessed thing to give, rather than to receive'" (Acts 20:35).

[108] To give a kingdom. Compare with the attitude of Judge Gideon when offered the kingship in ancient Israel: "And Gideon said unto them, 'I will not reign over you, neither shall my child reign over you, but the Lord shall reign over you" (Judges 8:23).

Greater and nobler done, and to lay down[109]
Far more magnanimous, than to assume.
Riches are needless, then, both for themselves,
And for thy reason why they should be sought
To gain a sceptre, oftest better missed

[109] To lay down a life for others. "As the Father knoweth me, so know I the Father: and I lay down my life for my sheep [...] Therefore doth my Father love me, because I lay down my life, that I might take it again" (John 10:15, 17).

BOOK THREE

SO spake the Son of God; and Satan stood
A while as mute, confounded what to say,
What to reply, confuted and convinced
Of his weak arguing and fallacious drift;
At length, collecting all his serpent wiles,[1]
With soothing words[2] renewed, him thus accosts:
"I see thou know'st what is of use to know,
What best to say canst say, to do canst do;
Thy actions to thy words accord; thy words
To thy large heart[3] give utterance due; thy heart
Contains of good, wise, just, the perfet shape.
Should kings and nations from thy mouth consult,
Thy counsel would be as the oracle
Urim and Thummim,[4] those oraculous gems

---

[1]Serpent wiles. "Put on the whole armor of God, that ye may be able to stand against the wiles of the devil" (Ephesians 6:11, AV). Not DR "deceits of the devil." Not GE, Bishops, GT, Coverdale, Tyndale "assaults of the devil." "And the great dragon, that old serpent, called the devil and Satan, was cast out, which deceiveth all the world: he was even cast into the earth, and his angels were cast out with him" (Revelation 12:9).

[2] Satan resorts to flattery: "For the eyes of his children shall fail, that speaketh flattery to his friends" (Job 17:5). "For no constancy is in their mouth: within, they are very corruption: their throat is an open sepulcher, and they flatter with their tongue. Destroy them, O God: let them fall from their counsels: cast them out for the multitude of their iniquities, because they have rebelled against thee" (Psalms 5:9, 10). "They speak deceitfully everyone with his neighbor, flattering with their lips, and speak with a double heart. The Lord cut off all flattering lips, and the tongue that speaketh proud things" (Psalms 12:2, 3).

[3] Compare with the "large heart" of wise King Solomon: "And God gave Solomon wisdom and understanding exceeding much, & a large heart, even as the sand that is on the seashore" (1 Kings 4:29).

[4] [Lines 12–14] The Urim and Thummim in the breastpiece of the High Priest of Israel were consulted in some unspecified manner when there were decisions of

On Aaron's breast, or tongue of Seers old[5]
Infallible; or, wert thou sought to deeds
That might require the array of war, thy skill
Of conduct would be such that all the world
Could not sustain thy prowess, or subsist
In battle, though against thy few in arms.[6]
These godlike virtues wherefore dost thou hide?
Affecting private life, or more obscure
In savage wilderness, wherefore deprive

---

national import to be made. "After he put the breastplate thereon, and put in the breastplate the Urim and the Thummim" (Leviticus 8:8). "And he shall stand before Eleazar the Priest, who shall ask counsel for him by the judgment of Urim before the Lord: at his word they shall go out, and at his word they shall come in, both he, and all the children of Israel with him and all the Congregation" (Numbers 27:21). "Also thou shalt put in the breastplate of judgment the Urim and the Thummim, which shall be upon Aaron's heart, when he goeth in before the Lord: and Aaron shall bear the judgment of the children of Israel upon his heart before the Lord continually" (Exodus 28:30). "And Tirshatha said unto them, that they should not eat of the most holy thing, until there rose up a Priest with Urim and Thummim" (Ezra 2:63). "And the Tirshatha said unto them, that they should not eat of the most holy, till there rose up a Priest with Urim & Thummim" (Nehemiah 7:65). Although oracular, the Urim and Thummim would only "work" if the consulter was a faithful priest: "And of Levi he said, 'Let thy Thummim and thine Urim be with thine Holy one, whom thou didst prove in Massah, and didst cause him to strive at the waters of Meribah'" (Deuteronomy 33:8). Jehovah cut off unfaithful King Saul from the Urim: "Therefore Saul asked counsel of the Lord, and the Lord answered him not, neither by dreams, nor by Urim, nor yet by Prophets" (1 Samuel 28:6).

[5] Prophets were also known as seers. "(Beforetime in Israel when a man went to seek an answer of God, thus he spoke, 'Come, and let us go to the Seer: for he that is called now a Prophet, was in the old time called a Seer')" (1 Samuel 9:9). The prophets owed their ability to God's spirit and not their own prowess: "For the prophecy came not in old time by the will of man: but holy men of God spoke as they were moved by the holy Ghost" (2 Peter 1:21).

[6] [Lines 17–20] Satan suggests that Jesus could gain fame and glory (line 25) from martial prowess. Contrast with the warning: "Thus saith the Lord, 'Let not the wise man glory in his wisdom, nor the strong man glory in his strength, neither the rich man glory in his riches'" (Jeremiah 9:23, 24).

All Earth her wonder at thy acts, thyself
The fame and glory—glory, the reward
That sole excites to high attempts the flame
Of most erected spirits, most tempered pure
AEthereal, who all pleasures else despise,
All treasures and all gain esteem as dross,
And dignities and powers, all but the highest?
Thy years are ripe, and over-ripe.[7] The son
Of Macedonian Philip had ere these
Won Asia, and the throne of Cyrus held
At his dispose; young Scipio had brought down
The Carthaginian pride; young Pompey quelled
The Pontic king, and in triumph had rode.
Yet years, and to ripe years judgment mature,
Quench not the thirst of glory, but augment.
Great Julius, whom now all the world admires,
The more he grew in years, the more inflamed
With glory, wept that he had lived so long
Ingloroious. But thou yet art not too late."
To whom our Saviour calmly thus replied:
"Thou neither dost persuade me to seek wealth
For empire's sake, nor empire to affect
For glory's sake,[8] by all thy argument.
For what is glory but the blaze of fame,
The people's praise, if always praise unmixed?
And what the people but a herd confused,
A miscellaneous rabble, who extol
Things vulgar, and, well weighed, scarce worth the praise?

---

[7] Thy years are ripe, and over ripe. Satan suggests that Jesus is of an age to become truly great and goads him by asserting that many notable rulers of antiquity had achieved greatness at much younger ages. "And Jesus himself began to be about thirty year of age, being as men supposed the son of Joseph, which was the son of Eli" (Luke 3:23).

[8] Satan is provoking Jesus to seek glory for glory's sake. "Let us not be desirous of vain glory, provoking one another, envying one another" (Galatians 5:26).

They praise and they admire they know not what,
And know not whom,[9] but as one leads the other;
And what delight to be by such extolled,
To live upon their tongues, and be their talk?
Of whom to be dispraised were no small praise[10]
His lot who dares be singularly good.
The intelligent among them and the wise
Are few, and glory scarce of few is raised.
This is true glory and renown—when God,
Looking on the Earth, with approbation marks
The just man, and divulges him through Heaven
To all his Angels, who with true applause
Recount his praises. Thus he did to Job,
When, to extend his fame through Heaven and Earth,
As thou to thy reproach may'st well remember,
He asked thee, 'Hast thou seen my servant Job?'[11]
Famous he was in Heaven; on Earth less known,
Where glory is false glory, attributed
To things not glorious, men not worthy of fame.[12]

---

[9] [Lines 52–54] They praise and they admire they know not what, / And know not whom. Compare with Jesus's words to the Samaritan woman: "Ye worship that which ye know not: we worship that which we know: for salvation is of the Jews" (John 4:22).

[10] Of whom to be dispraised were no small praise. Compare with Jesus's comments from the Sermon on the Mount: "Blessed are ye when men hate you, and when they separate you, & revile you, & put out your name as evil, for the Son of man's sake [...] Woe be to you when all men speak well of you: for so did their fathers to the false prophets" (Luke 6:22, 26).

[11] [Lines 64–70] "There was a man in the land of Uz called Job, & this man was an upright and just man, one that feared God, and eschewed evil [...] And the Lord said unto Satan, 'Hast thou not considered my servant Job, how none is like him in the earth? An upright and just man, one that feareth God, and escheweth evil'" (Job 1:1, 8). "And the Lord said unto Satan, 'Hast thou not considered my servant Job, how none is like him in the earth? an upright and just man, one that feareth God, and escheweth evil? for yet he continueth in his uprightness, although thou movedst me against him, to destroy him without cause'" (Job 2:3).

They err who count it glorious to subdue
By conquest far and wide, to overrun
Large countries, and in field great battles win,
Great cities by assault. What do these worthies
But rob and spoil, burn, slaughter, and enslave
Peaceable nations, neighbouring or remote,
Made captive, yet deserving freedom more
Than those their conquerors, who leave behind
Nothing but ruin wheresoe'er they rove,
And all the flourishing works of peace destroy;
Then swell with pride, and must be titled Gods,[13]
Great benefactors of mankind,[14] Deliverers,
Worshipped with temple, priest, and sacrifice?
One is the son of Jove, of Mars the other;[15]

---

[12] Men not worthy of fame. Consider the violent and monstrous offspring of the fallen angels before the Noahic Flood: "There were giants in the earth in those days: yea, and after that the sons of God came unto the daughters of men, and they had born them children, these were mighty men, which in old time were men of renown" (Genesis 6:4).

[13] They swell with pride, and must be counted Gods. When Jesus called himself God's son, a crowd attempted to stone him, but Jesus quieted them by quoting Psalm 82 which describes some human judges as "gods" due to their mighty status. "Then the Jews again took up stones, to stone him. Jesus answered them, 'Many good works have I showed you from my Father: for which of these works do ye stone me?' The Jews answered him, saying, 'For the good work we stone thee not, but for blasphemy, and that thou being a man, makest thyself God.' Jesus answered them, 'Is it not written in your Law, I said, Ye are gods? If he called them gods, unto whom the word of God was given, and the Scripture cannot be broken, Say ye of him, whom the Father hath sanctified, and sent into the world, Thou blasphemest, because I said, I am the Son of God?'" (John 10:31–36).

[14] Great benefactors of mankind. "And he said unto them, 'The Kings of the Gentiles exercise lordship over them, & they that exercise authority upon them, are called benefactors'" (Luke 22:25, AV). GE "are called bountiful." DR "beneficent." Bishops, GT, Tyndale, Coverdale "gracious."

[15] One is son of Jove, of Mars the other. In Lystra, the crowd believed Paul and Barnabus to be gods due to the powerful works that they performed. "Now there sat a certain man at Lystra, impotent in his feet, which was a cripple from his

Till conqueror Death discover them scarce men,
Rowling in brutish vices, and deformed,
Violent or shameful death their due reward.[16]
But, if there be in glory aught of good;
It may be means far different be attained,
Without ambition, war, or violence
By deeds of peace, by wisdom eminent,
By patience, temperance.[17] I mention still
Him whom thy wrongs, with saintly patience borne,
Made famous in a land and times obscure;
Who names not now with honor patient Job?[18]
Poor Socrates, (who next more memorable?)
By what he taught and suffered for so doing,
For truth's sake suffering death unjust, lives now

---

mother's womb, who had never walked. He heard Paul speak: who beholding him, and perceiving that he had faith to be healed, said with a loud voice, 'Stand upright on thy feet;' he leaped up, and walked. Then when the people saw what Paul had done, they lift up their voices, saying in the speech of Lycaonia, 'Gods are come down to us in the likeness of men. And they called Barnabas, Jupiter: and Paul, Mercurius, because he was the chief speaker. Then Jupiter's priest, which was before their city, brought bulls with garlands unto the gates, & would have sacrificed with the people. But when the Apostles, Barnabas and Paul heard it, they rent their clothes, and ran in among the people, crying, and saying, 'O men, why do ye these things? We are even men subject to the like passions that ye be, and preach unto you, that ye should turn from these vain things unto the living God, which made heaven and earth, and the sea, and all things that in them are" (Acts 14:8–15).

[16] Violent or shameful death their due reward. Herod is struck dead the moment he was acclaimed a god: "And upon a day appointed, Herod arrayed himself in royal apparel, and sat on the judgment seat, and made an oration unto them. And the people gave a shout, saying, 'The voice of God, and not of man.' But immediately the Angel of the Lord smote him, because he gave not glory unto God, so that he was eaten of worms, and gave up the ghost" (Acts 12:21–23).

[17] By patience, temperance. "And with knowledge, temperance: and with temperance, patience: and with patience, godliness" (2 Peter 1:6).

[18] Patient Job. "Behold, we count them blessed which endure. Ye have heard of the patience of Job, and have known what end the Lord made. For the Lord is very pitiful and merciful" (James 5:11).

Equal in fame to proudest conquerors.
Yet, if for fame and glory aught be done,
Aught suffered—if young African for fame
His wasted country freed from Punic rage—
The deed becomes unpraised, the man at least,
And loses, though but verbal, his reward.[19]
Shall I seek glory, then, as vain men seek,[20]
Oft not deserved? I seek not mine,[21] but His
Who sent me,[22] and thereby witness whence I am."[23]
To whom the Tempter,[24] murmuring, thus replied:

---

[19] "Take heed that ye give not your alms before men, to be seen of them, or else ye shall have no reward of your Father which is in heaven" (Matthew 6:1). "Look to yourselves, that we lose not the things which we have done, but that we may receive full reward" (2 John 8).

[20] "He that speaketh of himself, seeketh his own glory: but he that seeketh his glory that sent him, the same is true, and no unrighteousness is in him" (John 7:18). "And I seek not mine own praise: but there is one that seeketh it, and judgeth" (John 8:50).

[21] Jesus need not seek "mine" because all is given to him. "He shall glorify me: for he shall receive of mine, and shall show it unto you. All things that the Father hath, are mine: therefore said I, that he shall take of mine, and show it unto you" (John 16:14).

[22] [Lines 106–107] I seek not mine, but His / Who sent me. "I can do nothing of mine own self: as I hear, I judge: and my judgment is just, because I seek not mine own will, but the will of the Father who hath sent me. If I should bear witness of my self, my witness were not true. There is another that beareth witness of me, and I know that the witness, which he beareth of me, is true" (John 5:30–32).

[23] "Jesus answered, and said unto them, 'Though I bear record of my self, yet my record is true: for I know whence I came, and whither I go: but ye cannot tell whence I come, and whither I go. […] I am one that bear witness of myself, and the Father that sent me, beareth witness of me'" (John 8:14, 18). "If God be glorified in him, God shall also glorify him in himself, and shall straightway glorify him" (John 13:32).

[24] Satan the Tempter. "Then came to him the tempter" (Matthew 4:3a). "Even for this cause, when I could no longer forbear, I sent him that I might know of your faith, lest the tempter had tempted you in any sort, and that our labor had been in vain" (1 Thessalonians 3:5). "Let no man say when he is tempted, I am

"Think not so slight of glory, therein least
Resembling thy great Father. He seeks glory,
And for his glory all things made,[25] all things[26]
Orders and governs;[27] nor content in Heaven,[28]
By all his Angels glorified,[29] requires

---

tempted of God: for God can not be tempted with evil, neither tempteth he any man. But every man is tempted, when he is drawn away by his own concupiscence, and is enticed" (James 1:13, 14). "Brethren, if a man be suddenly taken in any offense, ye which are spiritual, restore such one with the spirit of meekness, considering thyself, least thou also be tempted" (Galatians 6:1). "There hath no temptation taken you, but such as appertain to man: and God is faithful, which will not suffer you to be tempted above that you be able, but will even give the issue with the temptation, that ye may be able to bear it" (1 Corinthians 10:13).

[25] And for his glory all things made. God is worthy of glory because he is the Creator. "Thou art worthy, O Lord, to receive glory and honor, and power: for thou hast created all things, and for thy will's sake they are, and have been created" (Revelation 4:11). "Give unto the Lord the glory of his Name: bring an offering, and enter into his courts" (Psalm 96:8).

[26] "And saying, 'O men, why do ye these things? We are even men subject to the like passions that ye be, and preach unto you, that ye should turn from these vain things unto the living God, which made heaven and earth, and the sea, and all things that in them are" (Acts 14:15).

[27] Orders and governs. For example, the span of human life: "Are not his days determined? The number of his months are with thee: thou hast appointed his bounds, which he can not pass" (Job 14:5).

[28] Nor content in Heaven. "The Lord looketh down from heaven, and beholdeth all the children of men. From the habitation of his dwelling he beholdeth all them that dwell in the earth. He fashioneth their hearts every one, and understandeth all their works" (Psalm 33:13–15). "Every one shall be called by my Name: for I created him for my glory, formed him and made him" (Isaiah 43:7). The culmination of earthly creation: "And God saw all that he had made, and lo, it was very good. So the evening and the morning were the sixth day" (Genesis 1:31). "To him that excelleth. A Psalm of David. The heavens declare the glory of God, and the firmament showeth the work of his hands" (Psalm 19:1).

[29] By all his angels glorified. Isaiah's vision of a heavenly court scene: "The Seraphim stood upon it: every one had six wings: with twain he covered his face, and with twain he covered his feet, and with twain he did fly. And one cried to another, and said, 'Holy, holy, holy is the Lord of hosts: the whole world is full of

Glory from men, from all men, good[30] or bad,[31]
Wise or unwise, no difference, no exemption.[32]

---

his glory" (Isaiah 6:2, 3). At the birth of Jesus: "And straightway there was with the Angel a multitude of heavenly soldiers, praising God, and saying, 'Glory be to God in the high heavens, and peace in earth, and towards men good will'" (Luke 2:13, 14). Angels are at times referred to as stars: "When the stars of the morning praised me together, and all the children of God rejoiced" (Job 38:7). "Praise ye him, all ye his Angels: praise him, all his army" (Psalm 148:2). "Thou art Lord alone: thou hast made heaven, and the heaven of all heavens, with all their host, the earth, and all things that are therein, the seas, & all that are in them, & thou preservest them all, and the host of the heaven worshippeth thee" (Nehemiah 9:6). "And the four beasts had each one of them six wings about him, and they were full of eyes within, and they ceased not day nor night, saying, 'Holy, holy, holy Lord God almighty, Which Was, and Which Is, and Which Is to come.' And when those beasts gave glory, and honor, and thanks to him that sat on the throne, which liveth for ever and ever, the four and twenty Elders fell down before him that sat on the throne and worshipped him that liveth for evermore, and cast their crowns before the throne, saying, 'Thou art worthy, O Lord, to receive glory and honor, and power: for thou hast created all things, and for thy will's sake they are, and have been created'" (Revelation 4:8–11). "Then I saw another Angel fly in the midst of heaven, having an everlasting Gospel, to preach unto them that dwell on the earth, and to every nation, and kindred, and tongue, and people, Saying with a loud voice, 'Fear God, and give glory to him: for the hour of his judgment is come: and worship him that made heaven & earth, and the sea, and the fountains of waters'" (Revelation 14:6, 7).

30 "For every creature of God is good, and nothing ought to be refused, if it be received with thanksgiving" (1 Timothy 4:4).

31 "The Lord hath made all things for his own sake: yea, even the wicked for the day of evil" (Proverbs 16:4). The unrighteous are still accountable to serve God because God's invisible qualities have been revealed to them through his creative works: "For the wrath of God is revealed from heaven against all ungodliness, and unrighteousness of men, which withhold the truth in unrighteousness. Forasmuch as that, which may be know of God, is manifest in them: for God hath showed it unto them. For the invisible things of him, that is, his eternal power & Godhead, are seen by the creation of the world, being considered in his works, to the intent that they should be without excuse" (Romans 1:18–20).

32 "Whether therefore ye eat, or drink, or whatsoever ye do, do all to the glory of God" (1 Corinthians 10:31). "Give unto the Lord, ye sons of the mighty: give unto the Lord glory and strength. Give unto the Lorde glory due unto his Name: worship the Lord in the glorious Sanctuary" (Psalm 29:1, 2). "Let them give glory

Above all sacrifice, or hallowed gift,
Glory he requires,[33] and glory he receives,[34]
Promiscuous from all nations, Jew, or Greek,
Or Barbarous,[35] nor exception hath declared;
From us, his foes pronounced, glory he exacts."[36]
To whom our Saviour fervently replied:
"And reason;[37] since his Word all things produced,[38]

---

unto the Lord, and declare his praise in the islands" (Isaiah 42:12). "For of him, and through him, and for him are all things: to him be glory forever. Amen" (Romans 11:36).

33 Consider God's demand of glory from apostate priests. "If ye will not hear it, nor consider it in your heart, to give glory unto my Name, saith the Lord of hosts, I will even send a curse upon you, and will curse your blessings: yea, I have cursed them already, because ye do not consider it in your heart" (Malachi 2:2).

34 "Give unto the Lord, ye families of the people: give unto the Lord glory and power. Give unto the Lorde the glory of his Name: bring an offering and come before him, and worship the Lord in the glorious Sanctuary" (1 Chronicles 16:28, 29).

35 [Lines 118–119] Promiscuous from all nations, Jew, or Greek, / Or Barbarous. "Where is neither Grecian nor Jew, circumcision nor uncircumcision, Barbarian, Scythian, bond, free: But Christ is all, and in all things" (Colossians 3:11). "I am debtor both to the Grecians, and to the Barbarians, both to the wisemen and unto the unwise" (Romans 1:14).

36 Glory he exacts. Contrary to Satan's claim, God does not demand nor require anything from humans. "God that made the world, and all things that are therein, seeing that he is Lord of heaven and earth, dwelleth not in temples made with hands, neither is worshipped with men's hands, as though he needed anything, seeing he giveth to all life and breath and all things" (Acts 17:24, 25).

37 "But sanctify the Lord God in your hearts: and be ready always to give an answer to every man that asketh you a reason of the hope that is in you, with meekness and reverence" (2 Peter 3:15).

38 Since his Word all things produced. God spoke celestial and earthly creation into existence. "Then God said, 'Let there be light: And there was light'" (Genesis 1:3). "For this they willingly know not, that the heavens were of old, and the earth that was of the water and by the water, by the word of God" (2 Peter 3:5). Jesus is referred to as "the Word" in his pre-human existence. "In the beginning was that Word, and that Word was with God, and that Word was God. This same was in the beginning with God. All things were made by it, and without it

Though chiefly not for glory as prime end,
But to shew forth his goodness, and impart
His good communicable to every soul[39]
Freely; of whom what could He less expect
Than glory and benediction that is, thanks
The slightest, easiest, readiest recompense
From them who could return him nothing else,[40]
And, not returning that, would likeliest render
Contempt instead, dishonour, obloquy?
Hard recompense, unsuitable return
For so much good, so much beneficience!
But why should man seek glory, who of his own
Hath nothing, and to whom nothing belongs[41]
But condemnation, ignominy, and shame
Who, for so many benefits received,
Turned recreant to God, ingrate and false,
And so of all true good himself despoiled;
Yet, sacrilegious, to himself would take
That which to God alone of right belongs?
Yet so much bounty is in God, such grace,
That who advances his glory, not their own,
Them he himself to glory will advance."
So spake the Son of God; and here again

---

was made nothing that was made" (John 1:1–3). In a sense, human's have nothing to say because God has spoken it all: "I should have been dumb, and not have opened my mouth, because thou didst it" (Psalm 39:9). "Who being the brightness of the glory, and the engraved form of his person, and bearing up all things by his mighty word, hath by himself purged our sins, and sitteth at the right hand of the Majesty in the highest places" (Hebrews 1:3).

[39] [Lines 124–125] "Let them therefore confess before the Lord his loving kindness, and his wonderful works before the sons of men. For he satisfied the thirsty soul, and filled the hungry soul with goodness" (Psalm 107:8, 9).

[40] "What shall I render unto the Lord for all his benefits toward me? I will take the cup of salvation, and call upon the Name of the Lord" (Psalm 116:12, 13).

[41] "For I know nothing by myself, yet am I not thereby justified: but he that judgeth me, is the Lord" (1 Corinthians 4:7).

Satan had not to answer, but stood struck
With guilt of his own sin for he himself,
Insatiable of glory, had lost all;
Yet of another plea bethought him soon:
"Of glory, as thou wilt," said he, "so deem;
Worth or not worth the seeking, let it pass.
But to a Kingdom thou art born ordained
To sit upon thy father David's throne,[42]
By mother's side thy father,[43] though thy right
Be now in powerful hands, that will not part
Easily from possession won with arms.
Judaea now and all the Promised Land,
Reduced a province under Roman yoke,[44]

---

[42] They father David's throne. "He shall be great, and shall be called the Son of the most High, and the Lord God shall give unto him the throne of his father David. And he shall reign over the house of Jacob forever, and of his kingdom shall be none end" (Luke 1:32, 33). "Men and brethren, I may boldly speak unto you of the Patriarch David, that he is both dead and buried, and his sepulcher remaineth with us unto this day. Therefore, seeing he was a Prophet, and knew that God had sworn with an oath to him, that of the fruit of his loins he would raise up Christ concerning the flesh, to set him upon his throne, He knowing this before, spoke of the resurrection of Christ, that his soul should not be left in grave, neither his flesh should see corruption" (Acts 2:29–31). "To a virgin affianced to a man whose name was Joseph, of the house of David, & the virgin's name was Mary" (Luke 1:27).

[43] Milton is referring to Luke's genealogy of seventy-seven generations which establishes that Jesus is a descendant of David though his maternal lineage (Eli being the father of Mary). "And Jesus himself began to be about thirty years of age, being as men supposed the son of Joseph, which was the son of Eli [...] The son of Melea, the son of Mainan, the son of Mattatha, the son of Nathan, the son of David [...] the son of Enos, the son of Seth, the son of Adam, the son of God" (Luke 3:23, 31, 38). Matthew's gospel follows the genealogy from the paternal side from Abraham forward: "The book of the generation of Jesus Christ the son of David, the son of Abraham. Abraham begat Isaac. And Isaac begat Jacob; Jacob begat Judas and his brethren [...] And Jesse begat David the King; David the King begat Solomon of her that was the wife of Uriah. [...] And Jacob begat Joseph the husband of Mary, of whom was born Jesus, that is called Christ" (Matthew 1:1, 2, 6, 16).

Obeys Tiberius,[45] nor is always ruled
With temperate sway: oft have they violated
The Temple, oft the Law, with foul affronts,
Abominations[46] rather, as did once
Antiochus.[47] And think'st thou to regain
Thy right by sitting still, or thus retiring?
So did not Machabeus. He indeed

---

44 Reduced a province under the Roman Yoke. Jesus refers to a bloody incident in which the Roman Proconsul of Judea, Pontius Pilate, disguised Roman soldiers to mix in a crowd of Jews and then signaled an attack. It appears that many Galileans were slain in the temple area. "There were certain men present at the same season, that showed him of the Galileans, whose blood Pilate had mingled with their sacrifices" (Luke 13:1).

45 Tiberius was the Roman Emperor during the three and half year ministry of Jesus. "Now in the fifteenth year of the reign of Tiberius Cæsar, Pontius Pilate being governor of Judea, and Herod being Tetrarch of Galilee, and his brother Philip Tetrarch of Iturea, and of the country of Trachonitis, and Lysanias the Tetrarch of Abilene" (Luke 3:1).

46 Abominations. Milton, along with many other English Renaissance church reformers, saw the attack by Antiochus as a fulfillment of verses in the book of Daniel. "And armies shall stand on his part, and they shall pollute the Sanctuary of strength, and shall take away the daily sacrifice, and they shall set up the abominable desolation" (Daniel 11:31). "And from the time that the daily sacrifice shall be taken away & the abominable desolation set up, there shall be a thousand, two hundred & ninety days" (Daniel 12:11).

47 Antiochus Epiphanes who desecrated the Temple in Jerusalem. "And after that Antiochus had smitten Egypt, he turned again in the hundredth, forty and three year, And went up toward Israel and Jerusalem with a mighty people, And entered proudly into the Sanctuary, & took away the golden altar, and the candlestick for the light, & all the instruments thereof, and the table of the showbread, and the pouring vessels, & the bowls, and the golden basins, & the veil, and the crowns, and the golden apparel, which was before the Temple, and broke all in pieces. He took also the silver and gold, and the precious jewels, & he took the secret treasures that he found, and when he had taken away all, he departed into his own land" (1 Maccabees 1:21–24). "Thus was there a slaughter of young men, and old men, and a destruction of men & women and children, and virgins, and infants were murdered: So that within three days were slain fourscore thousand, & forty thousand taken prisoners, and there were as many sold as were slain" (2 Maccabees 5:13, 14).

Retired unto the Desert, but with arms;[48]
And o'er a mighty king so oft prevailed
That by strong hand his family obtained,
Though priests, the crown, and David's throne usurped,[49]
With Modin and her suburbs once content.[50]
If kingdom move thee not, let move thee zeal[51]

---

[48] [Lines 165–166] Judas Maccabeus. "So the host removed, and pitched upon the Southside of Emmaus: And Judas said, 'Arm yourselves, and be valiant men, and be ready against the morning to fight with these nations, which are gathered together against us, to destroy us and our Sanctuary. For it is better for us to die in battle, than to see the calamities of our people & of our Sanctuary" (1 Maccabees 3:57–59). "Then Judas and his army suddenly turned their march into the desert, to Bosor, and took the city: and he slew every male by the edge of the sword, and took all their spoils, and burnt it with fire" (1 Maccabees 5:28, DR). AV, GE, Bishops "marched into the wilderness." "Then many that sought after judgment, and justice, went down into the desert and they abode there, they and their children, and their wives, and their cattle: because afflictions increased upon them. And it was told to the king's men, and to the army that was in Jerusalem, in the city of David, that certain men, who had broken the king's commandment, were gone away into the secret laces in the wilderness, and that many were gone after them" (1 Maccabees 2:29–31, DR). AV, GE, Bishops "into the wilderness).

[49] David's throne usurped. "'King Alexander to his brother Jonathan sendeth salutation. We have heard of thee, that thou art a very valiant man, and worthy to be our friend. Wherefore this day we ordain thee to be the high Priest of thy nation, and to be called the King's friend: (and he sent him a purple robe, and a crown of gold,) that thou mayst consider what is for our profit, and keep friendship toward us.' So in the seventh month of the hundredth and three score year, upon the feast day of the tabernacles, Jonathan put on the holy garment, and gathered an host, and prepared many weapons" (1 Maccabees 10:18–21).

[50] "In those days stood up Mattathias the Priest, the son of Joannes, the son of Simeon, of the sons of Joarib of Jerusalem, and dwelt in Modin" (1 Maccabees 2:1).

[51] Compare with the zeal for true worship shown by Jehonadab: "And when he was departed thence, he met with Jehonadab the son of Rechab coming to meet him, and he blessed him, and said to him, 'Is thine heart upright, as mine heart is toward thine?' And Jehonadab answered, 'Yea, doubtless.' 'Then give me thine hand;' when he had given him his hand, he took him up to him into the chariot.

And duty zeal and duty are not slow,
But on Occasion's forelock watchful wait:
They themselves rather are occasion best,
Zeal of thy Father's house,[52] duty to free
Thy country from her heathen servitude.
So shalt thou best fulfil, best verify,
The Prophets old, who sung thy endless reign,[53]
The happier reign the sooner it begins.
Rein then; what canst thou better do the while?"
To whom our Saviour answer thus returned.
"All things are best fulfilled in their due time;[54]
And time there is for all things,[55] Truth hath said.[56]

And he said, 'Come with me, and see the zeal that I have for the Lord:' so they made him ride in his chariot" (2 Kings 10:15, 16).

[52] Zeal of thy father's house. Jesus disciples applied the words of Psalm 69 after he removed the money changers from the temple for the first time. "Then he made a scourge of small cords, and drove them all out of the Temple with the sheep and oxen, and poured out the changers' money, and overthrew the tables, And said unto them that sold doves, 'Take these things hence: make not my father's house, a house of merchandise.' And his disciples remembered, that it was written, 'The zeal of thine house hath eaten me up'" (John 2:15–17). "For the zeal of thine house hath eaten me, and the rebukes of them that rebuked thee, are fallen upon me" (Psalm 69:9).

[53] The prophets old who sung thy endless reign. Isaiah the prophet: "For unto us a child is born, and unto us a Son is given: and the government is upon his shoulder, and he shall call his name Wonderful, Counselor, The mighty God, The everlasting Father, The prince of peace, The increase of his government & peace shall have none end: he shall sit upon the throne of David, and upon his kingdom, to order it, and to establish it with judgment and with justice, from henceforth, even for ever: the zeal of the Lord of hosts will perform this" (Isaiah 9:6, 7).

[54] All things are best fulfilled in their due time. "But hath made his word manifest in due time through the preaching, which is committed unto me, according to the commandment of God our Savior" (Titus 1:3). "The husbandman must labor before he receive the fruits" (2 Timothy 2:6). "For when we were yet without strength, in due time, Christ died for the ungodly" (Romans 5:6, AV). GE "at his time." Bishops, Coverdale, Tyndale, GT, DR "according to the time."

If of my reign Prophetic Writ hath told
That it shall never end, so, when begin
The Father in his purpose hath decreed
He in whose hand all times and seasons rowl.[57]
What if he hath decreed that I shall first
Be tried in humble state, and things adverse,
By tribulations, injuries, insults,
Contempts, and scorns, and snares, and violence,
Suffering,[58] abstaining, quietly expecting

---

[55] And time there is for all things. "To all things there is an appointed time, and a time to every purpose under the heaven" (Ecclesiastes 3:1).

[56] Truth has said, by which Milton means "God's word has said." "Sanctify them with thy truth: thy word is truth" (John 17:17).

[57] [Lines 185–187] "And he said unto them, 'It is not for you to know the times, or the seasons, which the Father hath put in his own power'" (Acts 1:7). "Jesus said unto her, 'Woman, what have I to do with thee? Mine hour is not yet come" (John 2:4). "The increase of his government & peace shall have none end: he shall sit upon the throne of David, and upon his kingdom, to order it, and to establish it with judgment and with justice, from henceforth, even forever: the zeal of the Lord of hosts will perform this" (Isaiah 9:7). "And in the days of these Kings, shall the God of heaven set up a kingdom, which shall never be destroyed: and this kingdom shall not be given to another people, but it shall break, and destroy all these kingdoms, and it shall stand forever" (Daniel 2:44).

[58] [Lines 188–192] "Saying, The Son of man must suffer many things and be reproved of the Elders, and of the High Priest and Scribes, and be slain, and the third day rise again" (Luke 9:22). "But first must he suffer many things, and be reproved of this generation" (Luke 17:25). "I gave my back unto the smiters, and my cheeks to the nippers: I hid not my face from shame and spitting" (Isaiah 50:6). "But he was wounded for our transgressions, he was broken for our iniquities: the chastisement of our peace was upon him, and with his stripes we are healed. All we like sheep have gone astray: we have turned every one to his own way, and the Lord hath laid upon him the iniquity of us all. He was oppressed and he was afflicted, yet did he not open his mouth: he is brought as a sheep to the slaughter, and as a sheep before her shearer is dumb, so he openeth not his mouth. He was taken out from prison, and from judgment: and who shall declare his age? For he was cut out of the land of the living: for the transgression of my people was he plagued. And he made his grave with the wicked, and with the rich in his death, though he had done no wickedness, neither was any deceit

Without distrust or doubt, that He may know
What I can suffer, how obey?[59] Who best
Can suffer best can do, best reign who first
Well hath obeyed just trial ere I merit
My exaltation without change or end.[60]
But what concerns it thee when I begin
My everlasting Kingdom? Why art thou
Solicitous? What moves thy inquisition?
Know'st thou not that my rising is thy fall,[61]

---

in his mouth. Yet the Lord would break him, and make him subject to infirmities: when he shall make his soul an offering for sin, he shall see his seed and shall prolong his days, and the will of the Lord shall prosper in his hand. He shall see of the travail of his soul, and shall be satisfied: by his knowledge shall my righteous servant justify many: for he shall bear their iniquities" (Isaiah 53:5–11). "But those things which God before had showed by the mouth of all his Prophets, that Christ should suffer, he hath thus fulfilled" (Acts 3:18). "Searching when or what time the Spirit which testified before of Christ which was in them, should declare the sufferings that should come unto Christ, and the glory that should follow" (1 Peter 1:11). "That the trial of your faith, being much more precious then gold that perisheth (though it be tried with fire) might be found unto your praise, and honor and glory at the appearing of Jesus Christ" (1 Peter 1:7). "Fear none of those things, which thou shalt suffer: behold, it shall come to pass, that the devil shall cast some of you into prison, that ye may be tried, and ye shall have tribulation ten days: be thou faithful unto the death, and I will give thee the crown of life" (Revelation 2:10).

59 [Lines 193–194] "And though he were the Son, yet learned he obedience, by the things which he suffered" (Hebrews 5:8).

60 [Lines 195–197] "But we see Jesus crowned with glory and honor, which was made little inferior to the Angels, through the suffering of death, that by Gods grace he might taste death for all men. For it became him, for whom are all these things, and by whom are all these things, seeing that he brought many children unto glory, that he should consecrate the Prince of their salvation through afflictions" (Hebrews 2:9, 10). "But it shall not be so among you: but whosoever will be great among you, let him be your servant. And whosoever will be chief among you, let him be your servant" (Matthew 20:26, 27).

61 Know'st thou not that my rising is thy fall. "And Simeon blessed them, and said unto Mary his mother, 'Behold, this child is appointed for the fall and rising again of many in Israel, and for a sign which shall be spoken against" (Luke

And my promotion will be thy destruction?"
To whom the Tempter, inly racked, replied:
"Let that come when it comes. All hope is lost
Of my reception into grace; what worse?
For where no hope is left is left no fear.
If there be worse, the expectation more
Of worse torments me than the feeling can.[62]
I would be at the worst; worst is my port,
My harbour, and my ultimate repose,
The end I would attain, my final good.
My error was my error, and my crime
My crime; whatever, for itself condemned,
And will alike be punished, whether thou
Reign or reign not though to that gentle brow
Willingly I could fly, and hope thy reign,[63]

2:34). "I Jesus have sent mine Angel, to testify unto you these things in the Churches: I am the root and the generation of David, and the bright morning star'" (Revelation 22:16). "How art thou fallen from heaven, O Lucifer, son of the morning? and cut down to the ground, which didst cast lots upon the nations?" (Isaiah 14:12).

[62] [Lines 204–208] Expectation post-poned and the loss of hope. "The hope that is deferred, is the fainting of the heart: but when the desire cometh, it is as a tree of life" (Proverbs 13:12).

[63] [Lines 215–216] Satan hopes that the millennial reign of Jesus will be easier for him than when God exercises sovereignty. His hope is in vain because Jesus will defeat him before transferring power back to the Father. "Then shall be the end, when he hath delivered up the kingdom to God, even the Father, when he hath put down all rule, and all authority and power. For he must reign until he hath put all his enemies under his feet" (1 Corinthians 15:24, 25). Christ's Millennial Reign described: "And I saw an Angel come down from heaven, having the key of the bottomless pit, and a great chain in his hand. And he took the dragon that old serpent, which is the devil and Satan, and he bound him a thousand years: And cast him into the bottomless pit, and he shut him up, and sealed the door upon him, that he should deceive the people no more, until the thousand years were fulfilled: for after that he must be loosed for a little season. And I saw seats: & they sat upon them, & judgment was given unto them, & I saw the souls of them that were beheaded for the witness of Jesus, and for the word of God, & which did not worship the beast, neither his image, neither had taken his mark

From that placid aspect and meek regard,
Rather than aggravate my evil state,
Would stand between me and thy Father's ire
(Whose ire I dread more than the fire of Hell)[64]
A shelter and a kind of shading cool
Interposition, as a summer's cloud.[65]
If I, then, to the worst that can be haste,
Why move thy feet so slow to what is best?
Happiest, both to thyself and all the world,
That thou, who worthiest art, shouldst be their King![66]
Perhaps thou linger'st in deep thoughts detained
Of the enterprise so hazardous and high!
No wonder; for, though in thee be united
What of perfection can in Man be found,
Or human nature can receive,[67] consider

---

upon their foreheads, or on their hands: and they lived, & reigned with Christ a thousand years. And the devil that deceived them, was cast into a lake of fire and brimstone, where that beast and that false prophet are, and shall be tormented even day and night for evermore" (Revelation 20:1–4, 10).

64 "Then shall he say unto them on the left hand, 'Depart from me ye cursed, into everlasting fire, which is prepared for the devil and his angels'" (Matthew 25:41).

65 [Lines 222–221] Compare with Isaiah's description of God: "For thou hast been a strength unto the poor, even a strength to the needy in his trouble, a refuge against the tempest, a shadow against the heat: for the blast of the mighty is like a storm against the wall. Thou shalt bring down the noise of the strangers, as the heat in a dry place: he will bring down the song of the mighty, as the heat in the shadow of a cloud" (Isaiah 25:4, 5).

66 That thou, who worthiest art, shouldst be their King! "And I saw a strong Angel which preached with a loud voice, 'Who is worthy to open the book, and to loose the seals thereof?' [...] Then I wept much, because no man was found worthy to open, and to read the Book, neither to look thereon. [...] And they sung a new song, saying, 'Thou art worthy to take the Book, and to open the seals thereof, because thou wast killed, and hast redeemed us to God by thy blood out of every kindred, and tongue, and people, and nation, And hast made us unto our God Kings and Priests, and we shall reign on the earth.' [...] Saying with a loud voice, 'Worthy is the Lamb that was killed to receive power, & riches, & wisdom, & strength, & honor, & glory, and praise'" (Revelation 5:2, 4, 9–10, 12).

Thy life hath yet been private, most part spent
At home, scarce viewed the Galilean towns,
And once a year Jerusalem, few days'[68]
Short sojourn; and what thence couldst thou observe?
The world thou hast not seen, much less her glory,
Empires, and monarchs, and their radiant courts—
Best school of best experience, quickest in sight
In all things that to greatest actions lead.
The wisest, unexperienced, will be ever
Timorous, and loth, with novice modesty
(As he who, seeking asses, found a kingdom)[69]

---

[67] [Lines 229–232] "For it pleased the Father, that in him should all fullness dwell, And through peace made by that blood of that his cross, to reconcile to himself through him, through him, I say, all things, both which are in earth, and which are in heaven" (Colossians 1:19, 20). "And when all things shall be subdued unto him, then shall the Son also himself be subject unto him, that did subdue all things under him, that God may be all in all" (1 Corinthians 15:28).

[68] "Now his parents went to Jerusalem every year, at the feast of the Passover" (Luke 2:41). Under the Mosaic Law, Israelite males were required to sojourn to the central sanctuary, wherever the tabernacle was initially, and later at the temple, three times each year to observe the festivals of Passover (pesach), Pentecost (shavuot), and Tabernacles (sukkot). That Jesus's entire family traveled for the Passover is perhaps an indication of their depth of godly devotion. "Three times in the year shall all the males appear before the Lord thy God in the place which he shall choose: in the feast of the unleavened bread, and in the feast of the weeks, and in the feast of the Tabernacles: and they shall not appear before the Lord empty" (Deuteronomy 16:16).

[69] As he who, seeking asses, found a kingdom. Referring to Saul the first King of Israel. "And the asses of Kish, Saul's father, were lost: therefore Kish said to Saul his son, 'Take now one of the servants with thee, and arise, go, and seek the asses.' So he passed through mount Ephraim, and went through the land of Shalishah, but they found them not. Then they went through the land of Shalim, and there they were not: he went also through the land of Benjamin, but they found them not. When they came to the land of Zuph, Saul said unto his servant that was with him, 'Come and let us return, lest my father leave the care of asses, and take thought for us.' And he said unto him, 'Behold now, in this city is a man of God, and he is an honorable man: all that he saith cometh to pass: let us now go thither, if so be that he can show us what way we may go.' Then said Saul to

Irresolute, unhardy, unadventrous.
But I will bring thee where thou soon shalt quit
Those rudiments, and see before thine eyes
The monarchies of the Earth, their pomp and state
Sufficient introduction to inform
Thee, of thyself so apt, in regal arts,
And regal mysteries;[70] that thou may'st know

---

his servant, 'Well then, let us go: but what shall we bring unto the man? For the bread is spent in our vessels, and there is no present to bring to the man of God: what have we? And the servant answered Saul again, and said, 'Behold, I have found about me the fourth part of a shekel of silver: that will I give the man of God, to tell us our way.' (Beforetime in Israel when a man went to seek an answer of God, thus he spoke, 'Come, and let us go to the Seer: for he that is called now a Prophet, was in the old time called a Seer) Then said Saul to his servant, 'Well said, come, let us go:' so they went into the city where the man of God was [...] 'And as for thine asses that were lost three days ago, care not for them: for they are found; on whom is set all the desire of Israel? is it not upon thee and on all thy father's house? But Saul answered, and said, 'Am not I the son of Benjamin of the smallest tribe of Israel? and my family is the least of all the families of the tribe of Benjamin. Wherefore then speakest thou so to me'" (1 Samuel 9:3–10, 20–21). "Then Samuel took a vial of oil and poured it upon his head, and kissed him, and said, 'Hath not the Lord anointed thee to be governor over his inheritance?'" (1 Samuel 10:1). Compare AV, Bishops and Tyndale "captain over his inheritance." DR and GT "prince over his inheritance."

[70] Regal mysteries. Nebuchadnezzar the King of Babylon had a dream about kingdoms and kingship that was mysterious and could only be revealed by Daniel. What is rendered in English Renaissance Bible's as "secret," appears in the Greek Septuagint as *musterion* (mystery). "That they should beseech the God of heaven for grace in this secret, that Daniel and his fellows should not perish with the rest of the wisemen of Babel. Then was the secret revealed unto Daniel in a vision by night: therefore Daniel praised the God of heaven [...] He discovereth the deep and secret things: he knoweth what is in darkness, and the light dwelleth with him [...] Daniel answered in the presence of the King, and said, 'The secret which the King hath demanded, can neither the wise, the astrologians, the enchanters, nor the soothsayers declare unto the King' (Daniel 2:18, 19, 22, 27). "He answered, and said unto them, 'Because it is given unto you to know the mysteries of the kingdom of heaven, but to them it is not given'" (Matthew 13:11, AV [see also Coverdale]). GE, Bishops, GT, DR, Tyndale "secrets."

How best their opposition to withstand."
With that (such power was given him then), he took
The Son of God up to a mountain high.[71]
It was a mountain at whose verdant feet
A spacious plain outstretched in circuit wide
Lay pleasant; from his side two rivers flowed,
The one winding, the other straight, and left between
Fair champaign, with less rivers interveined,
Then meeting joined their tribute to the sea.
Fertil of corn the glebe, of oil, and wine;
With herds the pasture thronged, with flocks the hills;
Huge cities and high-towered, that well might seem
The seats of mightiest monarchs; and so large
The prospect was that here and there was room
For barren desert, fountainless and dry.
To this high mountain-top the Tempter brought
Our Saviour, and new train of words began:[72]
"Well have we speeded, and o'er hill and dale,
Forest, and field, and flood, temples and towers,
Cut shorter many a league. Here thou behold'st
Assyria, and her empire's ancient bounds,
Araxes and the Caspian lake; thence on
As far as Indus east, Euphrates west,
And oft beyond; to south the Persian bay,
And, inaccessible, the Arabian drouth:
Here, Nineveh, of length within her wall

---

[71] "Again the devil took him up into an exceeding high mountain, and shewed him all the kingdoms of the world, and the glory of them' (Matthew 4:8). "Then the devil took him up into an high mountain, and showed him all the kingdoms of the world, in the twinkling of an eye" (Luke 4:5).

[72] New train of words began. That is to say, Satan is transitioning from the temptation of bread to the temptation of kingdoms: "Then the devil said unto him, 'If thou be the Son of God, command this stone that it be made bread' [...] Again the devil took him up into an exceeding high mountain, and shewed him all the kingdoms of the world, and the glory of them" (Luke 4:3, 8).

Several days' journey, built by Ninus[73] old,[74]
Of that first golden monarchy the seat,[75]

---

[73] Built by Ninus old. Milton understood the legendary Assyrian King Ninus to be the Nimrod of the Bible who was said to have founded Nineveh. "And Cush begat Nimrod, who began to be mighty in the earth. He was a mighty hunter before the Lord. wherefore it is said, 'As Nimrod the mighty hunter before the Lord.' And the beginning of his kingdom was Babel, and Erech, and Akkad, and Calneh, in the land of Shinar. Out of that land came Asshur, and builded Nineveh, and the city Rehoboth, and Calah: Resen also between Nineveh and Calah: this is a great city" (Genesis 10:8–12).

[74] [Lines 275–276] Nineveh the capital of Assyria. "And Jonah arose, and went to Nineveh, according to the word of the Lord: now Ninevah was a great city of three days' journey. And Jonah began to enter into the city one day's journey: and he cried and said: 'Yet forty days and Nineveh shall be destroyed" (Jonah 3:3, DR). *Douay-Rheims* note: "Of three days' journey [...] By the computation of some ancient historians, Nineveh was about fifty miles round: so that to go through all the chief streets and public places was three days' journey." The Israelite prophet Nahum prophesied against Nineveh: "And it shall come to pass, that all they that look upon thee, shall flee from thee, and say, Nineveh is destroyed, who will have pity upon her? where shall I seek comforters for thee" (Nahum 3:7). Zephaniah's prophecy against Nineveh: "And he will stretch out his hand against the North, and destroy Asshur, and will make Nineveh desolate, and waste like a wilderness. And flocks shall lie in the midst of her, and all the beasts of the nations, and the pelican, and the owl shall abide in the upper posts of it: the voice of birds shall sing in the windows, and desolation shall be upon the posts: for the cedars are uncovered. This is the rejoicing city that dwelt careless, that said in her heart, I am, and there is none besides me: how is she made waste, and the lodging of the beasts! every one that passeth by her, shall hiss and wag his hand" (Zephaniah 2:13–15).

[75] Of that first golden monarchy the seat. The "golden monarchy" is Babylon which grew out of the Assyrian Empire; hence, Nineveh is "the seat" of what would become Babylonia after the Assyrian governor of the city of Babylon, Nabopolassar (the father of Nebuchadnezzar), revolted and later destroyed the city of Nineveh. Consider Daniel's interpretation of the multi-metaled image of Nebuchadnezzar's dream of consecutive monarchies: "This images head was of fine gold, his breast and his arms of silver, his belly and his thighs of brass, His legs of iron, and his feet were part of iron, and part of clay [...] And in all places where the children of men dwell, the beasts of the field, and the fowls of the heaven hath he given into thine hand, and hath made thee ruler over them all: thou art this head of gold. And after thee shall rise another kingdom, inferior to

And seat of Salmanassar, whose success
Israel in long captivity still mourns;[76]
There Babylon, the wonder of all tongues,[77]

---

thee, of silver, and another third kingdom shall be of brass, which shall bear rule over all the earth. And the fourth kingdom shall be strong as iron: for as iron breaketh in pieces, and subdueth all things, and as iron bruiseth all these things, so shall it break in pieces, and bruise all. Where as thou sawest the feet and toes, part of potter's clay, and part of iron: the kingdom shall be divided, but there shall be in it of the strength of the iron, as thou sawest the iron mixt with the clay, and earth" (Daniel 2:32, 33, 38–41). The Geneva note describes the metals representing Babylon (gold), Medo-Persia (silver), Greece (brass), Roman (iron), that Rome would be weakened by civil wars and strife (iron mixed with clay).

[76] [Lines 278–279] Shalmanezar V, King of Assyria, laid siege to Samaria, the capital of the ten-tribe Kingdom of Israel, for three years. His successor, Sargon II, completed the conquest of Israel. "And in the fourth year of King Hezekiah, (which was the seventh year of Hoshea son of Elah King of Israel) Shalmaneser King of Asshur came up against Samaria, and besieged it" (2 Kings 18:9). "Those are the ten tribes, which were carried away prisoners out of their own land in the time of Hoshea the King whom Shalmanezer the King of Assyria led away captive, and he carried them over the waters, and so came they into another land" (2 Esdras 13:40). The Assyrians forcibly relocated Israelites to other lands and brought in new inhabitants to Samaria. The descendants of those brought in by the Assyrians who married into the local population became the Samaritans of Jesus's day. "And Shalmaneser king of Asshur came up against him, and Hoshea became his servant, and gave him presents. And the King of Asshur found treason in Hoshea: for he had sent messengers to So the King of Egypt, and brought no present unto the King of Asshur, as he had done yearly: therefore the king of Asshur shut him up, and put him in prison. Then the king of Asshur came up throughout all the land, and went against Samaria, and besieged it three years. For when the children of Israel sinned against the Lord their God, which had brought them out of the land of Egypt, from under the hand of Pharaoh king of Egypt, & feared other gods [...] And the King of Asshur brought folk from Babel, and from Cuthah, and from Aua, and from Hamath, and from Sepharvaim, & placed them in the cities of Samaria instead of the children of Israel: so they possessed Samaria, and dwelt in the cities thereof [...] And the Auims made Nibhaz, and Tartak: and the Sepharvaims burnt their children in the fire to Adrammelech, and Anammelech the gods of Sepharvaim" (2 Kings 17:3–6, 31).

As ancient, but rebuilt by him[78] who twice
Judah and all thy father David's house
Led captive,[79] and Jerusalem laid waste,

---

[77] Babylon, the wonder of all tongues. Nimrod founds Babylon. "He was a mighty hunter before the Lord. wherefore it is said, 'As Nimrod the mighty hunter before the Lord.' And the beginning of his kingdom was Babel, and Erech, and Accad, and Calneh, in the land of Shinar" (Genesis 10:9, 10). Nimrod keeps the post-flood population in one location at Babylon in order to dominate them and to erect an enormous tower. God frustrates his plans by confusing the sole language spoken at that time and creating new languages. "Then the whole earth was of one language and one speech. And as they went from the East, they found a plain in the land of Shinar, and there they abode. And they said one to another, 'Come, let us make brick, and burn it in the fire.' So they had brick for stone, and slime had they instead of mortar. Also they said, 'Go to, let us build us a city and a tower, whose top may reach unto the heaven, that we may get us a name, lest we be scattered upon the whole earth.' But the Lord came down, to see the city and tower, which the sons of men built. And the Lord said, 'Behold, the people is one, and they all have one language, and this they begin to do, neither can they now be stopped from whatsoever they have imagined to do. Come on, let us go down, and there confound their language, that every one perceive not another's speech.' So the Lord scattered them from thence upon all the earth, & they left off to build the city. Therefore the name of it was called Babel, because the Lord did there confound the language of all the earth: from thence then did the Lord scatter them upon all the earth" (Genesis 11:1–9).

[78] Babylon was rebuilt by Nebuchadnezzar. "And the King spoke and said, 'Is not this great Babel, that I have built for the house of the kingdom by the might of my power, and for the honor of my majesty" (Daniel 4:30).

[79] [Lines 281–283] Nebuchadnezzar twice led away captives from Jerusalem: once during the reign of King Jehoiachin and secondly when he ended the Davidic line of Kings ten years later by deposing King Zedekiah. Jehoiachin's revolt and the first group of Jewish exiles into Babylon: "Jehoiachin was eighteen years old, when he began to reign, and reigned in Jerusalem three months. His mother's name also was Nehushta, the daughter of Elnathan of Jerusalem. And he did evil in the sight of the Lord, according to all that his father had done. In that time came the servants of Nebuchadnezzar king of Babel up against Jerusalem: so the city was besieged. Then Jehoiachin the king of Judah came out against the King of Babel, he, and his mother and his servants, and his princes, & his eunuchs: and the King of Babel took him in the eighth year of his reign [...] And he carried away all Jerusalem, and all the princes, and all the strong men of war, even ten

Till Cyrus set them free;[80] Persepolis,

---

thousand into captivity, and all the workmen, and cunning men: so none remained saving the poor people of the land. And he carried away Jehoiachin into Babel, and the King's mother, and the King's wives, and his eunuchs, and the mighty of the land carried he away into captivity from Jerusalem to Babel, And all the men of war, even seven thousand, and carpenters, & locksmiths a thousand: all that were strong and apt for war, did the King of Babel bring to Babel captives. And the King of Babel made Mattaniah his uncle King in his stead, and changed his name to Zedekiah" (2 Kings 24:8–12, 14–17). Among the captives brought to Babylon after the rebellion of Jehoiachin, were Daniel and his three companions Hananiah, Azariah, and Mishael: "And the King spoke unto Ashpenaz the master of his Eunuchs, that he should bring certain of the children of Israel, of the King's seed, and of the princes: Children in whom was no blemish, but well favored, and instruct in all wisdom, and well seen in knowledge, and able to utter knowledge, & such as were able to stand in the king's palace, and whom they might teach the learning, and the tongue of the Chaldeans. And the King appointed them provision every day of a portion of the Kings meat, and of the wine, which he drank, so nourishing them three years, that at the end thereof, they might stand before the King. Now among these were certain of the children of Judah, Daniel, Hananiah, Mishael and Azariah" (Daniel 1:3–6). Zedekiah's revolt and the second round of captives: "And in the ninth year of his reign, the tenth month and tenth day of the month Nebuchadnezzar King of Babel came, he, and all his host against Jerusalem, & pitched against it, and they built forts against it round about it. [...] And the rest of the people that were left in the city, and those that were fled and fallen to the King of Babel, with the remnant of the multitude, did Nebuzaradan chief steward carry away captive" (2 Chronicles 36:1, 11). "Then Nebuzaradan the chief steward carried away captive into Babel the remnant of the people, that remained in the city, and those that were fled and fallen unto him, with the rest of the people that remained" (Jeremiah 1:9).

[80] Cyrus King of Persia, after capturing Babylon, frees the captive Jews and their descendants after seventy years of exile in Babylon and permits those who wish return to Jerusalem. "Now in the first year of Cyrus King of Persia (that the word of the Lord, spoken by the mouth of Jeremiah, might be accomplished) the Lord stirred up the spirit of Cyrus King of Persia, and he made a Proclamation through all his Kingdom, and also by writing, saying, Thus saith Cyrus King of Persia, 'The Lord God of heaven hath given me all the kingdoms of the earth, and he hath commanded me to build him a house in Jerusalem, which is in Judah. Who is he among you of all his people with whom his God is? let him go up to Jerusalem which is in Judah, and build the house of the Lord God of Israel:

His city, there thou seest, and Bactra there;
Ecbatana[81] her structure vast there shews,
And Hecatompylos her hunderd gates;
There Susa[82] by Choaspes, amber stream,
The drink of none but kings; of later fame,
Built by Emathian or by Parthian hands,
The great Seleucia, Nisibis, and there
Artaxata, Teredon, Ctesiphon,
Turning with easy eye, thou may'st behold.
All these the Parthian (now some ages past
By great Arsaces led, who founded first
That empire) under his dominion holds,
From the luxurious kings of Antioch won.
And just in time thou com'st to have a view
Of his great power; for now the Parthian king
In Ctesiphon hath gathered all his host
Against the Scythian, whose incursions wild
Have wasted Sogdiana; to her aid
He marches now in haste. See, though from far,
His thousands, in what martial equipage
They issue forth, steel bows and shafts their arms,
Of equal dread in flight or in pursuit
All horsemen, in which fight they most excel;

---

he is the God, which is in Jerusalem.' [...] These also are the sons of the province, that went up out of the captivity (whom Nebuchadnezzar King of Babel had carried away unto Babel) and returned to Jerusalem, and to Judah, every one unto his city," (Ezra 1:1–3; 2:1).

[81] "And there was found in Ecbatana, which is a castle in the province of Media, a book in which this record was written" Ezra 6:2, DR).

[82] Susa was a Persian royal city of residence. "In the second year of the reign of great Artaxerxes in the first day of the month Nisan, Mordecai the son of Jarus, the son of Semei, the son of Cis of the tribe of Benjamin had a dream, A Jew dwelling in the city of Susa, a noble man, that bore office in the King's court" (Esther 1:1, 2). "And I saw in a vision, and when I saw it, I was in the palace of Susa, which is in the province of Elam, and in a vision me thought I was by the river of Ulai" (Daniel 8:2).

See how in warlike muster they appear,
In rhombs, and wedges, and half-moons, and wings."
He looked, and saw what numbers numberless
The city gates outpoured, light-armed troops
In coats of mail and military pride.
In mail their horses clad, yet fleet and strong,
Prauncing their riders bore, the flower and choice
Of many provinces from bound to bound
From Arachosia, from Candaor east,
And Margiana, to the Hyrcanian cliffs
Of Caucasus, and dark Iberian dales;
From Atropatia, and the neighbouring plains
Of Adiabene, Media, and the south
Of Susiana, to Balsara's haven.
He saw them in their forms of battle ranged,
How quick they wheeled, and flying behind them shot
Sharp sleet of arrowy showers against the face
Of their pursuers, and overcame by flight;
The field all iron cast a gleaming brown.
Nor wanted clouds of foot, nor, on each horn,
Cuirassiers all in steel for standing fight,
Chariots,[83] or elephants indorsed with towers[84]

---

[83] Israel mostly fought as infantry, and reliance on chariots and horses was discourage by God. Egyptian chariots at the time of the Israelite captivity in Egypt. "And took six hundred chosen chariots, and all the chariots of Egypt, and captains over every one of them [...] And took six hundred chosen chariots, and all the chariots of Egypt, and captains over every one of them" (Exodus 14:7, 9). Israel defeats the Aramites, despite their advantage of using chariots. "And they slew everyone his enemy: and the Aramites fled, and Israel pursued them: but Benhadad the King of Aram escaped on an horse with his horsemen. And the King of Israel went out, & smote the horses and chariots, and with a great slaughter slew he the Aramites" (1 Kings 20:20, 21). God responds through the prophet Isaiah to the taunts of Sennacherib the King of Assyria's messengers: "By thy messengers thou hast railed on the Lord, and said, 'By the multitude of my chariots I am come up to the top of the mountains, by the sides of Lebanon, and will cut down the high cedars thereof, and the fair fir trees thereof, and I will

Of archers; nor of labouring pioners
A multitude, with spades and axes armed,
To lay hills plain, fell woods, or valleys fill,
Or where plain was raise hill, or overlay
With bridges rivers proud, as with a yoke:
Mules after these, camels and dromedaries,[85]
And waggons fraught with utensils of war.
Such forces met not, nor so wide a camp,
When Agrican, with all his northern powers,
Besieged Albracea, as romances tell,
The city of Gallaphrone, from thence to win
The fairest of her sex, Angelica,
His daughter, sought by many prowest knights,
Both Paynim and the peers of Charlemane.
Such and so numerous was their chivalry;
At sight whereof the Fiend yet more presumed,
And to our Saviour thus his words renewed:
"That thou may'st know I seek not to engage
Thy virtue, and not every way secure
On no slight grounds thy safety, hear and mark

---

go into the lodging of his borders, and into the forest of his Carmel'" (2 Kings 19:23). Isaiah sees a visionary watchman mark the approach of a chariot declaring that Babylon the treacherous betrayer of Israel is no more. "And behold, this man's chariot cometh with two horsemen; he answered and said, 'Babel is fallen: it is fallen, and all the images of her gods hath he broken unto the ground'" (Isaiah 21:9). Isaiah condemns those who would look to the military might of Egypt (symbolized by the chariot) instead of to God. "Woe unto them that go down into Egypt for help, and stay upon horses, and trust in chariots, because they are many, and in horsemen, because they be very strong: but they look not unto the holy one of Israel, nor seek unto the Lord" (Isaiah 31:1).

[84] Beasts equipped with towers in warfare. "And upon them were strong towers of wood that covered every beast, which were fastened thereon with instruments, and upon every one was two and thirty men that fought in them, and the Indian that ruled him" (1 Maccabees 6:37).

[85] The dromedaries of Persia. "And he wrote in the King Achashverosh name, and sealed it with the King's ring: and he sent letters by posts on horseback and that rode on beasts of price, as dromedaries and colts of mares" (Esther 8:10).

To what end I have brought thee hither, and shew
All this fair sight. Thy kingdom, though foretold
By Prophet or by Angel, unless thou
Endeavour[86], as thy father David did,[87]
Thou never shalt obtain: prediction still
In all things, and all men, supposes means;
Without means used, what it predicts revokes.
But say thou wert possessed of David's throne
By free consent of all, none opposite,
Samaritan or Jew;[88] how couldst thou hope

---

[86] [Lines 353–354] Satan urges Jesus to "endeavor" to seize rulership, but Jesus endeavors for peace. Compare the words of Paul: "Endeavoring to keep the unity of the Spirit in the bond of peace" (Ephesians 4:3).

[87] As thy father David did. "There was then long war between the house of Saul and the house of David: but David waxed stronger, and the house of Saul waxed weaker" (2 Samuel 3:1). "Then came all the tribes of Israel to David unto Hebron, and said thus, 'Behold, we are thy bones and thy flesh. And in time past when Saul was our King, thou leadest Israel in and out: and the Lord hath said to thee, Thou shalt feed my people Israel, and thou shalt be a captain over Israel.' So all the Elders of Israel came to the King to Hebron: and King David made a covenant with them in Hebron before the Lord: & they anointed David King over Israel" (2 Samuel 5:1–3).

[88] There was long standing animosity between Jews and Samaritans. The Samaritans were descendants of northern Ten-tribe Kingdom Israelites and foreigners who were imported by the Assyrians. The Jews considered them to be apostates because the only recognized the Pentateuch (Genesis, Exodus, Leviticus, Numbers, Deuteronomy) as sacred texts they and rejected the rest of the Jewish holy canon. Furthermore, and more seriously, they did not see the need to worship at the Temple in Jerusalem. A Samaritan woman is shocked when Jesus engages her in a conversation: "Then said the woman of Samaria unto him, 'How is it, that thou being a Jew, askest drink of me, which am a woman of Samaria? For the Jews meddle not with the Samaritans" (John 4:9). Samaritans, in the days when Israelites returned to rebuild the temple in Jerusalem, opposed and tried to block the project. "But the adversaries of Judah and Benjamin heard, that the children of the captivity built the Temple unto the Lord God of Israel [...] Wherefore the people of the land discouraged the people of Judah, and troubled them in building, And they hired counselors against them, to hinder their device, all the days of Cyrus King of Persia, even until the

Long to enjoy it quiet and secure
Between two such enclosing enemies,
Roman and Parthian? Therefore one of these
Thou must make sure thy own: the Parthian first,
By my advice, as nearer, and of late
Found able by invasion to annoy
Thy country, and captive lead away her kings,
Antigonus and old Hyrcanus, bound,

---

reign of Darius King of Persia. And in the reign of Ahashuerosh (in the beginning of his reign) wrote they an accusation against the inhabitants of Judah and Jerusalem. [...] Rehum the chancellor, and Shimshai the scribe wrote a letter against Jerusalem to Artahshashte the King, in this sort" (Ezra 4:1, 4–6, 8). Samaritans tried to prevent the rebuilding of Jerusalem walls after the Babylonian exile. "But when Sanballat, & Tobiah, and the Arabians, and the Ammonites, and the Ashdodims heard that the walls of Jerusalem were repaired, (for the breaches began to be stopped) then they were very wroth, And conspired all together to come & to fight against Jerusalem, and to hinder them" (Nehemiah 4:7–8). Jesus confined the ministry of his disciples, while he was on earth, to the Jews and forbid them to preach to Samaritans. "These twelve did Jesus send forth, & commanded them, saying, 'Go not into the way of the Gentiles, and into the cities of the Samaritans enter ye not'" (Matthew 10:5). When asked "who is my neighbor," Jesus teaches a lesson against racial and national prejudice by relating the parable of the Good Samaritan: "And Jesus answered, and said, 'A certain man went down from Jerusalem to Jericho, and fell among thieves, and they robbed him of his raiment, and wounded him, and departed, leaving him half dead. Now so it fell out, that there came down a certain Priest that same way, and when he saw him, he passed by on the other side. And likewise also a Levite, when he was come near to the place, went and looked on him, and passed by on the other side. Then a certain Samaritan, as he journeyed, came near unto him, and when he saw him, he had compassion on him, And went to him, & bound p his wounds, and poured in oil and wine, and put him on his own beast, and brought him to an Inn, and made provision for him. And on the morrow when he departed, he took out two pence, and gave them to the host, and said unto him, Take care of him, and whatsoever thou spendest more, when I come again, I will recompense thee. Which now of these three, thinkest thou, was neighbor unto him that fell among the thieves?' And he said, 'He that shewed mercy on him.' Then said Jesus unto him, 'Go, and do thou likewise'" (Luke 10:30–37).

Maugre the Roman. It shall be my task
To render thee the Parthian at dispose,
Choose which thou wilt, by conquest or by league.
By him thou shalt regain, without him not,
That which alone can truly reinstall thee
In David's royal seat, his true successor
Deliverance of thy brethren, those Ten Tribes[89]
Whose offspring in his territory yet serve
In Habor, and among the Medes dispersed:[90]
The sons of Jacob, two of Joseph, lost
Thus long from Israel, serving, as of old
Their fathers in the land of Egypt served,
This offer sets before thee to deliver.

---

[89] Kings Saul, David, and Solomon ruled over all Twelve Tribes of Israel. The ten northern tribes broke off from the tribes of Judah and Benjamin to form their own kingdom during the reign of Rehoboam the son of Solomon. "And the King hearkened not unto the people: for it was the ordinance of the Lord, that he might perform his saying, which the Lord had spoken by Ahijah the Shilonite unto Jeroboam the son of Nebat. So when all Israel saw that the King regarded them not, the people answered the King thus, saying, 'What portion have we in David? we have none inheritance in the son of Ishai. To your tents, O Israel: now see to thine own house, David.' So Israel departed unto their tents. Howbeit over the children of Israel, which dwelt in the cities of Judah, did Rehoboam reign still. Now the King Rehoboam sent Adoram the receiver of the tribute, and all Israel stoned him to death: then King Rehoboam made speed to get him up to his chariot, to flee to Jerusalem. And Israel rebelled against the house of David unto this day. And when all Israel had heard that Jeroboam was come again, they sent and called him unto the assembly, and made him King over all Israel: none followed the house of David, but the tribe of Judah only" (1 Kings 12:15–21).

[90] [Lines 374–376] The Israelites of the Ten Tribe Kingdom of Israel are dispersed to Media by the Assyrians: "In the ninth year of Hoshea, the King of Asshur took Samaria, and carried Israel away unto Asshur, and put them in Halah, and in Habor by the river of Gozan, & in the cities of the Medes" (2 Kings 17:6). "Then the King of Asshur did carry away Israel unto Asshur, and put them in Halah and in Habor, by the river of Gozan, and in the cities of the Medes, Because they would not obey the voice of the Lord their God, but transgressed his covenant: that is, all that Moses the servant of the Lord had commanded, and would neither obey nor do them" (2 Kings 18:11, 12).

These if from servitude thou shalt restore
To their inheritance, then, nor till then,
Thou on the throne of David in full glory,
From Egypt to Euphrates[91] and beyond,[92]
Shalt reign, and Rome or Caesar not need fear."
To whom our Saviour answered thus, unmoved:
"Much ostentation vain of fleshly arm[93]
And fragile arms, much instrument of war,
Long in preparing, soon to nothing brought,
Before mine eyes thou hast set, and in my ear
Vented much policy, and projects deep
Of enemies, of aids, battles, and leagues,
Plausible to the world, to me worth naught.
Means I must use, thou say'st; prediction else
Will unpredict, and fail me of the throne!
My time, I told thee (and that time for thee
Were better farthest off), is not yet come.[94]
When that comes, think not thou to find me slack[95]

---

[91] The land God promised to the descendants of Abraham: "In that same day the Lord made a covenant with Abram, saying, 'Unto thy seed have I given this land, from the river of Egypt unto the great river, the river Euphrates" (Genesis 15:18).

[92] And beyond. The extent of Solomon's kingdom: "And Solomon reigned over all kingdoms, from the River unto the land of the Philistines, and unto the border of Egypt, and they brought presents, & served Solomon all the days of his life" (1 Kings 4:21).

[93] Much ostentation vain of fleshly arm. An arm of flesh signifies human weakness and limitations: "With him is an arm of flesh, but with us is the Lord our God for to help us, & to fight our battles. Then the people were confirmed by the words of Hezekiah King of Judah" (2 Chronicles 32:8). "Thus saith the Lord, 'Cursed be the man that trusteth in man, and maketh flesh his arm, and withdraweth his heart from the Lord'" (Jeremiah 17:5).

[94] Compare with Jesus words to Mary Magdalene: "Jesus saith unto her, 'Touch me not: for I am not yet ascended to my Father: but go to my brethren, and say unto them, I ascend unto my Father, and to your Father, and to my God, and your God'" (John 20:17).

[95] Think not to find me slack. "The Lord of that promise is not slack (as some men count slackness) but is patient toward us, and would have no man to perish, but

On my part aught endeavouring, or to need
Thy politic maxims, or that cumbersome
Luggage of war there shewn me argument
Of human weakness rather than of strength.
My brethren, as thou call'st them, those Ten Tribes,
I must deliver, if I mean to reign
David's true heir, and his full sceptre sway
To just extent over all Israel's sons!
But whence to thee this zeal? Where was it then
For Israel, or for David, or his throne,
When thou stood'st up his tempter to the pride
Of numbering Israel[96] which cost the lives
of threescore and ten thousand Israelites[97]
By three days' pestilence?[98] Such was thy zeal
To Israel then, the same that now to me.
As for those captive tribes, themselves were they
Who wrought their own captivity,[99] fell off

---

would all men to come to repentance" (2 Peter 3:9). Not DR "the Lord delayeth not."

[96] [Lines 409–410] Satan tempts David to take a census in Israel which God had commanded David not to do. It was a lack of faith to rely on the number of men who could serve in David's armies. "And Satan stood up against Israel, and provoked Dauid to number Israel. Therefore Dauid said to Ioab, and to the rulers of the people, Go, and number Israel from Beer-sheba even to Dan, and bring it to me, that I may know the number of them."

[97] "So the Lord sent a pestilence in Israel, and there fell of Israel seventy thousand men" (1 Chronicles 21:14).

[98] "So Gad came to David, and showed him, and said unto him, 'Wilt thou that seven years famine come upon thee in thy land, or wilt thou flee three months before thine enemies, they following thee, or that there be three days pestilence in thy land? now advise thee, and see, what answer I shall give to him that sent me'" (2 Samuel 24:13).

[99] Israel and Jeroboam their king "wrought their own captivity" by worshipping other gods. The prophet Ahijah prophesies: "Go, tell Jeroboam, 'Thus saith the Lord God of Israel, Forasmuch as I have exalted thee from among the people, and have made thee prince over my people Israel, And have rent the kingdom away from the house of David, and have given it thee, and thou hast not been as

From God to worship calves,[100] the deities[101]
Of Egypt, Baal next and Ashtaroth,[102]

---

my servant David, which kept my commandments, and followed me with all his heart, and did only that which was right in mine eyes, But hast done evil above all that were before thee (for thou hast gone & made thee other gods, and molten images, to provoke me, & hast cast me behind thy back) Therefore behold, I will bring evil upon the house of Jeroboam, and will cut off from Jeroboam him that pisseth against the wall, as well him that is shut up, as him that is left in Israel, and will away the remnant of the house of Jeroboam, as a man sweepeth away doing, until it be all gone. The dogs shall eat him of Jeroboam's stock that dieth in the city, and the fowls of the air shall eat him that dieth in the field: for the Lord hath said it [...] For the Lord shall smite Israel, as when a reed is shaken in the water, and he shall weed Israel out of his good land, which he gave to their fathers, and shall scatter them beyond the River, because they have made them groves, provoking the Lord to anger. And he shall give Israel up, because of the sins of Jeroboam, who did sin, and made Israel to sin'" (2 Kings 14:7–11, 16, 17). "So they forsook the Lord, and served Baal, and Ashtaroth. And the wrath of the Lord was host against Israel, & he delivered them into the hands of spoilers, that spoiled them, and he sold them into the hands of their enemies round about them, so that they could no longer stand before their enemies" (Judges 2:13, 14).

100 [Lines 414–416] Calf worshipping Ten Tribe Kingdom: "Whereupon the King took counsel, and made two calves of gold, and said unto them, 'It is too much for you to go up to Jerusalem: behold, O Israel, thy gods, which brought thee up out of the land of Egypt.' And he set the one in Bethel, and the other set he in Dan. And this thing turned to sin: for the people went (because of the one) even to Dan. Also he made an house of high places, and made Priests of the lowest of the people, which were not of the sons of Levi. And Jeroboam made a feast the fifteenth day of the eight month, like unto the feast that is in Judah, and offered on the altar. So did he in Bethel and offered unto the calves that he had made: and he placed in Bethel the Priests of the high places, which he had made. And he offered upon the altar, which he had made in Bethel, the fifteenth day of the eight month, (even in the month which he had forged of his own heart) and made a solemn feast unto the children of Israel: and he went up to the altar, to burn incense" (1 Kings 12:28–33).

101 "But where are thy gods, that thou hast made thee? let them arise, if they can help thee in the time of thy trouble: for according to the number of thy cities, are thy gods, O Judah" (Jeremiah 2:28). "For according to the number of thy cities were thy gods, O Judah, and according to the number of the streets of Jerusalem have ye set up altars of confusion, even altars to burn incense unto Baal" (Jeremiah 11:13).

---

[102] The progression of Israel with Egypt, Baal, and Ashtaroth. "For when the children of Israel sinned against the Lord their God, which had brought them out of the land of Egypt, from under the hand of Pharaoh king of Egypt, & feared other gods, and walked according to the factions of the Heathen, whom the Lord had cast out before the children of Israel, and after the manners of the Kings of Israel, which they used, and the children of Israel had done secretly things that were not upright before the Lord their God, & throughout all their cities had built high places, both from the tower of the watch, to the defensed city, and had made them images and groves upon every high hill, and under every green tree, and there burnt incense in all the high places, as did the heathen, whom the Lord had taken away before them, and wrought wicked things to anger the Lord, and served idols: whereof the Lord had said unto them, 'Ye shall do no such thing', notwithstanding the Lord testified to Israel, and to Judah by all the Prophets, & by all the Seers, saying, 'Turn from your evil ways, and keep my commandments & my statutes, according to all the Law, which I commanded your fathers, and which I sent to you by my servants the Prophets.' Nevertheless they would not obey, but hardened their necks, like to the necks of their fathers, that did not believe in the Lord their God. And they refused his statutes and his covenant, that he made with their fathers, & his testimonies (wherewith he witnessed unto them) and they followed vanity, and became vain, and followed the heathen that were round about them: concerning whom the Lord had charged them, that they should not do like them. Finally they left all the commandments of the Lord their God, and made them molten images, even two calves, and made a grove, and worshipped all the host of heaven, and served Baal. And they made their sons and their daughters pass threw the fire, and used witchcraft and enchantments, yea, sold themselves to do evil in the sight of the Lord, to anger him. Therefore the Lord was exceeding wroth with Israel, and put them out of his sight, and none was left but the tribe of Judah only" (2 Kings 17:7–18). Solomon adopts the worship of the Canaanite goddess Ashtoroth. "For Solomon followed Ashtaroth the god of the Zidonians, and Milcom the abomination of the Ammonites" (1 Kings 11:5). Ahab the King of Israel marries Jezebel the daughter of King Ethbal of Sidon and introduces a new strand of Baal worship in the region. "For was it a light thing for him to walk in the sins of Jeroboam the son of Nebat, except he took Jezebel also the daughter of Ethbaal King of the Zidonians to wife, and went and served Baal, and worshipped him? Also he reared up an altar to Baal in the house of Baal, which he had built in Samaria. And Ahab made a grove, & Ahab proceeded, & did provoke the Lord God of Israel more then all the kings of Israel that were before him" (1 Kings 16:31–33). Elijah reprimands Ahab for his promotion of Baal worship. "And when Ahab saw Elijah, Ahab said unto him, 'Art thou he that troubleth Israel?' And he answered, 'I have not troubled Israel,

And all the idolatries of heathen round,[103]
Besides their other worse than heathenish crimes;[104]
Nor in the land of their captivity
Humbled themselves, or penitent besought
The God of their forefathers, but so died
Impenitent, and left a race behind
Like to themselves, distinguishable scarce
From Gentiles, but by circumcision vain,[105]

---

but thou, and thy father's house, in that ye have forsaken the commandments of the Lord, and thou hast followed Baals" (1 Kings 18:17, 19). "And the children of Israel wrought wickedness again in the sight of the Lord, and served Baalim and Ashtaroth, and the gods of Aram, and the gods of Sidon, and the gods of Moab, and the gods of the children of Ammon, and the gods of the Philistines, and forsook the Lord and served not him" (Judges 10:6).

[103] The idolatries of heathen round. "Beware, lest thou be taken in a snare after them, after that they be destroyed before thee, and lest thou ask after their gods, saying, 'How did these nations serve their gods, that I may do so likewise?" (Deuteronomy 12:30).

[104] Heathenish crimes. "And the Auims made Nibhaz, and Tartak: and the Sepharuims burnt their children in the fire to Adrammelech, and Anammelech the gods of Sepharvaim" (2 Kings 17:31) King Josiah made reforms in Judah including destroying altars that had been used for sacrificing children. "He defiled also Topheth, which was in the valley of the children of Hinnom, that no man should make his son or his daughter pass through the fire to Molech" (2 Kings 23:10). "Also thou shalt not give thy children to offer them unto Molech, neither shalt thou defile the name of thy God: for I am the Lord" (Leviticus 18:21). "Thou shalt not do so unto the Lord thy God: for all abomination, which the Lord hateth, have they done unto their gods: for they have burned both their sons and their daughters with fire to their gods" (Deuteronomy 12:31). "Because they have forsaken me, and profaned this place, and have burnt incense in it unto other gods, whom neither they, nor their fathers have known, nor the Kings of Judah (they have filled this place also with the blood of innocents, And they have built the high places of Baal, to burn their sons with fire for burnt offerings unto Baal, which I commanded not, nor spake it, neither came it into my mind) Therefore behold, the days come, saith the Lord, that this place shall no more be called Topheth, nor the valley of Ben-hinnom, but the valley of slaughter" (Jeremiah 19:4–6).

[105] Circumcision vain. "For circumcision verily is profitable, if thou do the Law: but if thou be a transgressor of the Law, thy circumcision is made

And God with idols in their worship joined.
Should I of these the liberty regard,
Who, freed, as to their ancient patrimony,
Unhumbled, unrepentant, unreformed,
Headlong would follow, and to their gods perhaps
Of Bethel and of Dan?[106] No; let them serve
Their enemies who serve idols with God.[107]
Yet He at length, time to himself best known,
Remembering Abraham, by some wondrous call
May bring them back, repentant and sincere,[108]

---

uncircumcision" (Romans 2:25, GE). Geneva note: "He precisely prevents their objection, who set a holiness in circumcision, and the outward observation of the law: so that he shows that the outward circumcision, if it is separated from the inward, does not justify, and also condemns those who are indeed circumcised, of whom it is required that they fulfil that which circumcision signifies, that is to say, cleanness of the heart and the whole life according to the commandment of the law, so that if there is a man uncircumcised according to the flesh, who is circumcised in heart, he is far better and to be more regarded than any Jew that is circumcised according to the flesh only. "For in Jesus Christ neither circumcision availeth anything, neither uncircumcision, but faith which worketh by love" (Galatians 5:6).

[106] King Jeroboam of Israel established calf worship centers in Dan and Bethel. "Whereupon the King took counsel, and made two calves of gold, and said unto them, 'It is too much for you to go up to Jerusalem: behold, O Israel, thy gods, which brought thee up out of the land of Egypt.' And he set the one in Bethel, and the other set he in Dan" (1 Kings 12:28, 29).

[107] [Lines 431–432] Let them serve / Their enemies who serve idols with God. The same sense of God's judgment upon apostate Judah through the mouth of Jeremiah: "And when ye shall say, 'Wherefore doth the Lord our God do these things unto us?' then shalt thou answer them, 'Like as ye have forsaken me and served strange gods in your land, so shall ye serve strangers in a land that is not yours'" (Jeremiah 5:19).

[108] [Lines 433–435] May bring them back repentant and sincere. "But now thus saith the Lord, that created thee, 'O Jacob: and he that formed thee, O Israel, Fear not: for I have redeemed thee: I have called thee by thy name, thou art mine. When thou passest through the waters, I will be with thee, & through the floods, that they do not overflow thee. When thou walkest through the very fire, thou shalt not be burnt, neither shall the flame kindle upon thee [...] Fear not, for I am

And at their passing cleave the Assyrian flood,
While to their native land with joy they haste,[109]
As the Red Sea and Jordan once he cleft,[110]

---

with thee: I will bring thy seed from the East, and gather thee from the West. I will say to the North, Give: and to the South, Keep not back: bring my sons from far, & my daughters from the ends of the earth'" (Isaiah 43:1, 2, 5, 6).

[109] [Lines 436–437] And at their passing cleave the Assyrian flood. The Israel exiles from the Ten Tribe kingdom are to be restored. "These are the ten tribes which were led away from their own land into captivity in the days of King Hoshea, whom Shalmaneser the king of the Assyrians led captive; he took them across the river, and they were taken into another land. But they formed this plan for themselves, that they would leave the multitude of the nations and go to a more distant region, where mankind had never lived, that there at least they might keep their statutes which they had not kept in their own land. And they went in by the narrow passages of the Euphrates river. For at that time the Most High performed signs for them, and stopped the channels of the river until they had passed over. Through that region there was a long way to go, a journey of a year and a half; and that country is called Arzareth. Then they dwelt there until the last times; now when they are about to come again, the Most High will stop the channels of the river again, so that they may be able to pass over" (2 Esdras 13:40–47). "The Lord also shall utterly destroy the tongue of the Egyptian's sea, and with his mighty wind shall lift up his hand over the river, and shall smite him in his seven streams, and cause men to walk therein with shoes. And there shall be a path to the remnant of his people, which are left of Asshur, like as it was unto Israel in the day that he came up out of the land of Egypt" (Isaiah 11:15, 16). "And the sixth Angel poured out his vial upon the great river Euphrates, and the water thereof dried up, that the way of the Kings of the East should be prepared" (Revelation 16:12).

[110] As the Red Sea and the Jordan once he cleft. "Thou breakest up the fountain and river: thou driest up mighty rivers" (Psalm 74:15). Crossing the Red Sea when Israel left bondage in Egypt. "Thou breakest up the fountain and river: thou driest up mighty rivers. Then the children of Israel went through the midst of the Sea upon the dry ground, and the waters were a wall unto them on their right hand, and on their left hand" (Exodus 14:21, 22). Israel crosses the Jordan River into the land promised to the descendants of Abraham after forty years of wandering in the wilderness: "Then when the people were departed from their tents to go over Jordan, the Priests bearing the Ark of the Covenant, went before people. And as they that bare the Ark came unto Jordan, and the feet of the Priests that bore the Ark were dipped in the brink of the water, (for Jordan used

When to the Promised Land their fathers passed.
To his due time[111] and providence I leave them."
So spake Israel's true King, and to the Fiend
Made answer meet, that made void all his wiles.
So fares it when with truth falsehood contends.

---

to fill all his banks all the time of harvest) then the waters that came down from above, stayed and rose upon an heap and departed far from the city of Adam, that was beside Zaretan: but the waters that came down toward the Sea of the wilderness, even the salt Sea, failed, and were cut off: so the people went right over against Jericho. But the Priests that bore the Ark of the covenant of the Lord, stood dry within Jordan ready prepared, and all the Israelites went over dry, until all the people were gone clean over through Jordan" (Joshua 3:14–17).

[111] To his due time. "But hath made his word manifest in due time through the preaching, which is committed unto me, according to the commandment of God our Savior" (Titus 1:3, GE). "Due times," AV. "Time appointed," Tyndale and GT. "At his time," Coverdale. "Appointed time," Bishops.

Book Four

Perplexed and troubled[1] at his bad success
The Tempter stood, nor had what to reply,
Discovered in his fraud, thrown from his hope
So oft, and the persuasive rhetoric
That sleeked his tongue, and won so much on Eve,
So little here, nay lost. But Eve was Eve;
This far his over-match, who, self-deceived
And rash, beforehand had no better weighed
The strength he was to cope with, or his own.
But as a man who had been matchless held
In cunning, over-reached where least he thought,[2]
To salve his credit, and for very spite,
Still will be tempting him who foils him still,

---

[1] Being defeated by God brings trouble and perplexity. "For it is a day of trouble, and of ruin, and of perplexity by the Lord God of hosts in the valley of vision, breaking down the city: and a crying unto the mountains" (Isaiah 22:5). "And the posts compelled by the Kings commandment went forth, and the commandment was given in the palace at Shushan: and the King & Haman sat drinking, but the city of Shushan was in perplexity" (Esther 3:15, GE). Not AV "perplexed." GT, Coverdale, Bishops "disquieted." "Weeping" DR. "The best of them is as a briar: the most upright is sharper then a thorn hedge: the day of thy watchmen, and thy visitation cometh; now shall be their perplexity" (Micah 7:4, AV). Not Geneva and Bishops "confusion." DR, "destruction." GT and Coverdale "wasted away." "Now Herod the Tetrarch heard of all that was done by him: and he was perplexed, because that it was said of some, that 'John was risen from the dead'" (Luke 9:7 AV). DR, "in doubt." "Doubted" GE, Bishops, GT, Coverdale, Tyndale. "Then there shall be signs in the sun, and in the moon, and in the stars, and upon the earth trouble among the nations with perplexity: the sea and the waters shall roar" (Luke 21:25 GE, Bishops, AV, Coverdale, Tyndale). Not GT "at wits end." Not DR "confusion."

[2] Strength overreached and overcome by one who is stronger. "When a strong man armed keepeth his palace, the things that he possesseth, are in peace. But when a stronger then he, cometh upon him, and overcometh him: he taketh from him all his armor wherein he trusted, and divideth his spoils" (Luke 11: 21, 22).

And never cease, though to his shame the more;
Or as a swarm of flies in vintage-time,
About the wine-press where sweet must is poured,[3]
Beat off, returns as oft with humming sound;
Or surging waves against a solid rock,[4]
Though all to shivers dashed, the assault renew,
(Vain battery!) and in froth or bubbles end
So Satan, whom repulse upon repulse
Met ever, and to shameful silence brought,[5]
Yet gives not o'er, though desperate of success,
And his vain importunity pursues.
He brought our Saviour to the western side
Of that high mountain, whence he might behold
Another plain, long, but in breadth not wide,
Washed by the southern sea, and on the north
To equal length backed with a ridge of hills
That screened the fruits of the earth and seats of men
From cold Septentrion blasts; thence in the midst
Divided by a river, off whose banks

---

[3] [Lines 15–16] "I am that true vine, and my Father is that husbandman" (John 15:1).

[4] Surging waves against a solid rock. "These are rocks in your feasts of charity when they feast with you, without all fear, feeding themselves: clouds they are without water, carried about of winds, corrupt trees & without fruit, twice dead, and plucked up by the roots. They are the raging waves of the sea, forming out their own shame: they are wandering stars, to whom is reserved the blackness of darkness forever" (Jude 12, 13). Christ as Rock: "And did all drink the same spiritual drink (for they drank of the spiritual Rock that followed them: and the Rock was Christ)" (1 Corinthians 10:4). "And I say also unto thee, that thou art Peter, and upon this rock I will build my Church: and the gates of hell shall not overcome it" (Matthew 16:18).

[5] [Lines 18–22] Compare the Milton's rock simile illustrating the futility of Satan's efforts with Jesus's parable of the man who built his house upon the rock mass. "Whosoever then heareth of me these words, & doth the same, I will liken him to a wiseman, which hath built his house on a rock: And the rain fell, and the floods came, and the winds blew, and beat upon that house, and it fell not: for it was grounded on a rock" (Matthew 7:24, 25).

On each side an Imperial City stood,
With towers and temples proudly elevate
On seven small hills, with palaces adorned,
Porches and theatres, baths, aqueducts,
Statues and trophies, and triumphal arcs,
Gardens and groves, presented to his eyes
Above the highth of mountains interposed.
By what strange parallax, or optic skill
Of vision, multiplied through air, or glass
Of telescope, were curious to enquire.
And now the Tempter thus his silence broke.
"The city which thou seest no other deem
Than great and glorious Rome, Queen of the Earth
So far renowned, and with the spoils enriched
Of nations.[6] There the Capitol thou seest,
Above the rest lifting his stately head
On the Tarpeian rock, her citadel
Impregnable; and there Mount Palatine,
The imperial palace, compass huge, and high
The structure, skill of noblest architects,
With gilded battlements, conspicuous far,
Turrets, and terraces, and glittering spires.
Many a fair edifice besides, more like
Houses of gods (so well I have disposed
My aerie microscope) thou may'st behold,
Outside and inside both, pillars and roofs
Carved work, the hand of famed artificers
In cedar, marble, ivory, or gold.
Thence to the gates cast round thine eye, and see

[6] [Lines 44–47] Compare with the description of the mysterious and Queenly Whore of Babylon whom early Christian apologists identified with the city of Rome but Protestant Reformers associated with Roman Catholicism: "In as much as she glorified herself, and lived in pleasure, so much give ye to her torment & sorrow: for she saith in her heart, 'I sit being a queen, and am no widow, and shall see no mourning'" (Revelation 18:7).

What conflux issuing forth, or entering in:
Praetors, proconsuls to their provinces
Hasting, or on return, in robes of state;
Lictors and rods, the ensigns of their power;
Legions and cohorts, turms of horse and wings;
Or embassies from regions far remote,
In various habits, on the Appian road,
Or on the Aemilian, some from farthest south,
Syene, and where the shadow both way falls,
Meroe, Nilotic isle, and, more to west,
The realm of Bocchus to the Blackmoor sea;
From the Asian kings (and Parthian among these),
From India and the Golden Chersoness,
And utmost Indian isle Taprobane,
Dusk faces with white silken turbants wreathed;
From Gallia, Gades, and the British west;
Germans, and Scythians, and Sarmatians north
Beyond Danubius to the Tauric pool.
All nations now to Rome obedience pay,
To Rome's great Emperor, whose wide domain,
In ample territory, wealth and power,
Civility of manners, arts and arms,
And long renown, thou justly may'st prefer
Before the Parthian. These two thrones except,
The rest are barbarous, and scarce worth the sight,
Shared among petty kings too far removed;
These having shewn thee, I have shewn thee all
The kingdoms of the world, and all their glory.[7]
This Emperor hath no son, and now is old,
Old and lascivious, and from Rome retired
To Capreae, an island small but strong

[7] [Lines 88–89] I have shown thee all / The Kingdoms of the world, and all their glory. "Again the devil took him up into an exceeding high mountain, and showed him all the kingdoms of the world, and the glory of them" (Matthew 4:8).

On the Campanian shore, with purpose there
His horrid lusts in private to enjoy;
Committing to a wicked favourite
All public cares, and yet of him suspicious;
Hated of all,[8] and hating. With what ease,
Endued with regal virtues as thou art,
Appearing, and beginning noble deeds,
Might'st thou expel this monster from his throne,
Now made a sty, and, in his place ascending,
A victor-people free from servile yoke![9]
And with my help thou may'st; to me the power
Is given, and by that right I give it thee.[10]

---

[8] [Lines 90–97] Satan is describing the Roman Emperor Tiberius who was reigning while Jesus was on earth. "Now in the fifteenth year of the reign of Tiberius Cæsar, Pontius Pilate being governor of Judea, and Herod being Tetrarch of Galilee, and his brother Philip Tetrarch of Iturea, and of the country of Trachonitis, and Lysanias the Tetrarch of Abilene [...] the word of God came unto John, the son of Zacharias in the wilderness" (Luke 3:1, 2). "Hated of all." English Renaissance Protestants identified the one the King's prophesied in Daniel who is described as a " vile person" to be Tiberius who came to the throne of Augustus "peaceably": "And in his place shall stand up a vile person, to whom they shall not give the honor of the kingdom: but he shall come in peaceably, and obtain the kingdom by flatteries" (Daniel 11:21).

[9] Compare with Jesus's use of "yoke" to denote degrees of servitude and note the sense stress upon the word "my" making it clear that there is an alternative yoke (likely that of the Roman's or the Jewish religious leaders.) "'Take my yoke on you, and learn of me that I am meek and lowly in heart: and ye shall find rest unto your souls. For my yoke is easy, & my burden light'" (Matthew 11:29, 30). King Rehoboam of Judah metaphorically uses "yoke" to refer to the oppressive burden placed upon the common people by rulers. "And speak to them after the counsel of the young men, saying, 'My father made your yoke grievous, and I will make your yoke more grievous: my father hath chastised you with rods, but I will correct you with scourges" (1 Kings 12:14). Consider also Isaiah's prophecy against the "yoke" of the King of Assyria who was persecuting Israel: "That I will break to pieces Asshur in my land, and upon my mountains will I tread him under foot: so that his yoke shall depart from them, and his burden shall be taken from off their shoulder" (Isaiah 14:25).

Aim, therefore, at no less than all the world;
Aim at the highest; without the highest attained,
Will be for thee no sitting, or not long,[11]
On David's throne, be prophesied what will."
To whom the Son of God, unmoved, replied.
"Nor doth this grandeur and majestic shew
Of luxury, though called magnificence,
More than of arms before, allure mine eye,
Much less my mind; though thou should'st add to tell
Their sumptuous gluttonies, and gorgeous feasts
On citron tables or Atlantic stone
(For I have also heard, perhaps have read),
Their wines of Setia, Cales, and Falerne,
Chios and Crete, and how they quaff in gold,
Crystal, and myrrhine cups, imbossed with gems
And studs of pearl—to me should'st tell, who thirst
And hunger still. Then embassies thou shew'st
From nations far and nigh! What honor that,
But tedious waste of time, to sit and hear
So many hollow compliments and lies,
Outlandish flatteries? Then proceed'st to talk
Of the Emperor, how easily subdued,
How gloriously. I shall, thou say'st, expel
A brutish monster: what if I withal
Expel a Devil who first made him such?[12]

---

[10] [Lines 103–104] To me the power / Is given, and by that right I give it thee. "And the devil said unto him, 'All this power will I give thee, and the glory of those kingdoms: for that is delivered to me: and to whomsoever I will, I give it'" (Luke 4:6).

[11] [Lines 105–108] The angel Gabriel's prophecy concerning Jesus that he delivered to Mary. "He shall be great, and shall be called the Son of the most High, and the Lord God shall give unto him the throne of his father David. And he shall reign over the house of Jacob forever, and of his kingdom shall be no end" (Luke 1:32, 33).

[12] [Lines 127–129] Jesus's power to expel the Devil. "Forasmuch then as the children are partakers of flesh and blood, he also himself likewise took part with

Let his tormentor, Conscience,[13] find him out;
For him I was not sent,[14] nor yet to free
That people, victor once, now vile and base,
Deservedly made vassal—who, once just,
Frugal, and mild, and temperate, conquered well,
But govern ill the nations under yoke,[15]
Peeling their provinces, exhausted all
By lust and rapine; first ambitious grown
Of triumph, that insulting vanity;
Then cruel, by their sports to blood inured
Of fighting beasts, and men to beasts exposed;[16]

---

them, that through death he might expel him that had lordship over death, that is the devil: And that he might deliver them, which through fear of death, were all their lifetime in danger of bondage" (Hebrews 2:14, 15 Bishops [see also GT]). Not AV or GE "destroy." "Put down through death" Tyndale. "Through death might take away the power of him" Coverdale. "And he called his twelve disciples unto him, and gave them power against unclean spirits, to cast them out, and to heal every sickness, and every disease" (Matthew 10:1). "And the seventy turned again with joy, saying, 'Lord, even the devils are subdued to us through thy Name'" (Luke 10:17).

13 His tormentor conscience, find him out. Even the Gentile rulers have a conscience and can be judged by God on that basis without knowing God's requirements otherwise: "For when the Gentiles which have not the Law, doe by nature, the things contained in the Law, they having not the Law, are a Law unto themselves, Which shows the effect of the Law written in their hearts, their conscience also bearing witness, and their thoughts accusing one another, or excusing)" (Romans 2:14, 15).

14 For him I was not sent. "But he answered, and said, 'I am not sent, but unto the lost sheep of the house of Israel'" (Matthew 15:24). For this he was sent: "But he said unto them, 'Surely I must also preach the kingdom of God to other cities: for therefore am I sent'" (Luke 4:43).

15 Whole nations can be subjected to "the yoke" of other nations. Consider the example from the prophet Jeremiah regarding Nebuchadnezzar the King of Babylon: "And the nation and kingdom which will not serve the same Nebuchadnezzar king of Babel, and that will not put their neck under the yoke of the King of Babel, the same nation will I visit, saith the Lord, with the sword, and with the famine, and with the pestilence, until I have wholly given them into his hands" (Jeremiah 27:8).

Luxurious by their wealth, and greedier still,
And from the daily Scene effeminate.[17]
What wise and valiant man would seek to free
These, thus degenerate, by themselves enslaved,[18]
Or could of inward slaves make outward free?
Know, therefore, when my season comes to sit
On David's throne, it shall be like a tree
Spreading and overshadowing all the earth,[19]

---

[16] Of fighting beasts, and men to beasts exposed. Compare with the arena experience of Paul: "If I have fought with beasts at Ephesus after the manner of men, what advantageth it me, if the dead be not raised up? let us eat and drink: for tomorrow we shall die" (1 Corinthians 15:32). Compare also with Daniel's ordeal in the lion's den of King Darius: "Then the King commanded, and they brought Daniel, and cast him into the den of lions: now the King spake, and said unto Daniel, 'Thy God, whom thou always servest, even he will deliver thee'" (Daniel 6:16).

[17] The understanding of the word "effeminate" in Renaissance English means to be under the influence of a woman; it does not mean to behave like a woman. Compare with the resurrected Jesus's words to the congregation in Thyatira: "Notwithstanding, I have a few things against thee, that thou sufferest the woman Jezabel, which calleth herself a prophetess, to teach and to deceive my servants to make them commit fornication, and to eat meats sacrificed unto idols" (Revelation 2:20).

[18] By themselves enslaved. "Jesus answered them, 'Verily, verily I say unto you, that whosoever committeth sin, is the servant of sin" (John 8:34).

[19] [Lines 146–148] Compare with the description of King Nebuchadnezzar's kingship revealed to him in a dream: "Thus were the visions of mine head in my bed; behold, I saw a tree in the midst of the earth and the height thereof was great: A great tree and strong, and the height thereof reached unto heaven, and the sight thereof to the ends of all the earth. The boughs thereof were fair & the fruit thereof much, and in it was meat for all: it made a shadow under it for the beasts of the field, and the fowls of the heaven dwelt in the boughs thereof, and all flesh fed of it […] The tree that thou sawest, which was great and mighty, whose height reached unto the heaven, and the sight thereof through all the world, whose leaves were fair & the fruit thereof much, and in it was meat for all, under the which the beasts of the field dwelt, and upon whose branches the fowls of the heaven did sit" (Daniel 4:10–12, 20, 21). Jesus compares the Kingdom of Heaven to such a large tree: "Another parable he put forth unto them, saying, 'The kingdom of heaven is like unto a grain of mustard seed,

Or as a stone that shall to pieces dash[20]
All monarchies besides throughout the world;
And of my Kingdom there shall be no end.[21]

---

which a man taketh and soweth in his field: Which indeed is the least of all seeds: but when it is grown, it is the greatest among herbs, and it is a tree, so that the birds of heaven come and build in the branches thereof'" (Matthew 13:31, 32).

[20] To pieces dash. God's Kingdom under the rule of his Son will dash all other kingdoms to pieces: "The Kings of the earth band themselves, and the princes are assembled together against the Lord, and against his Christ. 'Let us break their bands, and cast their cords from us' [...] Even I have set my King upon Zion mine holy mountain. I will declare the decree: that is, the Lord hath said unto me, 'Thou art my Son: this day have I begotten thee. Ask of me, and I shall give thee the heathen for thine inheritance, and the ends of the earth for thy possession. Thou shalt crush them with a scepter of iron, and break them in pieces like a potter's vessel'" (Psalm 2:2, 3, 6–9).

[21] [Lines 149–151] God's endless Kingdom under Jesus is like a stone that destroys an image that represents the human kingdoms of the world. This description in Daniel was read prophetically by English Puritans: "O King, thou sawest, and behold, there was a great image: this great image whose glory was so excellent, stood before thee, & the form thereof was terrible. This image's head was of fine gold, his breast and his arms of silver, his belly and his thighs of brass, His legs of iron, and his feet were part of iron, and part of clay. Thou beheldest it until a stone was cut without hands, which smote the image upon his feet, that were of iron and clay, and broke them to pieces. Then was the iron, the clay, the brass, the silver and the gold broken all together, and became like the chaff of the summer flowers, and the wind carried them away, that no place was found for them: and the stone that smote the image, became a great mountain, and filled the whole earth. This is the dream, and we will declare before the King the interpretation thereof. O King, thou art a king of Kings: for the God of heaven hath given thee a kingdom, power, and strength, and glory. And in all places where the children of men dwell, the beasts of the field, and the fowls of the heaven hath he given into thine hand, and hath made thee ruler over them all: thou art this head of gold. And after thee shall rise another kingdom, inferior to thee, of silver, and another third kingdom shall be of brass, which shall bear rule over all the earth. And the fourth kingdom shall be strong as iron: for as iron breaketh in pieces, and subdueth all things, and as iron bruiseth all these things, so shall it break in pieces, and bruise all. Where as thou sawest the feet and toes, part of potter's clay, and part of iron: the kingdom shall be divided, but there shall be in it of the strength of the iron, as thou sawest the iron mixed with the

Means there shall be to this; but what the means
Is not for thee to know,[22] nor me to tell."
To whom the Tempter, impudent, replied.
"I see all offers made by me how slight
Thou valuest, because offered, and reject'st.
Nothing will please the difficult and nice,
Or nothing more than still to contradict.
On the other side know also thou that I
On what I offer set as high esteem,[23]
Nor what I part with mean to give for naught,
All these, which in a moment thou behold'st,
The kingdoms of the world, to thee I give

---

clay, and earth. And as the toes of the feet were part of iron, and part of clay, so shall the kingdom be partly strong, and partly broken. And where as thou sawest iron mixed with clay and earth, they shall mingle themselves with the seed of men: but they shall not join one with another, as iron can not be mixed with clay. And in the days of these Kings, shall the God of heaven set up a kingdom, which shall never be destroyed: and this kingdom shall not be given to another people, but it shall break, and destroy all these kingdoms, and it shall stand forever" (Daniel 2:31–44). "And he shall reign over the house of Jacob forever, and of his kingdom shall be no end" (Luke 1:33).

[22] Not for thee to know. "And he said unto them, 'It is not for you to know the times, or the seasons, which the Father hath put in his own power'" (Acts 1:7). "But of that day and hour knoweth no man, no, not the Angels which are in heaven, neither the Son himself, but the Father" (Mark 13:32).

[23] On what I offer set as high esteem. Contrast with the exaltation that the Proverbs claim come from "wisdom" with Milton's Satan's claim about the effects of political power: "Wisdom is the beginning: get wisdom therefore: and above all thy possession get understanding. Exalt her, and she shall exalt thee: she shall bring thee to honor, if thou embrace her" (Proverbs 4:7, 8). Contrast Satan's argument with the rejection of the political power of Egypt by Moses and his "esteeming the rebuke of Christ": "By faith Moses when he was come to age, refused to be called the son of Pharaoh's daughter, And chose rather to suffer adversity with the people of God, then to enjoy the pleasures of sins for a season, Esteeming the rebuke of Christ greater riches then the treasures of Egypt: for he had respect unto the recompense of the reward. By faith he forsook Egypt, and feared not the fierceness of the king: for he endured, as he that saw him which is invisible" (Hebrews 11:24–27).

(For, given to me, I give to whom I please),
No trifle; yet with this reserve, not else,
On this condition, if thou wilt fall down,
And worship me as thy superior Lord[24]
(Easily done), and hold them all of me;
For what can less so great a gift deserve?"
Whom thus our Saviour answered with disdain.
"I never liked thy talk, thy offers less;
Now both abhor, since thou hast dared to utter
The abominable terms, impious condition.
But I endure[25] the time, till which expired
Thou hast permission[26] on me.[27] It is written,

---

[24] [Lines 162–167] "Again the devil took him up into an exceeding high mountain, and showed him all the kingdoms of the world, and the glory of them, and said to him, 'All these will I give thee, if thou will fall down, and worship me'" (Matthew 4:8, 9). In a moment of time: "And the devil led him into a high mountain and shewed him all the kingdoms of the world in a moment of time. And he said to him: To thee will I give all this power and the glory of them. For to me they are delivered: and to whom I will, I give them" (Luke 4:5, 6, DR [See also AV and Bishops]). GE, GT, Tyndale, Coverdale "in the twinkling of an eye." If thou will fall down and worship me: "If thou therefore wilt fall down before me, & worship me, they shall be all thine. (Luke 4:7, Bishops [See also GT). Not AV, GE, Tyndale, Coverdale "will worship." Not DR "adore before me."

[25] "Rejoicing in hope, patient in tribulation, continuing in prayer" (Romans 12:12).

[26] Compare with God's permission granted to Satan to persecute righteous Job: "Then the Lord said unto Satan, 'Lo, all that he hath is in thine hand: only upon himself shalt thou not stretch out thine hand.' So Satan departed from the presence of the Lord" (Job 1:12).

[27] [Lines 174–175] But I endure the time, till which expired / Thou has permission on me. "And all the temptation being ended, the devil departed from him for a time" (Luke 4:13, DR). AV, Bishops, GT, Coverdale, Tyndale "departed from him for a season." GE "departed from him for a little season." Jesus successfully endures all temptations: "Seeing then that we have a great high Priest, which is entered into heaven, even Jesus the Son of God, let us hold fast our profession. For we have not an high Priest, which cannot be touched with the feeling of our infirmities, but was in all things tempted in like sort, yet without sin" (Hebrews 4:14, 15).

The first of all commandments, 'Thou shalt worship
The Lord thy God, and only Him shalt serve.'[28]
And dar'st thou to the Son of God propound
To worship thee, accursed? now more accursed
For this attempt, bolder than that on Eve,
And more blasphemous; which expect to rue.
The kingdoms of the world to thee were given![29]
Permitted[30] rather, and by thee usurped;

---

[28] Jesus quotes from Deuteronomy to refute Satan. "Thou shalt fear the Lord thy God, and serve him, and shall swear by his Name" (Deuteronomy 6:13). "Then said Jesus unto him, 'Avoid Satan: for it is written, Thou shalt worship the Lord thy God, and him only shalt thou serve'" (Matthew 4:10). "But Jesus answered him, and said, 'Hence from me, Satan: for it is written, Thou shalt worship the Lord thy God, and him alone thou shalt serve'" (Luke 4:8). "Thou shalt have no other Gods before me. Thou shalt make thee no graven image, neither any similitude of things that are in heaven above, neither that are in the earth beneath, nor that are in the waters under the earth. Thou shalt not bow down to them, neither serve them: for I am the Lord thy God, a jealous God, visiting the iniquity of the fathers upon the children, upon the third generation and upon the fourth of them that hate me" (Exodus 20:3–5).

[29] Satan as the ruler of the world: "Hereafter will I not speak many things unto you: for the prince of this world cometh, and hath nought in me" (John 14:30). Tyndale "ruler of the world."

[30] God "permits" the existence of any government. "Let every soul be subject unto the higher powers: for there is no power but of God: and the powers that be, are ordained of God. Whosoever therefore resisteth the power, resisteth the ordinance of God: and they that resist, shall receive to themselves condemnation. For Magistrates are not to be feared for good works, but for evil. Wilt thou then be without fear of the power? do well: so shalt thou have praise of the same" (Romans 13:1–3). Satan as temporarily "permitted" ruler of the world. "And he took the dragon that old serpent, which is the devil and Satan, and he bound him a thousand years: And cast him into the bottomless pit, and he shut him up, and sealed the door upon him, that he should deceive the people no more, until the thousand years were fulfilled: for after that he must be loosed for a little season [...] And when the thousand years are expired, Satan shall be loosed out of his prison, And shall go out to deceive the people, which are in the four quarters of the earth: even Gog and Magog, to gather them together to battle, whose number is, as the sand of the sea. And they went up into the plain of the earth, and they compassed the tents of the Saints about, & the beloved city: but fire came down

Other donation none thou canst produce.
If given, by whom but by the King of kings,[31]
God over all[32] supreme? If given to thee,
By thee how fairly is the Giver now
Repaid! But gratitude in thee is lost
Long since. Wert thou so void of fear or shame
As offer them to me, the Son of God
To me my own,[33] on such abhorred pact,
That I fall down and worship thee as God?
Get thee behind me![34] Plain thou now appear'st

---

from God out of heaven, and devoured them. And the devil that deceived them, was cast into a lake of fire and brimstone, where that beast and that false prophet are, and shall be tormented even day and night for evermore" (Revelation 20:2, 3, 7–10). "Therefore yet a little while, and the wicked shall not appear, and thou shalt look after his place, and he shall not be found" (Psalm 37:10).

31 Jesus as King of Kings: "These shall fight with the Lamb, and the Lamb shall overcome them: for he is Lord of Lords, and King of Kings: and they that are on his side, called, and chosen, and faithful" (Revelation 17:14). DR "King of all Kings." "And he hath upon his garment, and upon his thigh a name written, The King of Kings, and Lord of Lords" (Revelation 19:16). Coverdale "King of all Kings." "Which in due time he shall show, that is blessed and Prince only, the King of Kings and Lord of Lords" (1 Timothy 6:15).

32 God over all. "Of whom are the fathers, and of whom concerning the flesh, Christ came, who is God over all, blessed forever, Amen" (Romans 9:5, GE [see also Tyndale and Coverdale]). Not AV "who is over all, God blessed." Not Bishops "which is God, in all things to be praised forever." Not DR "who is over all things, God blessed forever." Not GT "which is God in all things."

33 One cannot give to God what is already his or what he has granted to others. "God that made the world, and all things that are therein, seeing that he is Lord of heaven and earth, dwelleth not in temples made with hands, neither is worshipped with men's hands, as though he needed anything, seeing he giveth to all life and breath and all things" (Acts 17:24, 25). "The earth is the Lord's, and all that therein is: the world and they that dwell therein. For he hath founded it upon the seas: and established it upon the floods" (Psalm 24:1, 2).

34 Get thee behind me. "And Jesus answered and said unto him, 'Get thee behind me, Satan: for it is written, Thou shalt worship the Lord thy God, and him only shalt thou sere" (Luke 4:8). Not GE, Bishops, DR, Coverdale, Tyndale, GT "hence from me." Coverdale "Avoid thou from me, Satan." "Then said Jesus unto him,

That Evil One, Satan for ever damned."
To whom the Fiend, with fear abashed, replied.
"Be not so sore offended, Son of God;
Though Sons of God both Angels are and Men,[35]
If I, to try whether in higher sort
Than these thou bear'st that title, have proposed
What both from Men and Angels I receive,
Tetrarchs[36] of Fire, Air, Flood, and on the Earth
Nations besides from all the quartered winds—

'Avoid Satan: for it is written, Thou shalt worship the Lord thy God, and him only shalt thou serve" (Matthew 4:10). AV "get thee hence." DR "begone, Satan." Compare with Jesus's rebuke of Peter: "Then he turned back, and said unto Peter, 'Get thee behind me, Satan: thou art an offence unto me, because thou understandeth not the things that are of God, but the things that are of men'" (Matthew 16:23, GE [see also AV]). Bishops and GT "go after me Satan." Tyndale "come after me Satan." "Avoid from me Satan" Coverdale. "Go behind me, Satan" DR.

[35] [Lines 195–197] "I have said, 'Ye are gods, and ye all are children of the most High'" (Psalm 82:6). "Now on a day when the children of God came and stood before the Lord, Satan came also among them [...] Again there was a day when the sons of God came to present themselves before the Lord, and Satan came also among them to present himself before the Lord" (Job 1:6; 2:1, AV). "GE, Bishops, DR, GT, Coverdale, Tyndale "children of God." Geneva note on "children of God": "That is, the angels." "Yet the number of the children of Israel shall be as the sand of the sea, which cannot be measured nor told: and in the place where it was said unto them, 'Ye are not my people, it shall be said unto them, 'Ye are the sons of the living God" (Hosea 1:10). Bishops, GT, Tyndale "children of God." "There were giants in the earth in those days: yea, and after that the sons of God came unto the daughters of men, and they had born them children, these were mighty men, which in old time were men of renown" (Genesis 6:4). Coverdale and Tyndale "children of God." "But as many as received him, to them he gave prerogative to be the sons of God, even to them that believe in his Name" (John 1:12). Coverdale "children of God." "For as many as are led by the Spirit of God, they are the sons of God" (Romans 8:14). Coverdale "children of God." "When the morning stars sang together, and all the sons of God shouted for joy" (Job 38:7, AV [see also DR]). GT "angels of God." GE, Bishops, Tyndale, Coverdale "children of God."

[36] "At that time Herod the Tetrarch heard of the fame of Jesus" (Matthew 14:1).

God of this World[37] invoked, and World beneath.
Who then thou art, whose coming[38] is foretold
To me most fatal, me it most concerns.
The trial hath indamaged thee no way,
Rather more honor left and more esteem;
Me naught advantaged, missing what I aimed.
Therefore let pass, as they are transitory,
The kingdoms of this world;[39] I shall no more
Advise thee; gain them as thou canst, or not.
And thou thyself seem'st otherwise inclined
Than to a worldly crown,[40] addicted more
To contemplation and profound dispute;
As by that early action may be judged,
When, slipping from thy mother's eye, thou went'st
Alone into the Temple, there wast found
Among the gravest Rabbies,[41] disputant

---

[37] Satan as the "God of this World": "In whom the God of this world hath blinded the minds, that is, of the infidels, that the light of the glorious Gospel of Christ, which is the image of God, should not shine unto them" (2 Corinthians 4:4).

[38] The "coming" or advent of Jesus foretold. "And as he sat upon the mount of Olives, his disciples came unto him apart, saying, 'Tell us when these things shall be, and what sign shall be of thy coming, and of the end of the world'" (Matthew 24:3, GE).

[39] [Lines 209–210] Transitory kingdoms of the world. "And we speak wisdom among them that are perfect: not the wisdom of this world, neither of the princes of this world, which come to nought" (1 Corinthians 2:6).

[40] Jesus refuses to be a king, while on earth. "When Jesus therefore perceived that they would come, and take him to make him a King, he departed again into a mountain himself alone" (John 6:15). "Jesus answered, 'My kingdom is not of this world: if my kingdom were of this world, my servants would surely fight, that I should not be delivered to the Jews: but now is my kingdom not from hence" (John 13:36).

[41] [Lines 215–218] "And had finished the days thereof, as they returned, the child Jesus remained in Jerusalem, and Joseph knew not, nor his mother [...] And it came to pass three days after, that they found him in the Temple, sitting in the midst of the doctors, both hearing them, and asking them questions: And all that

On points and questions fitting Moses' chair,[42]
Teaching, not taught. The childhood shews the man,
As morning shews the day.[43] Be famous, then,
By wisdom;[44] as thy empire must extend,
So let extend thy mind o'er all the world
In knowledge;[45] all things in it comprehend.[46]
All knowledge is not couched in Moses' law,
The Pentateuch, or what the Prophets wrote;[47]

---

heard him, were astonished at his understanding and answers" (Luke 2:43, 46, 47). Coverdale "in the midst of the Teachers."

[42] Moses' chair. "Then spake Jesus to the multitude, and to his disciples, Saying, 'The Scribes and the Pharisees sit in Moses' seat" (Matthew 23:1, 2). "Now on the morrow, when Moses sat to judge the people, the people stood about Moses from morning unto evening. And when Moses' father in law saw all that he did to the people, he said, 'What is this that thou dost to the people? Why sittest thou thyself alone, and all the people stand about thee from morning unto evening?' And Moses said unto his father-in-law, 'Because the people come unto me to seek God. When they have a matter, they come unto me, and I judge between one and another, and declare the ordinances of God, and his laws" (Exodus 18:13–16).

[43] As morning shows the day. "And in the morning ye say, 'Today shall be a tempest: for the sky is red and lowering. O hypocrites, ye can discern the face of the sky, and can ye not discern the signs of the times" (Matthew 16:3).

[44] [Lines 220–222] Even as a child, Jesus showed great wisdom: "And Jesus increased in wisdom, and stature, and in favor with God and men" (Luke 2:52).

[45] [Lines 223–224] So let extend thy mind o'er all the world / In knowledge. "Then shall none hurt nor destroy in all the mountain of mine holiness: for the earth shall be full of the knowledge of the Lord, as the waters that cover the sea" (Isaiah 11:9).

[46] In knowledge; all things in it comprehend. Satan tempts Jesus with academic knowledge, yet the Bible describes the transitory nature of human knowledge: "Love doth never fall away, though that prophesyings be abolished, or the tongues cease, or knowledge vanish away" (1 Corinthians 13:8). "For the wisdom of this world is foolishness with God: for it is written, 'He catcheth the wise in their own craftiness.' And again, 'The Lord knoweth that the thoughts of the wise be vain'" (1 Corinthians 3:19, 20).

[47] [Lines 225–226] Contrast with what Jesus says summed up the Law and the Prophets: "Therefore whatsoever ye would that men should do to you, even so do ye to them: for this is the Law and the Prophets" (Matthew 7:12).

The Gentiles also know, and write, and teach
To admiration, led by Nature's light;
And with the Gentiles much thou must converse,
Ruling them by persuasion,[48] as thou mean'st.
Without their learning, how wilt thou with them,
Or they with thee, hold conversation meet?
How wilt thou reason with them, how refute
Their idolisms, traditions, paradoxes?
Error by his own arms is best evinced.
Look once more, ere we leave this specular mount,
Westward, much nearer by south-west; behold
Where on the AEgean shore a city stands,
Built nobly, pure the air and light the soil,
Athens, the eye of Greece, mother of arts
And Eloquence, native to famous wits
Or hospitable, in her sweet recess,
City or suburban, studious walks and shades.
See there the olive-grove of Academe,
Plato's retirement, where the Attic bird
Trills her thick-warbled notes the summer long;
There, flowery hill, Hymettus, with the sound
Of bees' industrious murmur, oft invites
To studious musing; there Ilissus rowls
His whispering stream. Within the walls then view
The schools of ancient sages; his who bred
Great Alexander[49] to subdue the world,

---

[48] Compare with Paul in Corinth: "And he went into the synagogue, and spoke boldly for the space of three months, disputing & persuading those things that appertain to the kingdom of God" (Acts 19:8, Bishops [see also AV]). "Disputing and exhorting" GE, DR, GT, Tyndale. "Teaching and giving them exhortations" Coverdale.

[49] Great Alexander. "And as I considered, behold, a goat came from the West over the whole earth, and touched not the ground: and this goat had an horn that appeared between his eyes [...] Therefore the goat waxed exceeding great, and when he was at the strongest, his great horn was broken: and for it came up four that appeared toward the four winds of ye heaven [...] And I heard a man's

Lyceum there; and painted Stoa next.
There thou shalt hear and learn the secret power
Of harmony, in tones and numbers hit
By voice or hand, and various-measured verse,
AEolian charms and Dorian lyric odes,
And his who gave them breath, but higher sung,
Blind Melesigenes, thence Homer called,
Whose poem Phoebus challenged for his own.
Thence what the lofty grave Tragedians taught
In chorus or iambic, teachers best
Of moral prudence, with delight received
In brief sententious precepts, while they treat
Of fate, and chance, and change in human life,
High actions and high passions best describing.
Thence to the famous Orators repair,
Those ancient whose resistless eloquence
Wielded at will that fierce democraty,
Shook the Arsenal,[50] and fulmined over Greece

---

voice between the banks of Ulai, which called, and said, 'Gabriel, make this man to understand the vision.' So he came where I stood: and when he came, I was afraid, and fell upon my face: but he said unto me, Understand, O son of man: for in the last time shall be the vision.' Now as he was speaking unto me, I being asleep fell on my face to the ground: but he touched me, and set me up in my place [...] 'And the goat is the King of Greece, and the great horn that is between his eyes, is the first King" (Daniel 8:5, 8, 16–18, 21). Geneva note: "Meaning Alexander that came from Greece with great speed and warlike undertaking. Even though he came in the name of all of Greece, yet he bore the title and dignity of the general captain, so that the strength was attributed to him, which is meant by this horn."

[50] Shook the arsenal. Compare: "They that see thee, shall look upon thee and consider thee, saying, 'Is this the man that made the earth to tremble, and that did shake the kingdoms?" (Isaiah 14:16). "He stretched out his hand upon the sea: he shook the kingdoms: the Lord hath given a commandment concerning the place of merchandise, to destroy the power thereof" (Isaiah 23:11). "I made the nations to shake at the sound of his fall, when I cast him down to hell with them that descend into the pit, & all the excellent trees of Eden, and the best of Lebanon: even all that are nourished with waters, shall be comforted in the

To Macedon and Artaxerxes' throne.
To sage Philosophy[51] next lend thine ear,
From heaven descended to the low-roofed house
Of Socrates—see there his tenement,
Whom, well inspired, the Oracle pronounced
Wisest of men; from whose mouth issued forth
Mellifluous streams, that watered all the schools
Of Academics old and new, with those
Surnamed Peripatetics, and the sect
Epicurean, and the Stoic severe.
These here revolve, or, as thou likest, at home,
Till time mature thee to a kingdom's weight;
These rules will render thee a king complete
Within thyself, much more with empire joined."
To whom our Saviour sagely thus replied.
"Think not but that I know these things; or, think
I know them not, not therefore am I short
Of knowing what I ought. He who receives
Light from above, from the Fountain of Light,
No other doctrine needs,[52] though granted true;

---

nether parts of the earth" (Ezekiel 31:16). "For thus saith the Lord of hosts: yet once more will I shake heaven and earth, the sea, and the dry land" (Haggai 2:7, GT [see also AV]). GE, Bishops, Coverdale, DR "move heaven and earth."

[51] Philosophy or literally "love of wisdom." Compare with Solomon's personification of wisdom as a woman: "Get wisdom: get understanding: forget not, neither decline from the words of my mouth. Forsake her not, and she shall keep thee: love her and she shall preserve thee. Wisdom is the beginning: get wisdom therefore: and above all thy possession get understanding. Exalt her, and she shall exalt thee: she shall bring thee to honor, if thou embrace her" (Proverbs 4:5–8). "But ye are of him in Christ Jesus, who of God is made unto us wisdom and righteousness, and sanctification, and redemption" (1 Corinthians 1:30). "Seeing also that the Jews require a sign, and the Greeks seek after wisdom" (1 Corinthians 1:22). Compare with Paul's encounter with certain philosophers: "Then certain Philosophers of the Epicureans, and of the Stoics, disputed with him, and some said, 'What will this babbler say?' Others said, 'He seemeth to be a setter forth of strange gods (because he preached unto them Jesus, and the resurrection)" (Acts 17:18).

But these are false, or little else but dreams,
Conjectures, fancies, built on nothing firm.
The first and wisest of them all professed
To know this only, that he nothing knew;
The next to fabling fell and smooth conceits;
A third sort doubted all things, though plain sense;
Others in virtue placed felicity,
But virtue joined with riches and long life;
In corporal pleasure he, and careless ease;
The Stoic last in philosophic pride,
By him called virtue, and his virtuous man,
Wise, perfect in himself, and all possessing,
Equal to God, oft shames not to prefer,
As fearing God nor man, contemning all
Wealth, pleasure, pain or torment, death and life,

---

[52] [288–290] That is to say, more learning is not necessary. Light from above: "Every good giving, and every perfect gift is from above, and cometh down from the Father of lights, with whom is no variableness, neither shadow of turning" (James 1:17). "For with thee is the well of life, and in thy light shall we see light" (Psalm 36:9). "And of other things beside these, my son, take thou heed: for there is no end in making many books, and much reading is a weariness of the flesh" (Ecclesiastes 12:12). "For the wisdom of this world is foolishness with God: for it is written, 'He catcheth the wise in their own craftiness" (1 Corinthians 3:19). "If any of you lack wisdom, let him ask of God, which giveth to all men liberally, & reproacheth no man, and it shall be given him" (James 1:5). "This wisdom descendeth not from above, but is earthly, sensual, and devilish. For where envying and strife is, there is sedition, and all manner of evil works. But the wisdom that is from above, is first pure, then peaceable, gentle, easy to be entreated, full of mercy & good fruits, without judging, and without hypocrisy" (James 3:15–17). "For it is written, I will destroy the wisdom of the wise, and will cast away the understanding of the prudent. Where is the wise? where is the Scribe? where is the disputer of this world? hath not God made the wisdom of this world foolishness? For seeing the world by wisdom knew not God in the wisdom of God, it pleased God by the foolishness of preaching to save them that believe" (1 Corinthians 1:19–21). "Which things also we speak, not in the words which mans wisdom teacheth, but which the holy Ghost teacheth, comparing spiritual things with spiritual things" (1 Corinthians 2:13).

Which, when he lists, he leaves, or boasts he can;
For all his tedious talk is but vain boast,
Or subtle shifts conviction to evade.
Alas! what can they teach, and not mislead,
Ignorant of themselves, of God much more,[53]
And how the World began, and how Man fell,
Degraded by himself, on grace depending?
Much of the Soul they talk, but all awry;
And in themselves seek virtue; and to themselves
All glory arrogate, to God give none;[54]
Rather accuse him under usual names,
Fortune and Fate, as one regardless quite
Of mortal things. Who, therefore, seeks in these
True wisdom finds her not, or, by delusion

---

[53] [Lines 309–310] Compare with Paul among the philosophers at the Athenian Areopagus: "Then Paul stood in the midst of Mars street, and said, 'Ye men of Athens, I perceive that in all things ye are too superstitious. For as I passed by, and beheld your devotions, I found an altar wherein was written, Unto The Unknown God. Whom ye then ignorantly worship, him show I unto you. God that made the world, and all things that are therein, seeing that he is Lord of heaven and earth, dwelleth not in temples made with hands, Neither is worshipped with men's hands, as though he needed anything, seeing he giveth to all life and breath and all things, And hath made of one blood all mankind, to dwell on all the face of the earth, and hath assigned the seasons which were ordained before, and the bounds of their habitation, That they should seek the Lord, if so be they might have groped after him, and found him though doubtless he be not far from everyone of us. For in him we live, and move, and have our being, as also certain of your own Poets have said, for we are also his generation. Forasmuch then, as we are the generation of God, we ought not to think that the Godhead is like unto gold, or silver, or stone graven by art and the invention of man. And the time of this ignorance God regarded not: but now he admonisheth all men everywhere to repent'" (Acts 17:22–30).

[54] [Lines 314–315] "He that speaketh of himself, seeketh his own glory: but he that seeketh his glory that sent him, the same is true, and no unrighteousness is in him" (John 7:18). "That, according as it is written, 'He that rejoiceth, let him rejoice in the Lord'" (1 Corinthians 1:31). "Not that we are sufficient of ourselves, to think anything, as of ourselves: but our sufficiency is of God" (2 Corinthians 3:5).

Far worse, her false resemblance only meets,
An empty cloud. However, many books,
Wise men have said, are wearisome;[55] who reads
Incessantly, and to his reading brings not
A spirit and judgment equal or superior,
(And what he brings what needs he elsewhere seek?)
Uncertain and unsettled still remains,
Deep-versed in books and shallow in himself,
Crude or intoxicate, collecting toys
And trifles for choice matters, worth a sponge,
As children gathering pebbles on the shore.
Or, if I would delight my private hours
With music or with poem, where so soon
As in our native language can I find
That solace? All our Law and Story strewed
With hymns, our Psalms with artful terms inscribed,[56]

---

[55] [Lines 321–322] "And of other things beside these, my son, take thou heed: for there is no end in making many books, and much reading is a weariness of the flesh" (Ecclesiastes 12:12). Geneva note: "These things cannot be comprehended in books or learned by study, but God must instruct your heart that you may only know that wisdom is the true happiness and the way to it is to fear God."

[56] Consider the artful terms used by Jacob to describe the lives of his sons who would become the patriarchs of Israel's twelve tribes: "Judah, as a Lion's whelp shalt thou come up from the spoil, my son. He shall lie down and couch as a Lion, and as a Lioness: Who shall stir him up? […] He shall bind his Ass foal unto the vine, and his Ass's colt unto the best vine. he shall wash his garment in wine, and his cloak in the blood of grapes […] Issachar shall be a strong ass, couching down between two burdens: […] Dan shall be a serpent by the way, an adder by the path, biting the horse heels, so that his rider shall fall backward […] Concerning Asher, his bread shall be fat, and he shall give pleasures for a king. Naphtali shall be a hind let go, giving goodly words. Joseph shall be a fruitful bough, even a fruitful bough by the well side: the small boughs shall run upon the wall. […] Benjamin shall ravine as a wolf: in the morning he shall devour the prey, and at night he shall divide the spoil" (Genesis 49:9, 11, 14, 17, 20–22, 27). The song of Moses: "Hearken, ye heavens, and I will speak: and let the earth hear the words of my mouth. My doctrine shall drop as the rain, and my speech shall still as the dew, as the shower upon the herbs, and as the great rain upon the

Our Hebrew songs[57] and harps, in Babylon[58]
That pleased so well our victor's ear, declare

---

grass" (Deuteronomy 32:1, 2). The song of Deborah "Then sang Deborah, and Barak the son of Abinoam the same day, saying, 'Praise ye the Lord for the avenging of Israel, and for the people that offered themselves willingly. Hear, ye Kings, hearken ye princes: I, even I will sing unto the Lord: I will sing praise unto the Lord God of Israel'" (Judges 5:1–3). "And David spake the words of this song unto the Lord, what time the Lord had delivered him out of the hands of all his enemies, and out of the hand of Saul. And he said, 'The Lord is my rock and my fortress, and he that delivereth me. God is my strength, in him will I trust: my shield, and the horn of my salvation, my high tower and my refuge: my Savior, thou hast saved me from violence" (2 Samuel 22:1–3). King David's song of rejoicing when the Ark of the Covenant finally arrived in Jerusalem: "Let the heavens rejoice, and let the earth be glad, and let them say among the nations, The Lorde reigneth. Let the sea roar, and all that therein is: Let the field be joyful and all that is in it. Let the trees of the wood then rejoice at the presence of the Lord: for he cometh to judge the earth'" (1 Chronicles 16:31–33). The song of King Hezekiah upon recovering from a deadly illness and having his life extended by God: "I said in the cutting off of my days, I shall go to the gates of the grave: I am deprived of the residue of my years. I said, I shall not see the Lord, even the Lord in the land of the living: I shall see man no more among the inhabitants of the world. Mine habitation is departed, and is removed from me, like a shepherd's tent: I have cut off like a weaver my life: he will cut me off from the height: from day to night, thou wilt make an end of me. I reckoned to the morning: but he broke all my bones, like a lion: from day to night wilt thou make an end of me. Like a crane or a swallow, so did I chatter: I did mourn as a dove: mine eyes were lift up on high: O Lord, it hath oppressed me, comfort me" (Isaiah 38:10–14).

[57] [Lines 334–336] "And his brothers name was Jubal, who was the father of all that play on the harp and organs. And Zillah also bore Tubal-cain, who wrought cunningly every craft of brass and of iron: and the sister of Tubal-cain was Naamah. Then Lamech said unto his wives Adah and Zillah, 'Hear my voice, ye wives of Lamech: hearken unto my speech: for I would slay a man in my wound, and a young man in mine hurt. If Cain shall be avenged seven-fold, truly Lamech, seventy times seven-fold'" (Genesis 4:21–24).

[58] Harps in Babylon. "By the rivers of Babylon we sat, and there we wept, when we remembered Zion. We hanged our harps upon the willows in the midst thereof. Then they that led us captives, required of us songs and mirth, when we had hanged up our harps, saying, 'Sing us one of the songs of Zion'" (Psalm 137:1–3).

That rather Greece from us these arts derived;
Ill imitated while they loudest sing
The vices of their deities, and their own,
In fable, hymn, or song, so personating
Their gods ridiculous, and themselves past shame.
Remove their swelling epithetes, thick-laid[59]
As varnish on a harlot's cheek, the rest,
Thin-sown with aught of profit or delight,
Will far be found unworthy to compare
With Sion's songs, to all true tastes excelling,
Where God is praised aright and godlike men,
The Holiest of Holies and his Saints
Such are from God inspired,[60] not such from thee;
Unless where moral virtue is expressed
By light of Nature, not in all quite lost.[61]
Their orators thou then extoll'st as those
The top of eloquence, statists indeed,
And lovers of their country, as may seem;
But herein to our Prophets far beneath,
As men divinely taught,[62] and better teaching

---

[59] [Lines 340–343] Their swelling epithets, thick laid. "These are murmurers complainers, walking after their own lusts, and their mouth speaketh great swelling words, having men's persons in admiration because of advantage" (Jude 16, AV). "Proud words" (GE, Bishops, GT, DR, Coverdale, Tyndale).

[60] God inspired. "For the whole Scripture is given by inspiration of God, and is profitable to teach, to convince, to correct, and to instruct in righteousness, that the man of God may be absolute, being made perfect unto all good works" (2 Timothy 3:16). "For the prophecy came not in old time by the will of man: but holy men of God spoke as they were moved by the holy Ghost" (2 Peter 1:21).

[61] By light of Nature, not in all quite lost. "For when the Gentiles which have not the Law, do by nature, the things contained in the Law, they having not the Law, are a Law unto themselves, Which show the effect of the Law written in their hearts, their conscience also bearing witness, and their thoughts accusing one another, or excusing)" (Romans 2:14, 15).

[62] [Lines 356–357] "At the same time, saith the Lord, will I be the God of all the families of Israel, and they shall be my people. Thus saith the Lord, The people which escaped the sword, found grace in the wilderness: he walked before Israel

The solid rules of civil government,
In their majestic, unaffected style,
Than all the oratory of Greece and Rome.
In them is plainest taught, and easiest learnt,
What makes a nation happy, and keeps it so,[63]
What ruins kingdoms, and lays cities flat;[64]
These only, with our Law, best form a king."
So spake the Son of God; but Satan, now
Quite at a loss (for all his darts[65] were spent),
Thus to our Saviour, with stern brow, replied.
"Since neither wealth nor honor, arms nor arts,

---

to cause him to rest. The Lord hath appeared unto me of old, say they: 'Yea, I have loved thee with an everlasting love, therefore with mercy I have drawn thee. Again I will build thee, and thou shalt be built, O virgin Israel: thou shalt still be adorned with thy timbrels, and shalt go forth in the dance of them that be joyful'" (Jeremiah 31:1–4). "Whom the heaven must contain until the time that all things be restored, which God had spoken by the mouth of all his holy Prophets since the world began" (Acts 3:21). "Surely the Lord God will do nothing, but he revealed his secret unto his servants the Prophets" (Amos 3:7). "At sundry times and in divers manners God spake in the old time to our fathers by the Prophets: in these last days he hath spoken unto us by his Son" (Hebrews 1:1). "It is written in the Prophets, And they shall be all taught of God. Every man therefore that hath heard, and hath learned of the Father, cometh unto me" (John 6:45). "And he began at Moses, & at all the Prophets, and interpreted unto them in all the Scriptures the things which were written of him" (Luke 24:27).

[63] [Lines 361–362] "Wisdom resteth in the heart of him that hath understanding, and is known in the midst of fools. Justice exalteth a nation, but sin is a shame to the people" (Proverbs 14:34).

[64] What ruins kingdoms and lays cities flat. Consider Jericho: "And when they make a long blast with the rams horn, and ye hear the sound of the trumpet, all the people shall shout with a great shout: then shall the wall of the city fall down flat, and the people shall ascend up, every man straight before him [...] So the people shouted, when they had blown trumpets: for when the people had heard the sound of the trumpet, they shouted with a great shout: and the wall fell down flat: so the people went up into the city, every man straight before him: and they took the city" (Joshua 6:5, 20).

[65] Satan's "darts." "Above all, take the shield of faith, wherewith ye may quench all the fiery darts of the wicked" (Ephesians 6:16).

Kingdom nor empire, pleases thee, nor aught
By me proposed in life contemplative
Or active, tended on by glory or fame,
What dost thou in this world? The Wilderness
For thee is fittest place: I found thee there,
And thither will return thee. Yet remember
What I foretell thee; soon thou shalt have cause
To wish thou never hadst rejected, thus
Nicely or cautiously, my offered aid,
Which would have set thee in short time with ease[66]
On David's throne, or throne of all the world,
Now at full age,[67] fulness of time,[68] thy season,
When prophecies of thee are best fulfilled.
Now, contrary, if I read aught in heaven,
Or heaven write aught of fate—by what the stars
Voluminous, or single characters
In their conjunction met, give me to spell,[69]

---

[66] Note the response of Jesus to Peter when he suggested that Jesus should ease up. "From that time forth Jesus began to show unto his disciples, that he must go unto Jerusalem, and suffer many things of the Elders, and of the high Priests, and Scribes, and be slain, and be raised again the third day. Then Peter took him aside, and began to rebuke him, saying, 'Master, pity thyself: this shall not be unto thee.' Then he turned back, and said unto Peter, 'Get thee behind me, Satan: thou art an offence unto me, because thou understandest not the things that are of God, but the things that are of men.' Jesus then said to his disciples, 'If any man will follow me, let him forsake himself: and take up his cross, and follow me'" (Matthew 16:21–24).

[67] "And Jesus himself began to be about thirty year of age, being as men supposed the son of Joseph, which was the son of Eli" (Luke 3:23).

[68] "But when the fullness of time was come, God sent forth his Son made of a woman, and made under the Law" (Galatians 4:4).

[69] [Lines 382–385] Satan predicts the future by astrology which the Bible condemns. Notice the language of derision in Isaiah's strong denunciation of the magic practicing diviners of the Chaldeans: "Therefore shall evil come upon thee, and thou shalt not know the morning thereof: destruction shall fall upon thee, which thou shalt not be able to put away: destruction shall come upon thee suddenly, or thou beware. Stand now among thine enchanters, and in the

Sorrows and labours, opposition, hate,
Attends thee; scorns, reproaches, injuries,
Violence and stripes, and, lastly, cruel death.[70]

---

multitude of thy soothsayers (with whom thou hast wearied thy self from thy youth) if so be thou mayest have profit, or if so be thou mayest have strength. Thou art wearied in the multitude of thy counsels: let now the astrologers, the star gazers, and prognosticators stand up, & save thee from these things, that shall come upon thee" (Isaiah 47:11–13). "Hear ye the word of the Lord that he speaketh unto you, O house of Israel. Thus saith the Lord, Learn not the way of the heathen, & be not afraid for the signs of heaven, though the heathen be afraid of such" (Jeremiah 10:1, 2). Geneva note: "God forbids his people to give credit or fear the constellations and conjunctions of stars and planets which have no power of themselves but are governed by him, and their secret motions and influences are not known to man and therefore there can be no certain judgment of it."

[70] [Lines 386–388] The description of Jesus as the suffering and rejected Messiah foretold by Isaiah. "He is despised and rejected of men: he is a man full of sorrows and hath experience of infirmities: we hide as it were our faces from him: he was despised and we esteemed him not. Surely he hath born our infirmities, and caried our sorrows: yet we did judge him, as plagued, and smitten of God, and humbled. But he was wounded for our transgressions, he was broken for our iniquities: the chastisement of our peace was upon him, and with his stripes we are healed. All we like sheep have gone astray: we have turned every one to his own way, and the Lord hath laid upon him the iniquity of us all. He was oppressed and he was afflicted, yet did he not open his mouth: he is brought as a sheep to the slaughter, and as a sheep before her shearer is dumb, so he openeth He was taken out from prison, and from judgment: and who shall declare his age? For he was cut out of the land of the living: for the transgression of my people was he plagued. And he made his grave with the wicked, and with the rich in his death, though he had done no wickedness, neither was any deceit in his mouth. Yet the Lord would break him, and make him subject to infirmities: when he shall make his soul an offering for sin, he shall see his seed and shall prolong his days, and the will of the Lord shall prosper in his hand" (Isaiah 53:3–10). "And platted a crown of thorns, and put it upon his head, and a reed in his right hand, and bowed their knees before him, and mocked him, saying, 'God save thee King of the Jews' [...] And they that passed by, reviled him, wagging their heads" (Matthew 27:29, 39). "Let Christ the King of Israel now come down from the cross, that we may see, and believe. They also that were crucified with him, reviled him" (Mark 15:32). "And shall

A kingdom they portend thee, but what kingdom,
Real or allegoric, I discern not;
Nor when: eternal sure—as without end,
Without beginning; for no date prefixed[71]
Directs me in the starry rubric set."
So saying, he took (for still he knew his power
Not yet expired), and to the Wilderness
Brought back, the Son of God, and left him there,[72]
Feigning to disappear. Darkness now rose,
As daylight sunk, and brought in louring Night,
Her shadowy offspring, unsubstantial both,
Privation mere of light and absent day.
Our Saviour, meek, and with untroubled mind
After hisaerie jaunt, though hurried sore,
Hungry and cold, betook him to his rest,
Wherever, under some concourse of shades,
Whose branching arms thick intertwined might shield
From dews and damps of night his sheltered head;
But, sheltered, slept in vain; for at his head
The Tempter[73] watched, and soon with ugly dreams

---

deliver him to the Gentiles, to mock, and to scourge, and to crucify him, but the third day he shall rise again" (Matthew 20:19).

[71] [Lines 391–392] Perhaps unwittingly, Satan aptly describes the role of Jesus as a High Priest in the order of Melchizedek as does the author of Hebrews: "For this Melchizedek was King of Salem, the Priest of the most high God, who met Abraham, as he returned from the slaughter of the Kings, and blessed him: To whom also Abraham gave the tithe of all things: who first is by interpretation King of righteousness: after that, he is also King of Salem, that is, King of peace, Without father, without mother, without kindred, and hath neither beginning of his days, neither end of life: but is likened unto the Son of God, and continueth a Priest forever [...] For he testifieth thus, Thou art a Priest forever, after the order of Melchizedek [...] For he testifieth thus, Thou art a Priest forever, after the order of Melchizedek [...] But this man, because he endureth ever, hath a Priesthood, which cannot pass from one to another" (Hebrews 7:1–3, 17, 24).

[72] Left him there. "Then the devil left him: and behold, the Angels came, and ministered unto him" (Matthew 4:11). "And when the devil had ended all the temptation, he departed from him for a little season" (Luke 4:13).

Disturbed his sleep. And either tropic now
'Gan thunder, and both ends of heaven; the clouds
From many a horrid rift abortive poured
Fierce rain with lightning mixed, water with fire,
In ruin reconciled; nor slept the winds[74]
Within their stony caves, but rushed abroad
From the four hinges of the world, and fell
On the vexed wilderness, whose tallest pines,
Though rooted deep as high, and sturdiest oaks,
Bowed their stiff necks, loaden with stormy blasts,
Or torn up sheer. Ill wast thou shrouded then,
O patient Son of God, yet only stood'st
Unshaken![75] Nor yet staid the terror[76] there:

---

[73] Satan The Tempter. "Then came to him the tempter, and said, If thou be the Sonne of God, command that these stones be made bread" (Matthew 4:3). "Even for this cause, when I could no longer forbear, I sent him that I might know of your faith, lest the tempter had tempted you in any sort, and that our labor had been in vain" (1 Thessalonians 3:5). "He that tempteth" DR.

[74] Nor slept the winds. "Wherein, in times past ye walked, according to the course of this world, and after the prince that ruleth in the air, even the spirit, that now worketh in the children of disobedience" (Ephesians 2:2). God can judge and is in control even during storms, despite the ill reasoning of Satan which resonates with the claim Eliphaz one of the false-comforters of Job. "But thou sayest, 'How should God know? can he judge through the dark cloud? The clouds hide him that he cannot see, and he walketh in the circle of heaven'" (Job 22:13, 14).

[75] [Lines 419–421] The composure of Jesus during horrific storms. "And when he was entered into the ship, his disciples followed him And behold, there arose a great tempest in the sea, so that the ship was covered with waves: but he was asleep. Then his disciples came, and awoke him, saying, 'Master, save us: we perish.' And he said unto them, 'Why are ye fearful, O ye of little faith? Then he arose, & rebuked the winds & the sea: & so there was a great calm" (Matthew 8:23–26). "And they left the multitude, and took him as he was in the ship, and there were also with him other little ships. And there arose a great storm of wind, and the waves dashed into the ship, so that it was now full. And he was in the stern asleep on a pillow: and they awoke him, and said to him, 'Master, carest thou not that we perish?' And he rose up, and rebuked the wind, and said unto the sea, 'Peace, and be still.' So the wind ceased, and it was a great calm" (Mark

Infernal ghosts and hellish furies round
Environed thee; some howled, some yelled, some shrieked,
Some bent at thee their fiery darts,[77] while thou
Sat'st unappalled in calm and sinless peace.[78]
Thus passed the night so foul, till Morning fair
Came forth with pilgrim steps, in amice grey,
Who with her radiant finger stilled the roar
Of thunder, chased the clouds, and laid the winds,
And griesly spectres, which the Fiend had raised
To tempt the Son of God with terrors dire.
And now the sun with more effectual beams
Had cheered the face of earth, and dried the wet
From drooping plant, or dropping tree; the birds,
Who all things now behold more fresh and green,
After a night of storm so ruinous,
Cleared up their choicest notes in bush and spray,
To gratulate the sweet return of morn.
Nor yet, amidst this joy and brightest morn,

4:36–39). "And it came to pass on a certain day, that he went into a ship with his disciples, and he said unto them, Let us go over unto the other side of the lake; they launched forth. And as they sailed, he fell asleep, and there came down a storm of wind on the lake, and they were filled with water, and were in jeopardy. Then they went to him, and awoke him, saying, 'Master, Master, we perish;' he arose, and rebuked the wind, and the waves of water: and they ceased, and it was calm" (Luke 8:22–25).

[76] "Thou shalt not be afraid of the fear of the night, nor of the arrow that flyeth by day: Nor of the pestilence that walketh in the darkness: nor of the plague that destroyeth at noon day" (Psalm 91:5).

[77] Fiery darts. "Above all, take the shield of faith, wherewith ye may quench all the fiery darts of the wicked" (Ephesians 6:16).

[78] "By an assured purpose wilt thou preserve perfect peace, because they trusted in thee" (Isaiah 26:3). "But now in Christ Jesus, ye which once were far off, are made near by the blood of Christ. For he is our peace, which hath made of both one, and hath broken the stop of the partition wall, in abrogating through his flesh the hatred, that is, the Law of commandments which standeth in ordinances, for to make of twain one new man in himself, so making peace" (Ephesians 2:14).

Was absent, after all his mischief done,
The Prince of Darkness;[79] glad would also seem
Of this fair change, and to our Saviour came;
Yet with no new device[80] (they all were spent),
Rather by this his last affront resolved,
Desperate of better course, to vent his rage[81]
And mad despite to be so oft repelled.
Him walking on a sunny hill he found,
Backed on the north and west by a thick wood;
Out of the wood he starts in wonted shape,
And in a careless mood thus to him said.
"Fair morning yet betides thee, Son of God,
After a dismal night. I heard the wrack,
As earth and sky would mingle; but myself
Was distant; and these flaws, though mortals fear them,
As dangerous to the pillared frame of Heaven,[82]
Or to the Earth's dark basis underneath,
Are to the main as inconsiderable
And harmless, if not wholesome, as a sneeze
To man's less universe, and soon are gone.
Yet, as being ofttimes noxious where they light
On man, beast, plant, wasteful and turbulent,

---

[79] The Prince of Darkness. "For we wrestle not against flesh and blood, but against principalities, against powers, and against the worldly governors, the princes of the darkness of this world, against spiritual wickedness, which are in the high places" (Ephesians 6:12, GE). Not AV, DR, Coverdale, GT, Tyndale "rulers of darkness." Bishops "governors of darkness."

[80] Satan's devices. "Lest Satan should get an advantage of vs: for wee are not ignorant of his devices" (2 Corinthians 2:11, AV [see also DR]). Not GE "enterprises." Not Coverdale, Bishops, Tyndale, GT "thoughts."

[81] The rage of Satan. "Therefore rejoice, ye heavens, and ye that dwell in them. Woe to the inhabitants of the earth, and of the sea: for the devil is come down unto you, which hath great wrath, knowing that he hath but a short time" (Revelation 12:12).

[82] The pillared frame of Heaven. "The pillars of heaven tremble and quake at his reproof" (Job 26:11).

Like turbulencies in the affairs of men,
Over whose heads they roar, and seem to point,
They oft fore-signify and threaten ill.
This tempest at this desert most was bent;
Of men at thee, for only thou here dwell'st.
Did I not tell thee, if thou didst reject
The perfect season offered with my aid
To win thy destined seat, but wilt prolong
All to the push of fate, pursue thy way
Of gaining David's throne no man knows when
(For both the when and how is nowhere told),
Thou shalt be what thou art ordained, no doubt;
For Angels have proclaimed it, but concealing
The time and means? Each act is rightliest done
Not when it must, but when it may be best.
If thou observe not this, be sure to find
What I foretold thee, many a hard assay
Of dangers, and adversities, and pains,
Ere thou of Israel's sceptre[83] get fast hold;
Whereof this ominous night that closed thee round,
So many terrors, voices, prodigies,
May warn thee, as a sure foregoing sign."
So talked he, while the Son of God went on,
And staid not, but in brief him answered thus.
"Me worse than wet thou find'st not; other harm
Those terrors which thou speak'st of did me none.
I never feared they could, though noising loud
And threatening nigh: what they can do as signs
Betokening or ill-boding I contemn
As false portents, not sent from God, but thee;
Who, knowing I shall reign past thy preventing,

[83] Israel's scepter. "Thy throne, O God, is forever and ever: the scepter of thy kingdom is a scepter of righteousness" (Psalm 45:6). "But unto the Son he saith, 'O God, thy throne is forever and ever: the scepter of thy kingdom is a scepter of righteousness'" (Hebrews 1:8).

Obtrud'st thy offered aid, that I, accepting,
At least might seem to hold all power of thee,[84]
Ambitious Spirit! and would'st be thought my God;
And storm'st, refused, thinking to terrify
Me to thy will! Desist (thou art discerned,
And toil'st in vain), nor me in vain molest."
To whom the Fiend, now swoln with rage, replied.
"Then hear, O Son of David,[85] virgin-born![86]
For Son of God to me is yet in doubt.
Of the Messiah I have heard foretold[87]
By all the Prophets; of thy birth, at length
Announced by Gabriel,[88] with the first I knew,

---

[84] To hold all power of thee. "Again the devil took him up into an exceeding high mountain, and showed him all the kingdoms of the world, and the glory of them, And said to him, 'All these will I give thee, if thou wilt fall down, and worship me'" (Matthew 4:8, 9).

[85] "Then said he unto them, 'How say they that Christ is David's son? And David himself saith in the book of the Psalms, The Lord said unto my Lord, Sit at my right hand, till I shall make thine enemies thy footstool. Seeing David called him Lord, how is he then his son?'" (Luke 20:41–44).

[86] Virgin-born. "Therefore the Lord himself will give you a sign. Behold, the virgin shall conceive and bear a son, and she shall call his name Immanuel" (Isaiah 7:14). "Behold, a virgin shall be with child, and shall bear a son, & they shall call his name Emmanuel, which is by interpretation, God with us" (Matthew 1:23). "Then said Mary unto the Angel, 'How shall this be, seeing I know not man?'" (Luke 1:34).

[87] Of the Messiah I have heard foretold. Compare with response of the Samaritan woman at the well when Jesus spoke with her: "The woman said unto him, I know well that Messiah shall come which is called Christ: when he is come, he will tell us all things" (John 4:25).

[88] "And in the sixth month, the Angel Gabriel was sent from God unto a city of Galilee, named Nazareth, to a virgin affianced to a man whose name was Joseph, of the house of David, & the virgins name was Mary. And the Angel went in unto her, and said, 'Hail thou that art freely beloved: the Lord is with thee: blessed art thou among women.' And when she saw him, she was troubled at his saying, and thought what manner of salutation that should be. Then the Angel said unto her, 'Fear not, Mary: for thou hast found favor with God. For lo, thou

And of the angelic song in Bethlehem field,
On thy birth-night, that sung thee Saviour born.[89]
From that time seldom have I ceased to eye
Thy infancy, thy childhood, and thy youth,
Thy manhood last, though yet in private bred;
Till, at the ford of Jordan, whither all
Flocked to the Baptist,[90] I among the rest
(Though not to be baptized), by voice from Heaven[91]
Heard thee pronounced the Son of God beloved.
Thenceforth I thought thee worth my nearer view
And narrower scrutiny, that I might learn
In what degree or meaning thou art called
The Son of God, which bears no single sense.
The Son of God I also am, or was;
And, if I was, I am;[92] relation stands:
All men are Sons of God;[93] yet thee I thought

---

shalt conceive in thy womb, and bear a son, and shalt call his name Jesus'" (Luke 1:26–31).

[89] [Lines 505–506] "And there were in the same country shepherds, abiding in the field, and keeping watch by night over their flock. And lo, the Angel of the Lord came upon them, and the glory of the Lord shone about them, and they were sore afraid. Then the Angel said unto them, 'Be not afraid: for behold, I bring you glad tidings of great joy, that shall be to all the people, that is, that unto you is born this day in the city of David, a Savior, which is Christ the Lord. And this shall be a sign to you, ye shall find the babe swaddled, and laid in a cratch. And straightway there was with the Angel a multitude of heavenly soldiers, praising God, and saying, Glory be to God in the high heavens, and peace in earth, and towards men good will'" (Luke 2:8–14).

[90] [Lines 510–511] "Then went out to him Jerusalem and all Judea, and all the region round about Jordan. And they were baptized of him in Jordan, confessing their sins" (Matthew 3:5, 6).

[91] By voice from heaven: "And lo, a voice came from heaven, saying, 'This is my beloved Son, in whom I am well pleased'" (Matthew 3:17).

[92] Satan plays with God's designation as "I Am." "And God answered Moses, 'I Am That I Am. Also he said, Thus shalt thou say unto the children of Israel, I Am hath sent me unto you'" (Exodus 3:14).

In some respect far higher so declared.
Therefore I watched thy footsteps from that hour,
And followed thee still on to this waste wild,
Where, by all best conjectures, I collect
Thou art to be my fatal enemy.[94]
Good reason, then, if I beforehand seek
To understand my adversary,[95] who
And what he is; his wisdom, power, intent;
By parle or composition, truce or league,
To win him, or win from him what I can.
And opportunity I here have had
To try thee, sift thee,[96] and confess have found thee
Proof against all temptation,[97] as a rock[98]

---

[93] [Lines 517–520] All are sons of God. "I have said, 'Ye are gods, and ye all are children of the most High but ye shall die as a man, and ye princes, shall fall like others'" (Psalm 82:6–7). "Jesus answered them, 'Is it not written in your Law, I said, Ye are gods? If he called them gods, unto whom the word of God was given, and the Scripture cannot be broken, say ye of him, whom the Father hath sanctified, and sent into the world, thou blasphemest, because I said, I am the Son of God?'" (John 10:34–36). "Now there was a day, when the sons of God came to present themselves before the Lord, and Satan came also among them" (Job 1:6 [see also DR]). GE, Bishops, Coverdale, Tyndale, GT "children of God." Geneva note: "Meaning the angels who are called the sons of God because they are willing to execute his will."

[94] Thou art to be my fatal enemy. "I will also put enmity between thee and the woman, and between thy seed & her seed. He shall break thine head, and thou shalt bruise his heel" (Genesis 3:15).

[95] "Be sober, and watch: for your adversary the devil as a roaring lion walketh about, seeking whom he may devour" (1 Peter 5:8).

[96] Satan tries to "sift" his victims. "And the Lord said, 'Simon, Simon, behold, Satan hath desired to have you, that he may sift you as wheat'" (Luke 22:31, AV, et al except GE "winnow as wheat").

[97] "Because thou hast kept the word of my patience, therefore I will deliver thee from the hour of temptation, which will come upon all the world, to try them that dwell upon the earth" (Revelation 3:10). "For we have not an high Priest, which cannot be touched with the feeling of our infirmities, but was in all things tempted in like sort, yet without sin" (Hebrews 4:15).

Of adamant and as a centre, firm
To the utmost of mere man both wise and good,
Not more; for honours, riches, kingdoms, glory,
Have been before contemned, and may again.
Therefore, to know what more thou art than man,
Worth naming the Son of God by voice from Heaven,[99]
Another method I must now begin."
So saying, he caught him up, and, without wing
Of hippogrif, bore through the air sublime,
Over the wilderness and o'er the plain,
Till underneath them fair Jerusalem,[100]
The Holy City, lifted high her towers,
And higher yet the glorious Temple reared
Her pile, far off appearing like a mount
Of alablaster, topt with golden spires:
There, on the highest pinnacle, he set[101]

---

[98] "And did all drink the same spiritual drink (for they drank of the spiritual Rock that followed them: and the Rock was Christ)" (1 Corinthians 10:4). "And I say also unto thee, that thou art Peter, and upon this rock I will build my Church: and the gates of hell shall not overcome it" (Matthew 16:18).

[99] "While he yet spake, behold, a bright cloud shadowed them: and behold, there came a voice out of the cloud, saying, 'This is that my beloved Son, in whom I am well pleased: hear him" (Matthew 17:5).

[100] [Lines 544–545] Fair Jerusalem the Holy City. "Arise, arise: put on thy strength, O Zion: put on thy garments of thy beauty, O Jerusalem, the holy city: for henceforth there shall no more come into thee the uncircumcised and the unclean" (Isaiah 52:1). Coverdale and DR "holy one." "So shall ye know that I am the Lord your God dwelling in Zion, mine holy Mountain: then shall Jerusalem be holy, and there shall no strangers go threw her any more" (Joel 3:17). "But the court which is without the temple cast out, and mete it not: for it is given unto the Gentiles, and the holy city shall they tread under foot, two and forty months" (Revelation 11:2). "And I John saw the holy city new Jerusalem come down from God out of heaven, prepared as a bride trimmed for her husband" (Revelation 21:2).

[101] There on the highest pinnacle, he set. "Then the devil took him up into the holy City, and set him on a pinnacle of the temple" (Matthew 4:5). "Then he

The Son of God, and added thus in scorn:
"There stand, if thou wilt stand; to stand upright[102]
Will ask thee skill. I to thy Father's house[103]
Have brought thee, and highest placed: highest is best.
Now shew thy progeny; if not to stand,
Cast thyself down. Safely, if Son of God;
For it is written, 'He will give command
Concerning thee to his Angels; in their hands
They shall uplift thee, lest at any time
Thou chance to dash thy foot against a stone.'"[104]
To whom thus Jesus: "Also it is written,
'Tempt not the Lord thy God.'"[105] He said, and stood;[106]

---

brought him to Jerusalem, and set him on a pinnacle of the Temple, and said unto him, 'If thou be the Son of God, cast thyself down from hence'" (Luke 4:9).

[102] There stand, if thou wilt stand; to stand upright. To stand against the Devil three times: "Put on the whole armor of God, that ye may be able to stand against the assaults of the devil. For we wrestle not against flesh and blood, but against principalities, against powers, and against the worldly governors, the princes of the darkness of this world, against spiritual wickedness, which are in the high places. For this cause take unto you the whole armor of God, that ye may be able to resist in the evil day, and having finished all things, stand fast. Stand therefore, and your loins girded about with verity, and having on the breastplate of righteousness" (Ephesians 6:11–14).

[103] To thy father's house or the Temple. "And said unto them that sold doves, 'Take these things hence: make not my father's house, an house of merchandise'" (John 2:16).

[104] [Lines 553–559] "Then the devil took him up into the holy City, and set him on a pinnacle of the temple, And said unto him, 'If thou be the Son of God, cast thyself down: for it is written, that he will give his Angels charge over thee, and with their hands they shall lift thee up, lest at any time thou shouldst dash thy foot against a stone'" (Matthew 4:5, 6). "Then he brought him to Jerusalem, and set him on a pinnacle of the Temple, and said unto him, 'If thou be the Son of God, cast thyself down from hence, For it is written, That he will give his Angels charge over thee to keep thee: And with their hands they shall lift thee up, least at any time thou shouldst dash thy foot against a stone'" (Luke 4:9–11). "For he shall give his Angels charge over thee to keep thee in all thy ways. They shall bear thee in their hands, that thou hurt not thy foot against a stone" (Psalm 91:11, 12).

But Satan, smitten with amazement, fell.[107]
As when Earth's son, Antaeus (to compare
Small things with greatest), in Irassa strove
With Jove's Alcides, and, oft foiled, still rose,
Receiving from his mother Earth new strength,
Fresh from his fall, and fiercer grapple joined,
Throttled at length in the air expired and fell,
So, after many a foil, the Tempter proud,
Renewing fresh assaults, amidst his pride
Fell whence he stood to see his victor fall;[108]
And, as that Theban monster that proposed
Her riddle, and him who solved it not devoured,
That once found out and solved, for grief and spite
Cast herself headlong from the Ismenian steep,
So, strook with dread and anguish, fell the Fiend,
And to his crew, that sat consulting, brought

---

[105] Tempt not the Lord thy God. "Jesus said unto him, 'It is written again, Thou shalt not tempt the Lord thy God'" (Matthew 4:7). "And Jesus answered, and said unto him, 'It is said, Thou shalt not tempt the Lord thy God'" (Luke 4:13). "Ye shall not tempt the Lord your God, as ye did tempt him in Massah" (Deuteronomy 6:16). "And he called the name of the place, Massah and Meribah, because of the contention of the children of Israel, and because they had tempted the Lorde, saying, 'Is the Lord among us, or no?'" (Exodus 17:7).

[106] "Who art thou that condemnest another man's servant? He standeth or falleth to his own master: yea, he shall be established: for God is able to make him stand" (Romans 14:4).

[107] But Satan smitten with amazement, fell. Compare with the response upon those who came to seize Jesus in the Garden of Gethsemane: "Judas then, after he had received a band of men and officers of the high Priests, and of the Pharisees, came thither with lanterns and torches, and weapons. Then Jesus, knowing all things that should come unto him, went forth and said unto them, 'Whom seek ye?' They answered him, 'Jesus of Nazareth.' Jesus said unto them, 'I am he.' Now Judas also which betrayed him, stood with them. As soon then as he had said unto them, 'I am he,' they went away backwards, and fell to the ground" (John 18:4–6).

[108] "Wherefore, let him that thinketh he standeth, take heed lest he fall" (1 Corinthians 10:12).

Joyless triumphals of his hoped success,
Ruin, and desperation, and dismay,
Who durst so proudly tempt the Son of God.
So Satan fell; and straight a fiery globe
Of Angels on full sail of wing flew nigh,
Who on their plumy vans received Him soft[109]
From his uneasy station, and upbore,
As on a floating couch, through the blithe air;
Then, in a flowery valley, set him down
On a green bank, and set before him spread
A table of celestial food, divine
Ambrosial fruits fetched from the Tree of Life,
And from the Fount of Life[110] ambrosial drink,[111]
That soon refreshed him wearied, and repaired
What hunger, if aught hunger, had impaired,

---

[109] [Lines 582–583] The angels minister to Jesus. "Then the devil left him: and behold, the Angels came, and ministered unto him" (Matthew 4:11). "And he was there in the wilderness forty days, and was tempted of Satan: he was also with the wild beasts, and the Angels ministered unto him" (Mark 1:13).

[110] Fount of Life. "And he said to me: 'It is done. I am Alpha and Omega: the Beginning and the End. To him that thirsteth, I will give of the fountain of the water of life, freely'" (Revelation 21:6, DR [see also AV]). GE, Bishops, GT, Coverdale, Tyndale "well of life."

[111] [Lines 589–590] "And he showed me a pure river of water of life, clear as crystal, proceeding out of the throne of God, and of the Lamb. In the midst of the street of it, and of either side of the river, was the tree of life, which bare twelve manner of fruits, and gave fruit every month: and the leaves of the tree served to heal the nations with […] Blessed are they, that do his commandments, that their right may be in the tree of life, and may enter in through the gates into the city" (Revelation 22:1, 2, 14). "(For out of the ground made the Lord God to grow every tree pleasant to the sight, and good for meat: the tree of life also in the midst of the garden, and the tree of knowledge of good and of evil" (Genesis 2:9). "And the Lord God said, Behold, the man is become as one of us, to know good and evil; now lest he put forth his hand, and take also of the tree of life & eat & live forever […] Thus he cast out man, and at the East side of the garden of Eden he set the Cherubim, and the blade of a sword shaken, to keep the way of the tree of life" (Genesis 3:22, 24).

Or thirst; and, as he fed, Angelic quires
Sung heavenly anthems of his victory
Over temptation and the Tempter[112] proud.
"True Image of the Father, whether throned
In the bosom[113] of bliss, and light[114] of light[115]
Conceiving, or, remote from Heaven, enshrined
In fleshly[116] tabernacle[117] and human form,[118]
Wandering the wilderness—whatever place,
Habit, or state, or motion, still expressing

---

[112] Over temptation and the Tempter. "For we have not an high Priest, which cannot be touched with the feeling of our infirmities, but was in all things tempted in like sort, yet without sin" (Hebrews 4:15). "Then came to him the tempter, and said, 'If thou be the Son of God, command that these stones be made bread'" (Matthew 4:3).

[113] "No man hath seen God at any time: that only begotten Son, which is in the bosom of the Father, he hath declared him" (John 1:18).

[114] "This was that true light, which lighteth every man that cometh into the world" (John 1:9).

[115] [Lines 596–597] True Image of the Father, whether throned / In the bosom of bliss, and light of light. "Who being the brightness of the glory, and the engraved form of his person, and bearing up all things by his mighty word, hath by himself purged our sins, and sitteth at the right hand of the Majesty in the highest places […] But unto the Son he saith, 'O God, thy throne is forever and ever: the scepter of thy kingdom is a scepter of righteousness" (Hebrews 1:3, 8).

[116] "And that Word was made flesh, and dwelt among us, (and we saw the glory thereof, as the glory of the only begotten Son of the Father) full of grace and truth" (John 1:14). "Hereby shall ye know the Spirit of God, every spirit which confesseth that Jesus Christ is come in the flesh, is of God" (1 John 4:2, 3).

[117] "For we know that if our earthly house of this tabernacle be destroyed, we have a building given of God, that is, an house not made with hands, but eternal in the heavens" (2 Corinthians 5:1). "Seeing I know that the time is at hand that I must lay down this my tabernacle, even as our Lord Jesus Christ hath showed me" (2 Peter 1:14).

[118] "But he made himself of no reputation, & took on him the form of a servant, & was made like unto men, and was found in shape as a man" (Philippians 2:7). "For (that that was impossible to the Law, in as much as it was weak, because of the flesh) God sending his own Son, in the similitude of sinful flesh, & for sin, condemned sin in the flesh" (Romans 8:3).

The Son of God, with Godlike[119] force endued
Against the attempter of thy Father's throne
And thief of Paradise![120] Him long of old
Thou didst debel, and down from Heaven cast[121]
With all his army; now thou hast avenged
Supplanted Adam,[122] and, by vanquishing
Temptation, hast regained lost Paradise,
And frustrated the conquest fraudulent.
He never more henceforth will dare set foot
In paradise to tempt; his snares[123] are broke.
For, though that seat of earthly bliss be failed,
A fairer Paradise[124] is founded now
For Adam and his chosen sons, whom thou,

---

[119] "Yet thou saidst in thine heart, 'I will ascend into heaven, and exalt my throne above beside the stars of God: I will sit also upon the mount of the Congregation in the sides of the North. I will ascend above the height of the clouds, and I will be like the most high'" (Isaiah 14:13, 14). "For it pleased the Father, that in him should all fullness dwell [...] For in him dwelleth all the fullness of the Godhead bodily" (Colossians 1:19; 2:9). "And to know the love of Christ, which passeth knowledge, that ye may be filled with all fullness of God" (Ephesians 3:19).
[120] Thief of Paradise. Compare: "Verily, verily I say unto you, He that entereth not in by the door into the sheepfold, but climbeth up another way, he is a thief and a robber" (John 10:1).
[121] Down from heaven cast. "And he said unto them, 'I saw Satan, like lightning, fall down from heaven" (Luke 10:18). "And the great dragon, that old serpent, called the devil and Satan, was cast out, which deceiveth all the world: he was even cast into the earth, and his angels were cast out with him" (Revelation 12:9).
[122] Supplanted Adam. "For as in Adam all die, even so in Christ shall all be made alive" (1 Corinthians 15:22). "But death reigned from Adam to Moses, even over them also that sinned not after the like manner of that transgression of Adam, which was the figure of him that was to come" (Romans 5:14).
[123] Satan as the bird catcher. "Our soul is escaped, even as a bird out of the snare of the fowlers: the snare is broken, and we are delivered" (Psalm 124:7).
[124] A fairer paradise. "In the midst of the street of it, and of either side of the river, was the tree of life, which bore twelve manner of fruits, and gave fruit every month: and the leaves of the tree served to heal the nations with. And there shall be no more curse, but the throne of God and of the Lamb shall be in it, and his servants shall serve him" (Revelation 22:2, 3).

A Saviour, art come down to reinstall;
Where they shall dwell secure, when time shall be,
Of tempter and temptation without fear.[125]
But thou, Infernal Serpent! shalt not long
Rule in the clouds. Like an autumnal star,
Or lightning, thou shalt fall[126] from Heaven, trod down[127]
Under his feet. For proof, ere this thou feel'st
Thy wound (yet not thy last and deadliest wound)[128]
By this repulse received, and hold'st in Hell[129]
No triumph; in all her gates[130] Abaddon[131] rues[132]

---

125 "And the devil that deceived them, was cast into a lake of fire and brimstone, where that beast and that false prophet are, and shall be tormented even day and night for evermore" (Revelation 20:10). "And the great dragon, that old serpent, called the devil and Satan, was cast out, which deceiveth all the world: he was even cast into the earth, and his angels were cast out with him" (Revelation 12:9).
126 "And he said unto them, 'I saw Satan, like lightning, fall down from heaven. Behold, I give unto you power to tread on Serpents, and Scorpions, & over all the power of the enemy, and nothing shall hurt you'" (Luke 10:18, 19).
127 "And ye shall tread down the wicked: for they shall be dust under the soles of your feet in the day that I shall do this, saith the Lorde of hosts" (Malachi 4:3). "The God of peace shall tread Satan under your feet shortly. The grace of our Lord Jesus Christ be with you" (Romans 16:20).
128 Compare: "And I saw one of his heads as it were wounded to death, but his deadly wound was healed, and all the world wondered and followed the beast" (Revelation 13:3). "But the beast was taken, & with him that false prophet that wrought miracles before him, whereby he deceived them that received the beast's mark, and them that worshipped his image. These both were alive cast into a lake of fire, burning with brimstone" (Revelation 19:20). "And the devil that deceived them, was cast into a lake of fire and brimstone, where that beast and that false prophet are, and shall be tormented even day and night for evermore" (Revelation 20:10). The foretold "last and deadliest wound" for Satan. "I will also put enmity between thee and the woman, and between thy seed & her seed. He shall break thine head, and thou shalt bruise his heel" (Genesis 3:15).
129 "Hell is naked before him, and destruction hath no covering" (Job 26:6, AV et al except GE "the grave." "Shall thy loving kindness be declared in the grave? or thy faithfulness in destruction?" (Psalm 88:11).

Thy bold attempt. Hereafter learn with awe
To dread the Son of God. He, all unarmed,
Shall chase thee, with the terror of his voice,[133]
From thy demoniac holds,[134] possession foul
Thee and thy legions; yelling they shall fly,
And beg to hide them in a herd of swine,[135]
Lest he command them down into the Deep,[136]

---

[130] Gates of Hell. "And I say also unto thee, that thou art Peter, and upon this rock I will build my Church: and the gates of hell shall not overcome it" (Matthew 16:18). "Then shall her gates mourn and lament, and she, being desolate, shall sit upon the ground" (Isaiah 3:26).

[131] Abaddon. "And they have a King over them, which is the Angel of the bottomless pit, whose name in Hebrew is Abaddon, and in Greek he is named Apollyon, that is, destroying" (Revelation 9:11).

[132] "Destruction and death say, 'We have heard the fame thereof with our ears'" (Job 28:22). "Yea, this is a fire that shall devour to destruction, & which shall root out all mine increase" (Job 31:12).

[133] With the terror of his voice. "And then shall that wicked man be revealed, whom the Lord shall consume with the Spirit of his mouth, and shall abolish with the brightness of his coming" (2 Thessalonians 2:8).

[134] Demoniac holds. "And he cried out mightily with a loud voice, saying, 'It is fallen, it is fallen, Babylon that great city, and is become the habitation of devils, and the hold of all foul spirits, and a cage of every unclean and hateful bird'" (Revelation 18:2).

[135] [Lines 629–630] "And when he was come to the other side into the country of the Gergesenes, there met him two possessed with devils, which came out of the graves very fierce, so that no man might go by that way. And behold, they cried out, saying, Jesus the son of God, what have we to do with thee? Art thou come hither to torment us before the time? Now there was, afar off from them, a great heard of swine feeding. And the devils besought him, saying, 'If thou cast us out, suffer us to go into the heard of swine.' And he said unto them, 'Go.' So they went out and departed into the heard of swine: and behold, the whole herd of swine ran headlong into the sea, and died in the water. Then the herdmen fled: and when they were come into the city, they told all things, and what was become of them that were possessed with the devils" (Matthew 8:28–33).

[136] "And I saw an Angel come down from heaven, having the key of the bottomless pit, and a great chain in his hand. And he took the dragon that old serpent, which is the devil and Satan, and he bound him a thousand years: And cast him into the bottomless pit, and he shut him up, and sealed the door upon

Bound, and to torment sent before their time.[137]
Hail, Son of the Most High, heir of both Worlds,[138]
Queller of Satan![139] On thy glorious work[140]
Now enter, and begin to save Mankind."[141]
Thus they the Son of God, our Saviour meek,
Sung victor, and, from heavenly feast refreshed,[142]
Brought on his way with joy.[143] He, unobserved,
Home to his mother's house[144] private returned.

END.

---

him, that he should deceive the people no more, until the thousand years were fulfilled: for after that he must be loosed for a little season" (Revelation 20:1–3).

[137] "And cried with a loud voice, and said, 'What have I to do with thee, Jesus the Son of the most high God? I will that thou swear to me by God, that thou torment me not'" (Mark 5:7).

[138] Jesus the heir of "both worlds." "Whom he hath made heir of all things, by whom also he made the worlds" (Hebrews 1:2).

[139] "And whosoever was not found written in the book of life, was cast into the lake of fire" (Revelation 20:15).

[140] Thy glorious work. "Jesus said unto them, 'My meat is that I may do the will of him that sent me, and finish his work" (John 4:34). "I have glorified thee on the earth: I have finished the work which thou gavest me to do" (John 17:4).

[141] To save mankind. "For the Son of man is come to save that which was lost" (Matthew 18:11). "For the Son of man is not come to destroy men's lives, but to save them. Then they went to another town" (Luke 9:56). "For the Son of man is come to seek, and to save that which was lost" (Luke 19:10). "And we have seen, & do testify, that the Father sent that Son to be the Savior of the world" (1 John 4:14).

[142] From heavenly feast refreshed. "Then the devil left him: and behold, the Angels came, and ministered unto him" (Matthew 4:11). "Take my yoke on you, and learn of me that I am meek and lowly in heart: and ye shall find rest unto your souls" (Matthew 11:29).

[143] "Thus being brought forth by the Church, they passed through Phoenicia and Samaria, declaring the conversion of the Gentiles, and they brought great joy unto all the brethren" (Acts 15:3).

[144] Mary's house. Compare with Mary returning to her own home after visiting with her cousin Elizabeth the mother of John the Baptist. "And Mary abode with her about three months: after, she returned to her own house" (Luke 1:56). As Jesus also did after returning from the Temple as a teenager. "Then he went down with them, and came to Nazareth, and was subject to them: and his mother kept all these sayings in her heart" (Luke 2:51).

BIBLIOGRAPHY

Primary Sources:

Anglo-Rhemish New Testament. 1582.

Augustine, Saint, Bishop of Hippo. *Arianism and Other Heresies: Heresies, Memorandum to Augustine, To Orosius in refutation of the Priscillianists and Origenists, Arian Sermon, Answer to an Arian Sermon, Debate with Maximinus, Answer to Maximinus, Answer to an Enemy of the Law and the Prophets.* Ed. Roland J. Teske. Trans. John E. Rotelle. New York: New City, 1995.

_____. *The City of God.* Marcus Dods, trans. New York: Modern Library, 1993.

Authorized Version of the Bible. 1611. 1612.

Biblia Sacra. Vulgate Editionis, Sixti V. et Clementis VII.Londoni: Sumptibus Samuelis

Bagster, n.d.

Bishops Bible. 1595.

Calvin, John. *A commentarie of Iohn Caluine, upon the first booke of Moses called Genesis: translated out of Latine into English,* by Thomas Tymme, minister. London: Henry Middleton, 1578.

Coverdale Bible. 1535.

Geneva Bible. 1560.

Great Bible. 1539. 1540.

Luther, Martin. "Lectures on Genesis Chapters 6-14." *Luther's Works.* Vol. 2. Saint Louis: Concordia, 1960.

Milton, John. *De Doctrina Christiana.* Trans. Charles R. Sumner. *De Doctrina Christiana: Christian Doctrine.* Vol. 16-18 of *The Works of John Milton.* 22 vols. Ed. Frank Allen Patterson. New York: Columbia University Press, 1934.

_____. *Paradise Lost.* 1667. 1674. Vol. 2-3 of *John Milton's Complete Poetical Works Reproduced in Photographic Facsimile.* Ed. Harris Francis Fletcher. Urbana: University of Illinois Press, 1945.

_____. *Paradise Regained.* 1671. 1680. Vol. 4 of John Milton's Complete Poetical Works Reproduced in Photographic Facsimile. Ed. Harris Francis Fletcher. Urbana: University of Illinois Press, 1945.

Scholz, Johann Martin Augustin. *The English Hexapla*. London: Bagster, 1841.

Septuagint.

Stephens, Robert. *Textus Receptus*. 1624.

Tyndale New Testament. 1534.

Victorinus, Marius. *Theological Treatises on the Trinity*. Trans. Mary T. Clark.

Washington, D. C.: Catholic University of America Press, 1981.

The Latin Vulgate.

Wiclif New Testament. 1380.

Wilson, Benjamin. *The Emphatic Diaglott Containing the Original Greek Text of What Is Commonly Styled the New Testament according to the Recension of Dr. J. J. Griesbach*. Brooklyn: IBSA, 1942.

Secondary Sources:

Achinstein, Sharon. *Literature and Dissent in Milton's England*. Cambridge: Cambridge University Press, 2003.

Allen, D. C. "Milton and Rabbi Eliezer." *Modern Language Notes* 63.2 (1948): 262-63.

_____. "Milton and the Sons of God." Modern Language Notes 61.2 (1946): 75.

Alter, Robert. *The Five Books of Moses: A Translation with Commentary*. New York: Norton, 2004.

Baxter, Wynne E. "Milton's Bibles." *Notes and Queries* 3 (1911): 109-10.

Bauman, Michael E. *Milton's Arianism*. Frankfurt: Lang, 1987.

_____. "Milton's Theological Vocabulary and the Nicene Anathemas." *Milton Studies* 21 (1986): 71-92.

_____. "Naming Satan's Heresies." *English Language Notes* 23.1 (1985): 31-35.

Belloc, Hilaire. *The Great Heresies*. Freeport: Books for Libraries Press, 1968.

Bentley, Jerry H. *Humanists and Holy Writ: New Testament Scholarship in the Renaissance*. Princeton: Princeton University Press, 1983.

Bissel, Edwin Cone. *Genesis Printed in Colors Showing the Original Sources from Which It Is Supposed to Have Been Compiled with An Introduction*. Hartford : Belknap and Warfield, 1892.

Blondel, Jacques. "Milton: Poete de la Bible dans *le Paradis Perdu*." *Etudes de Critique et d'Histoire Litteraire* 22 (1959): 43-86.

Boehrer, Bruce Thomas. "*Paradise Lost* and the General Epistle of James: Milton, Augustine, Lacan." *Exemplaria* 4 (1992): 295-316.

Bozeman, Theodore Dwight. *The Precisionist Strain: Disciplinary Religion and Antinomian Backlash in Puritanism to 1638*. Chapel Hill: University of North Carolina Press, 2004.

Broadbent, John. "The Poet's Bible." *John Milton: Introductions*. Ed. John Broadbent.

Cambridge: Cambridge University Press, 1973.

Bruce, F. F. *The English Bible: A History of Translations*. New York: Oxford University Press, 1961.

Burnet, R. A. L. "Some Echoes of the *Genevan Bible* in Shakepeare and Milton." *Notes and Queries: For Readers and Writers, Collectors and Librarians* 27.2 (1980):

179-81.

_____. "Two Further Echoes of the Genevan Margin in Shakespeare and Milton." *Notes and Queries: For Readers and Writers, Collectors and Librarians* 28.1 (1981): 129.

Butterworth, Charles C. *The Literary Lineage of the King James Bible*. Philadelphia: University of Pennsylvania Press, 1941.

Christie-Murray, David. *A History of Heresy*. Oxford: Oxford University Press, 1989.

Coffey, John. *Persecution and Toleration in Protestant England, 1558-1689*. London: Longman, 2000.

Colligan, J. Hay. *The Arian Movement in England*. Manchester: Manchester University Press, 1913.

Como, David R. *Blown by the Spirit: Puritanism and the Emergence of an Antinomian Underground in Pre-Civil-War England*. Stanford: Stanford University Press, 2004.

Christopher, Georgia B. *Milton and the Science of the Saints*. Princeton: Princeton University Press, 1982.

Clark, Ira. *Christ Revealed: The History of the Neotypological Lyric in the English Renaissance*. Gainesville: University Press of Florida, 1982.

Cohen, Kitty. *The Throne and the Chariot: Studies in Milton's Herbraism*. The Hague: Mouton, 1975.

Collette, Carolyn P. "Milton's Psalm Translations: Petition and Praise." *English Literary Renaissance* 2 (1972): 243-59.

Conklin, George Newton. *Biblical Criticism and Heresy in Milton*. New York: Octagon, 1972.

Coolidge, John S. *The Pauline Renaissance in England: Puritanism and the Bible*. Oxford: Clarendon, 1970.

Daiches, David. *The King James Version of the English Bible: An Account of the Development and Sources of the English Bible of 1611 with Special Reference to the Hebrew Tradition*. Chicago: Archon, 1968.

Daniells, Roy. *John Milton: Introductions*. Cambridge: Cambridge University Press, 1973.

Davidson, Robert. "Genesis 1-11." *The Cambridge Bible Commentary*. Ed. P. R. Acroyd, A.R.C. Leaney, and J.W. Packer, 70 vols. Cambridge: Cambridge, University Press, 1973.

Dobbins, Austin. *Milton and the Book of Revelation: The Heavenly Cycle.*. University: University of Alabama Press, 1975.

Dobranksi, Stephen B. and John P. Rumrich, ed. *Milton and Heresy*. Cambridge: Cambridge University Press, 1998.

Ericson, Edward E. "The Sons of God in *Paradise Lost* and *Paradise Regained*." *Milton Quarterly* 25.3 (1991): 88-101.

Elliot, T. G. "Constantine and 'the Arian Reaction after Nicaea.'" *Journal of Ecclesiastical History* 43.2 (1992): 160-94.

Entzminger, Robert L. *Divine Word: Milton and the Redemption of Language*. Pittsburgh: Duquesne University Press, 1985.

Evans, J. Martin. *Paradise Lost and the Genesis Tradition*. Oxford: Clarendon, 1968.

Evans, G. R. *The Language and Logic of the Bible: The Road to Reformation*. Cambridge: Cambridge University Press, 1985.

Fisch, Harold. *The Biblical Presence in Shakespeare, Milton, and Blake: A Comparative Study*. Oxford: Clarendon, 1999.

Fixler, Michael. *Milton and the Kingdoms of God*. Chicago: Northwestern University Press, 1964.

Fletcher, Harris Francis. *Milton, Semitic Studies and Some Manifestations of Them in His Poetry*. Chicago: University of Chicago Press, 1926.

---. *The Use of the Bible in Milton's Prose*. New York: Haskell, 1929.

Firth, Katharine. *The Apocalyptic Tradition in Reformation Britain, 1530-1645*. Oxford: Oxford University Press, 1979.

Flannagan, Roy. *The Riverside Milton*. Boston: Houghton Mifflin, 1998.

Force, James E. and Richard H. Popkin, ed. *Essays on the Context, Nature, and Influence of Isaac Newton's Theology*. Dordrecht: Kluwer, 1990.

_____. *William Whiston: Honest Newtonian*. Cambridge: Cambridge University Press, 1985.

Forsyth, Neil. "Having Done All to Stand: Biblical and Classical Allusion in *Paradise Regained*." *Milton Studies* 21 (1986): 199-214.

Foster, Donald W. "Milton and the Universalists." *Notes and Queries: For Readers and Writers and Collectors and Librarians* 27.4 (1980): 334.

Fowler, Alastair, ed. *Milton: Paradise Lost*. 2nd ed. New York: Longman, 2006.

Frank, Mortimer H. *Milton and the Art of Sacred Song: Essays*. Madison: University s of WisconsinPress, 1979.

Fresch, Cheryl H. "'As the Rabbines expound': Milton, Genesis, and the Rabbis." *Milton Studies* 15 (1981): 59-80.

Frye, Northrop. *The Great Code: The Bible and Literature*. New York: Harcourt, 1982.

Gallagher, Philip J. *Milton, the Bible, and Misogyny*. Columbia: University of Missouri Press, 1990.

Gay, David. *The Endless Kingdom: Milton's Scriptural Society*. Newark: University of Delaware Press, 2002.

Giamatti, A. Bartlett. *The Earthly Paradise and the Renaissance Epic*. Princeton: Princeton University Press, 1966.

Gilman, Ernest B. *Iconoclasm and Poetry in the English Reformation: Down Went Dagon*. Chicago: University of Chicago Press, 1986.

Graves, Robert and Raphael Patai. *Hebrew Myths: The Book of Genesis*. Garden City: Doubleday, 1963.

Green, Jay P., ed. *The Pocket Interlinear Old Testament*. Vol 1. Grand Rapids: Baker, 1987.

Greenslade, S. L., ed. *Cambridge History of the Bible*. Vol. 1-3. Cambridge: Cambridge University Press, 1963.

Gribben, Crawford. *The Puritan Millennium: Literature and Theology, 1550-1682*. Portland: Four Courts, 2000.

Hammond, Gerald. *The Making of the English Bible*. Manchester: Carcanet, 1982.

Hannay, Margaret. "Milton's Doctrine of the Holy Scriptures." *Christian Scholars Review* 5 (1976): 339-49.

Hamilton, Donna B. and Richard Strier, ed. *Religion, Literature, and Politics in Post-Reformation England, 1540-1688*. Cambridge: Cambridge University Press, 1996.

Hanson, R. P. C. "New Light on Arianism." *Journal of Ecclesiastical History* 33.3 (1982): 491-97.

Haskin, Dayton. "Milton's Strange Pantheon: *The Apparent Tritheism of the* De Doctrina Christiana." *The Heythrop Journal: A Quarterly Review of Philosophy and Theology* 16.2 (1975): 129-48.

Haycock, David Boyd. "'The Long-Lost Truth': Sir Isaac Newton and the Newtonian Pursuit of Ancient Knowledge." *Studies in History and Philosophy of Science* 35.3 (2004): 605-23.

Hill, Christopher. *Antichrist in Seventeenth-Century England*. London: Oxford University Press, 1971.

Haskin, Dayton. *Milton's Burden of Interpretation*. Philadelphia: University of Pennsylvania Press, 1994.

Haublein, Ernst. "Milton's Paraphrase of Genesis: A Stylistic Reading of *Paradise Lost*, Book VII." *Milton Studies* 7 (1975): 101-25.

Hill, Christopher. *The English Bible and the Seventeenth-Century Revolution*. London: Penguin, 1993.

Hill, John Spencer. *John Milton: Poet, Priest, and Prophet*. Towtowa: Rowman, 1979.

Honeygosky, Stephen R. *Milton's House of God: The Invisible and Visible Church*. Columbia: University of Missouri Press, 1993.

Hughes, Merritt Y. *John Milton: Complete Poems and Major Prose*. New York: Odyssey, 1957.

Hunter, William B. *Visitation Unimplor'd: Milton and the Authorship of* De Doctrina Christiana. Pittsburgh: Duquesne University Press, 1998.

Hunter, William B, C. A. Patrides, and J. H. Adamson. *Bright Essence*. Salt Lake City: University of Utah Press, 1971.

Jones, G. Lloyd. *The Discovery of Hebrew in Tudor England: A Third Language*. Manchester: Manchester University Press, 1983.

Katz, David S. *God's Last Words: Reading the English Bible from the Reformation to Fundamentalism*. New Haven: Yale University Press, 2004.

Kelley, Mark R., Michael Lieb, and John T. Shawcross. *Milton and the Grounds of Contention*. Pittsburgh: Duquesne University Press, 2003.

Kelly, Maurice. *This Great Argument: A Study of Milton's* De Doctrina Christiana *as a Gloss upon* Paradise Lost. Gloucester: Smith, 1962.

Kernohan, R. D. "Britain and Italy's Waldensian Church." *Contemporary Review* 283.1653 (2003): 223-28.

Kopecek, Thomas A. *A History of Neo-Arianism*. Philadelphia: Philadelphia Patristic Foundation, 1979.

Kerrigan, William. *The Prophetic Milton*. Charlottesville: University Press of Virginia, 1974.

King, John N. *Milton and Religious Controversy: Satire and Polemic in* Paradise Lost. Cambridge: Cambridge University Press, 2000.

_____. *Voices of the English Reformation: A Sourcebook*. Philadelphia: University of Pennsylvania Press, 2004.

Kurth, Burton O. *Milton and Christian Heroism: Biblical Epic Themes and Forms in Seventeenth Century England*. Berkeley: U of California P, 1959.

Lares, Jameela. *Milton and the Preaching Arts*. Pittsburgh: Duquesne UP, 2001.

_____. A Variorum Commentary on The Poems of John Milton, Vol 5 "Paradise Lost Books 11-12" Ed. Paul Klemp. Pittsburg: Duquesne University Press, 2012).

Lauter, Paul. "Milton's 'Siloa's Brook.'" *Notes and Queries* 5 (1958): 204-03.

Lake, Peter. "Moving the Goal Posts? Modified Subscription and the Construction of Conformity in the Early Stuart Church." *Conformity and Orthodoxy in the English Church, c.1560-1660*. Ed. Peter Lake and Michael Questier. Woodbridge: Boydnell, 2000. 179-205.

Lamont, William. *Puritanism and Historical Controversy*. London: UCL, 1996.

Laymon, Charles M. *The Interpreter's One-Volune Commentary on the Bible: Introduction and Commentary for Each Book of the Bible Including the Apocrypha with General Articles*. Nashville: Abingdon, 1971.

Lewalski, Barbara K, ed. *John Milton: Paradise Lost*. New York: Wiley-Blackwell, 2007.

Loewenstein, David. *Representing Revolution in Milton and His Contemporaries: Religion, Politics, and Polemics in Radical Puritanism*. Cambridge: Cambridge University Press, 2001.

Lyman, Rebecca. "A Topography of Heresy: Mapping the Rhetorical Creation of Arianism." *Arianism after Arius: Essays on the Development of the Fourth-Century Trinitarian Conflicts*. Ed. Michael R. Barnes and Daniel H. Williams. Edinburgh: Clark, 1993.

Lieb, Michael. *Poetics of the Holy: A Reading of* Paradise Lost. Chapel Hill: University of North Carolina Press, 1981.

Lim, Walter S. H. "Adam, Eve, and Biblical Analogy in *Paradise Lost*." *Studies in English Literature, 1500-1900* 30 (1990): 115-31.

Loewenstein, David and James Grantham Turner, ed. *Politics, Poetics, and Hermeneutics in Milton's Prose*. Cambridge: Cambridge University Press, 1990.

MacCallum, H. R. "Milton and Figurative Interpretation of the Bible." *University of Toronto Quarterly* 31.4 (1962): 397-415.

_____. "Milton and Sacred History: Books XI and XII of *Paradise Lost*." *Essays in English Literature Presented to A. S. P. Woodhouse*. Toronto: University of Toronto Press, 1964, 149-68.

MacKellar, Walter. *A Variorum Commentary on the Poems of John Milton,* "Paradise Regained" Vol. 4. New York: Columbia University Press, 1975.

Madsen, William G. From *Shadowy Types to Truth: Studies in Milton's Symbolism*. New Haven: Yale University Press, 1968.

McBride, Kari Boyd and John C. Ulreich. "Answerable Styles: Biblical Poetics and Biblical Politics in the Poetry of Lanyer and Milton." *Journal of English and Germanic Philology* 100.3 (2001): 333-54.

McColley, Grant. Paradise Lost*: An Account of Its Growth and Major Origins with a Discussion of Milton's Use of Sources and Literary Patterns*. Chicago: Packard, 1940.

McDowell, Nicholas. *The English Radical Imagination: Culture, Religion, and Revolution, 1630-1660*. Oxford: Clarendon, 2003.

McGrath, Alister. *In the Beginning: The Story of the King James Bible and How It Changed a Nation, a Language, and a Culture*. London: Hodder, 2001.

Manuel, Frank. *The Religion of Isaac Newton: The Fremantle Lectures, 1973.* Oxford: Clarendon, 1974.

McGregor, J. F. and B. Reay, ed. *Radical Religion in the English Revolution*. Oxford: Oxford University Press, 1984.

McLachlan, H. John. *Socianism in Seventeenth-Century England.* Oxford: Oxford University Press, 1951.

Migne, J. P., ed. *Patrologia Latina.* 221 vols. Paris: Migne, 1844-1864.

_____. *Patrologia Graeca.* 166 vols. Paris: Migne, 1857-1886.

Mohl, Ruth. *John Milton and His Commonplace Book.* New York: Ungar, 1969.

Nicholson, Adam. *God's Secretaries: The Making of the King James Bible.* New York: Harper, 2003.

Nicholson, Marjorie Hope. "Milton and the Bible." *The Bible and Its Literary Associations.* Ed. Margaret B. Crook. New York: Abingdon, 1937. 35-72.

Norton, David. *A History of the English Bible as Literature.* Cambridge: Cambridge University Press, 2000.

Nuttall, A. D. *The Alternative Trinity: Gnostic Heresy in Marlowe, Milton, and Blake.* New York: Clarendon, 1998.

O'Keefe, Timothy J. *Milton and the Pauline Tradition: A Study of Theme and Symbolism.* Washington, D.C.: University Press of America, 1982.

Park, Youngwon. *Milton and Isaiah: A Journey through the Drama of Salvation in Paradise Lost.* New York: Lang, 2000.

Patrides, C. A. *Milton and the Christian Tradition.* Oxford: Clarendon, 1966.

_____. "The 'Protevangelium' in Renaissance Theology and *Paradise Lost.*" *Studies in English Literature* 3 (1963): 1930.

Partridge, A. C. *English Biblical Translation.* London: Deutsch, 1973.

Patrick, J. Max and Roger H. Sundell, ed. *Milton and the Art of Sacred Song.* Madison: University of Wisconsin Press, 1979.

Pelikan, Jaroslav. *Reformation of Church and Dogma, 1300-1700.* Chicago: University of Chicago Press, 1984.

Pettersen, Alvyn. "The Arian Context of Athanasius of Alexandria's *Tomus ad Antiochenos VII.*" *Journal of Ecclesiastical History* 41.2 (1990): 216-32.

Poole, Kristen. *Radical Religion from Shakespeare to Milton: Figures of Nonconformity in Early Modern England.* Cambridge: Cambridge University Press, 2000.

Potter, George. "Milton Bibles." *Notes and Queries* 3 (1911): 70.

Potts, James B., Jr. "Milton's 'Two-Fold Scripture' and the Seventeenth-Century Search for Certitude." *Explorations in Renaissance Culture* 18 (1992): 93-110.

Questier, Michael. "Conformity, Catholicism and the Law." *Conformity and Orthodoxy in the English Church, c.1560-1660*. Ed. Peter Lake and Michael Questier. Woodbridge: Boydnell, 2000. 237-61.

Radzinowicz, Mary Ann. *Milton's Epics and the Book of Psalms*. Princeton: Princeton University Press, 1989.

Reichart, John. *Milton's Wisdom: Nature and Scripture in Paradise Lost*. Ann Arbor: University of Michigan Press, 1992.

Richie, Daniel E. *Reconstructing Literature in an Ideological Age: A Biblical Poetics and Literary Studies from Milton to Burke*. Grand Rapids: Eerdmans, 1996.

Riggs, William. *The Christian Poet in* Paradise Lost. Berkeley: University of California Press, 1972.

Robins, Harry F. *If This Be Heresy: A Study of Milton and Origen*. Urbana: University of Illinois Press, 1963.

Roberts, Alexander and James Donaldson, ed. *The Ante-Nicene Fathers*. 1885-1887. Repr. 10 Vols. Peabody: Hendrickson, 1994.

Rosenblatt, Jason P. *Torah and Law in Paradise Lost*. Princeton: Princeton University Press, 1994.

Rowse, A. L. *Milton the Puritan: Portrait of a Mind*. London: Macmillan, 1977.

Rubenstein, Richard E. *When Jesus Became God: The Epic Fight over Christ's Divinity in the Last Days of Rome*. New York: Harcourt, 1999.

Ryken, Leland. *The Apocalyptic Vision in Paradise Lost*. Ithaca: Cornell University Press, 1970.

Ryken, Leland and James H. Sims, ed. *Milton and Scriptural Tradition: The Bible into Poetry*. Columbia: University of Missouri Press, 1984.

Schwartz, Regina M. *Remembering and Repeating: Biblical Creation in* Paradise Lost. Cambridge: Cambridge University Press, 1988.

Shawcross, John T. "*Paradise Lost* and the Theme of Exodus." *Milton Studies* 2 (1970): 3-26.

Sherwin, Oscar. "Milton for the Masses: John Wesley's Edition of *Paradise Lost*." *Modern Language Quarterly* 12 (1951): 267-85.

Shuger, Deborah K. *The Renaissance Bible: Scholarship, Sacrifice, Subjectivity*. Berkeley: University of California Press, 1994.

_____. *Sacred Rhetoric: The Christian Grand Style in the English Renaissance*. Princeton: Princeton University Press, 1988.

Sims, James H. *The Bible in Milton's Epics*. Gainesville: University of Florida Press, 1962.

Smalley, Beryl. *The Study of the Bible in the Middle Ages*. South Bend: University of Notre Name Press, 1952.

Smith, Nigel. *Perfection Proclaimed: Language and Literature in English Radical Religion, 1640-1660*. Oxford: Clarendon, 1989.

Spurr, John. *The Restoration Church of England, 1646-1689*. New Haven: Yale University Press, 1991.

Stachniewski, John. *The Persecutory Imagination: English Puritanism and the Literature of Religious Despair*. Oxford: Clarendon, 1990.

Stallard, Matthew, ed. *John Milton,* Paradise Lost: *The Biblically Annotated Edition*. Macon: Mercer University Press, 2011.

Steadman, John M. *Milton's Biblical and Classical Imagery*. Pittsburgh: Duquesne, 1984.

Steinmetz, David, ed. *The Bible in the Sixteenth Century*. Durham: Duke University Press, 1990.

Sullivan, Ernest W. "The Bible and Satanic Deceit: *Paradise Lost* X.460-572." *English Studies: A Journal of English Language and Literature* 61 (1980): 127-29.

Teskey, Gordon, ed. *Paradise Lost: A Norton Critical Edition*. New York: Norton, 2004.

Todd, Margaret, ed. *Reformation to Revolution: Politics and Religion in Early Modern England*. London: Routledge, 1995.

Tyack, Nicholas. *Aspects of English Protestantism, c.1530-1700*. Manchester: Manchester University Press, 2001.

Von Rad, Gerhard. *Genesis: A Commentary*. Philadelphia: Westminster, 1972.

Wackernagel, Wolfgang. "Two Thousand Years of Heresy: An Essay." *Diogenes* 47.3 (1999): 134-48.

Wallace, Dewey D. "Socinianism, Justification by Faith and the Sources of John Locke's *The Reasonableness of Christianity*." *Philosophy, Religion and Science in the Seventeenth and Eighteenth Centuries*. Ed. J. W. Yolton. Rochester: U of Rochester P, 1994. 152-69.

West, Robert H. "Milton's Sons of God." *Modern Language Notes* 65/3 (1950) 187-191.

Westfall, Richard. *The Life of Isaac Newton*. Cambridge: Cambridge University Press, 1993.

Whiston, William, trans. *The Works of Josephus Complete and Unabridged.* "The Antiquities of the Jews." 1748. Peabody: Hendrickson, 1988.

Wiles, Maurice. *Archetypal Heresy: Arianism through the Centuries*. Oxford: Clarendon, 1996.

Williams, Arnold. *The Common Expositor: An Account of the Commentaries of Genesis, 1527-1633*. Chapel Hill: University of North Carolina Press, 1948.

Williams, George Huntston. *The Radical Reformation*. 3rd ed. Ann Arbor: Edwards Brothers, 1992.

Williams, Rowan. *Arius: Heresy and Tradition*. 2nd ed. Grand Rapids: Eerdmans, 2001.

Wise, Michael, Martin Abegg, and Edward Cook, ed. *The Dead Sea Scrolls: A New Translation*. London: Harper Collins, 1996.

Woodhead, Abraham. *The Protestants Plea for a Socinian*. 1686. Ed. Richard Knoll. Pasadena: Castle, 1987.

Werman, Golda. *Milton and Midrash*. Washington, D. C.: Catholic U of America P, 1995.

Willoughby, Harold R. *The First Authorized English Bible and the Cranmer Preface*. Chicago: University of Chicago Press, 1942.

Wittreich, Joseph Anthony. *Visionary Poetics: Milton's Tradition and His Legacy*. San Marino: Kingsport, 1979.

Wollaeger, Mark A. "Apocryphal Narration: Milton, Raphael, and the Book of Tobit." *Milton Studies* 21 (1986): 137-156.

Woodhouse, A. S. P. *The Heavenly Muse: A Preface to Milton*. Ed. Hugh MacCallum. Toronto: University of Toronto Press, 1963.

Young, Brian. "Newtonianism and the Enthusiasm of Englightenment." *Studies in History and Philosophy of Science* 35.4 (2004): 645-63.

Young, R. V. *Doctrine and Devotion in Seventeenth-Century Poetry: Studies in Donne, Herbert, Crashaw, and Vaughn*. Cambridge: Brewer, 2000.

INDEX

1 Corinthians (Bible Book), 1, 10, 13, 18, 21, 43, 44, 47, 48, 49, 73, 92, 93, 95, 102, 104, 126, 132, 140, 143, 144, 145, 160, 162, 165
1 Chronicles (Bible Book), xiv, 94, 118, 147
1 Enoch (Apocryphal), xvi
1 John (Bible Book), 9, 14, 164, 168
1 Kings (Bible Book), 40, 41, 45, 53, 64, 65, 68, 69, 72, 85, 108, 112, 116, 117, 119, 120, 121, 122, 129
1 Maccabees (Apocrypha), 71, 97, 98, 113
1 Peter (Bible Book), xviii, Appendix D, 39, 44, 56, 159
1 Samuel (Bible Book), 49, 80, 86, 105
1 Thessalonians (Bible Book), 1, 14, 91, 153
1 Timothy (Bible Book), Appendix D, 11, 13, 24, 25, 43, 45, 46, 56, 79, 93, 137
2Corinthians (Bible Book), 11, 17, 36, 44, 80, 139, 145, 155, 164
2 Chronicles (Bible Book), 42, 110, 117
2 Esdras (Apocrypha), 108, 123
2 John (Bible Book), 91
2 Kings (Bible Book), xxviii, Appendix D, 8, 39, 53, 81, 99, 108, 109, 113, 116, 119, 120, 121
2 Maccabees (Apocrypha), 97
2 Peter (Bible Book), Appendix D, 7, 12, 17, 44, 49, 86, 90, 94, 118, 148, 164
2 Samuel (Bible Book), Appendix D, 114, 118, 147
2 Thessalonians (Bible Book), 46, 167
2 Timothy (Bible Book), 23, 45, 99, 148
Abegg, Martin, xvi
Ackroyd, P. R., xxvi
Acts (Bible Book), 6, 37, 43, 47, 55, 56, 74, 83, 90, 92, 94, 96, 100, 137, 141, 143, 145, 149, 168
Ages of the World (Apocryphal), xvii
Allen, Don Cameron, xxxii, xxxix
Amos (Bible Book), 82, 149
Alter, Robert, xiv, xxv
Ambrose, xxiv
Aramaic Targums, xxvi
Athenagoras, xxiv
Aquinas, Thomas, xxxii
Augustine of Hippo, xxxi, xxxii, xxxiv, xlii, xlviii
Babbington, Gervase, xxxvi
Bissel, Edwin Cone, xvi
Book of Giants (Apocryphal), xvii
Calvin, John, xxxiv, xxxv, xxxviii
Canaanites, xxvi
Colossians (Bible Book), 17, 19, 23, 72, 94, 104, 165
Commodianus, xxi
Cook, Edward, xvi
Corpus Christianorum, xxv
Cyprian, xxiv
Daniel (Bible Book), xlii, 15, 70, 74, 97, 100, 105, 107, 108, 109, 111, 129, 132, 133, 134, 141, 142
Davidson, Robert, xxvi
Dead Sea Scrolls, xvi
Deuteronomy (Bible Book) Appendix D, 2, 13, 17, 28, 35, 38, 42, 53, 73, 79, 86, 104, 114, 121, 136, 147, 162
Disputation of Achelaus and Manes, xxiii
Donaldson, James, xx
Ecclesiastes (Bible Book), 66, 100, 144, 146
Ephem the Syrian, xxx
Ephesians (Bible Book), 1, 6, 14, 20, 40, 45, 60, 83, 85, 114, 149, 153, 154, 155, 161, 165

Eliezer, Pirqe Rabbi, xxix, xxx
Ellwood, Thomas, ix, x
Ericson, Edward E., xl
Esther (Bible Book), 111, 113
Exodus (Bible Book), 11, 23, 28, 29, 38, 52, 53, 71, 86, 112, 114, 123, 125, 136, 140, 158, 162
Ezekiel (Bible Book), 35, 41, 81, 143
Ezra (Bible Book), 86, 111, 115
Forsyth, Neil, xvi
Flannagan, Roy, xiv
Fowler, Alastair, xv
Gay, David, ii
Galatians (Bible Book), 7, 16, 33, 48, 87, 92, 122, 150
Genesis (Bible Book), xii, xxiv, xxv, xxix, xxxii, xxxiii, xxxv, xxxvi, xxviii, xlii, xliii, xlvi, xlvii, xlviii, (Appendices A, B, C, D), 2, 7, 13, 14, 16, 23, 24, 36, 53, 60, 63, 64, 71, 75, 89, 92, 94, 107, 109, 114, 117, 138, 146, 147, 159, 163, 166
Genesis Rabba, xxix
Gibbens, Nicholas, xxxvi, xxxvii
Graves, Robert, xviii, xix, xxix, xxx
Green, Jay P., Appendix A
Haggai (Bible Book), 79, 143
Hebrews (Bible Book), Appendix D, 1, 3, 16, 18, 19, 26, 27, 47, 53, 72, 95, 101, 131, 134, 135, 149, 152, 156, 159, 164, 168
Heywood, Thomas, xxiv
Hooke, Robert, xliv
Hosea (Bible Book), 138,
Hughes, Merritt Y., xv, xxxviii, xli
Hyrcanos, Rabbi Eliezer ben, xxix
Incubi, xxxiii, xxxiv
Isaiah (Bible Book), 2, 3, 4, 12, 14, 19, 24, 29, 30, 31, 35, 49, 51, 56, 59, 81, 82, 92, 93, 99, 100, 101, 102, 103, 113, 123, 125, 129, 140, 142, 147, 150, 151, 154, 157, 160, 165, 167
James (Bible Book), 16, 44, 46, 90, 92, 144
Jeremiah (Bible Book), xlii, Appendix D, 23, 25, 29, 79, 86, 110, 117, 119, 120, 121, 122, 131, 149, 150,
Jerome, Appendix C
Job (Bible Book), xliii, 6, 11, 14, 16, 40, 44, 68, 78, 85, 88, 92, 93, 135, 138, 153, 155, 159, 166, 167
Joel (Bible Book), 160
Jonah (Bible Book), 107
John (Bible Book), 4, 5, 9, 10, 11, 14, 17, 19, 20, 22, 23, 25, 28, 30, 31, 32, 33, 34, 36, 37, 41, 42, 43, 47, 50, 51, 52, 53, 55, 57, 58, 60, 68, 78, 82, 84, 88, 89, 91, 95, 99, 100, 114, 117, 126, 132, 136, 138, 139, 145, 149, 157, 159, 161, 162, 164, 165, 168
Josephus, Flavius, xviii, xxx
Joshua (Bible Book), 8, 56, 124, 149
Julius, Africanus, xxii, xxx
Justin Martyr, xx, xlvii
Jude (Bible Book), xviii, xliv, Appendix D, 12, 39, 44, 126, 148
Judges (Bible Book), 62, 80, 83, 119, 121, 147
Jubilees (Apocryphal), xvii, 46
Klemp, Paul J., xv
Lactantius, xxiii, xxxvi
Laymon, Charles, xxvi
Leaney, A. R. C., xxvi
Leptogenesis (Apocryphal), xvii
Leviticus (Bible Book), 24, 42, 73, 86, 114, 121
Lares, Jameela, xv, xli
Lewalski, Barbara K., xv
Luke (Bible Book), xiv, xxiv, Appendix D, 1, 2, 4, 5, 8, 9, 10, 13, 14, 15, 16, 20, 21, 22, 23, 24, 25, 26, 27, 28, 29, 31, 33, 34, 36, 37, 38, 39, 51, 52, 54, 56, 57, 58, 59, 61, 66, 67, 76, 77, 82, 87, 88, 89, 93, 96, 97, 100, 101, 104, 106, 115, 125, 129, 130, 131, 134, 135, 136, 137, 140, 149, 150, 152, 154, 157, 158, 159, 161, 162, 165, 166, 168
Leasure, T. Ross, ii

Luther, Martin, xxxiii, xxxviii
MacKellar, Walter, xl
Malachi (Bible Book), 54, 94
Mark (Bible Book), 3, 4, 5, 8, 9, 10, 13, 21, 29, 30, 33, 34, 51, 52, 54, 67, 76, 82, 134, 151, 153, 163, 166, 168
Masoretic Text, xiv, Appendix A
Matthew (Bible Book), 1, 2, 3, 4, 5, 6, 7, 8, 9, 10, 12, 14, 17, 20, 21, 23, 26, 27, 28, 30, 31, 32, 33, 34, 36, 37, 38, 39, 42, 46, 48, 51, 52, 54, 57, 58, 66, 67, 68, 76, 77, 78, 82, 91, 96, 101, 103, 105, 106, 115, 126, 128, 129, 133, 135, 136, 138, 139, 140, 150, 151, 152, 153, 157, 158, 160, 162, 163, 164, 167, 168
Micah (Bible Book), 24, 125
Migne, J. P., xxiv
Nahum (Bible Book), 107
Nehemiah (Bible Book), 86, 93, 115
Nephilim, xxvii
Nicholas of Lyra, xxxii
Numbers (Bible Book), 13, 17, 35, 37, 49, 86, 114
Of Reformation, xlvii
Origen, xxiv
On Noah, xxiv
Packer, J. W., xxvi
Parker, William Riley, x
Patai, Raphael, xviii
Patterson, Frank Allen, xlvii
Patrologia Latina, xxiv
Philippians (Bible Book), 11, 18, 24, 42, 72, 164
Psalms (Bible Book), xlii, Appendix D, 7, 9, 13, 15, 18, 22, 24, 32, 37, 44, 50, 55, 56, 61, 68, 77, 78, 80, 85, 89, 92, 93, 95, 99, 123, 133, 137, 138, 144, 147, 154, 156, 159, 161, 165, 166
Proverbs (Bible Book), xlii, 79, 83, 93, 102, 134, 143, 149
Qorha, Joshua ben, xxx
Revelation (Bible Book), xxiv, 3, 10, 17, 18, 19, 20, 34, 40, 43, 44, 50, 62, 85, 92, 93, 101, 102, 103, 123, 127, 132, 137, 155, 159, 160, 163, 165, 166, 167
Roberts, Alexander, xx
Romans (Bible Book) 1, 11, 12, 16, 17, 19, 25, 46, 48, 61, 93, 94, 99, 122, 131, 135, 136, 137, 138, 148, 162, 164, 165, 166
Samson Agonistes, ix
Septuagint, xx, Appendix B
Shoulson, Jeffrey, ii
Song of Solomon (Bible Book), 63
Speiser, E. A., xxv
Swift, Edgar, Appendix C
Tanakh, xxvi
Tertullian, xxi
Teskey, Gordon, xv
Titans, xxvii
Titus (Bible Book), 99, 124
Tobit, (Apocrypha), 45, 62, 63
Tostado, Alphonso, xxxii
Trinity Manuscript, ix
Tymme, Thomas, xxxv
Ugaritic, xxvi, xxx
Von Rad, Gerhard, xxviii
Vulgate, Appendix C
West, Robert H., xxxix, xl, xli, xlvii
Wise, Michael, xvi
Whiston, William, xix
Williams, Arnold, xxv, xxxii
Wolfe, Don M., x
Wycliffe, John, xliv
Yohai, Rabbi Shimon ben, xxix
Zephaniah (Bible Book), 107